Creating Tomorrow

Andrew Parry

Published by Andrew Parry, 2024.

While every precaution has been taken in the preparation of this book, the publisher assumes no responsibility for errors or omissions, or for damages resulting from the use of the information contained herein.

CREATING TOMORROW

First edition. November 6, 2024.

Copyright © 2024 Andrew Parry.

ISBN: 979-8227714961

Written by Andrew Parry.

Table of Contents

The Blueprint of Sci-Fi Screenplays: Format and Structure Essentials 1

Setting the Scene: Building Visual Worlds on the Page 3

Crafting Compelling Openings: Hooking the Audience from Scene One 5

Visualizing the Impossible: Describing Futuristic and Alien Elements 7

Momentum and Pacing: Keeping the Sci-Fi Story Engaging 9

Subtext and Symbolism: Elevating Sci-Fi Themes Visually 11

Action as Storytelling: Choreographing Visual Impact 13

From Page to Screen: Ensuring Cinematic Flow in Every Scene 15

Building Tomorrow: Crafting Futuristic Concepts and Settings 17

Science Meets Story: Integrating Technology and Plot Progression 19

Beyond the Stars: Exploring Sci-Fi Themes of Exploration and Discovery 22

In the Mind's Eye: Creating Believable Alien and Artificial Intelligences 25

The Catalyst: Establishing Tech-Driven Conflict and Tension 28

The Science of Wonder: Balancing Realism and Speculation 30

Epic Sagas and Timelines: Shaping Long-Arc Sci-Fi Narratives 33

The 'What If' Factor: Plotting with Scientific Hypotheses 36

Creating Characters for a Sci-Fi World: Beyond Stereotypes 39

The Hero's Evolution: Building a Sci-Fi Protagonist with Depth" 42

Alien Minds: Crafting Non-Human Characters with Relatable Traits 45

Technological Transformations: When Machines and Humans Collide 48

Psychology of the Future: Understanding Character Motivations in Sci-Fi 51

Heroes and Anti-Heroes: Moral Complexity in a Sci-Fi Setting 54

Relationships in Space: Exploring Connections across Dimensions 57

Arcs in Alien Worlds: Character Growth amidst Futuristic Challenges 60

Speaking the Future: Crafting Dialogue for a Sci-Fi Setting 63

Beyond Technobabble: Balancing Jargon and Clarity 65

Voices from Other Worlds: Creating Distinctive Alien and AI Dialogue 67

Emotion in the Unknown: Conveying Humanity through Sci-Fi Dialogue 70

Dialect and Diction: Developing a Unique Linguistic Style 73

Exposition through Dialogue: Revealing the Sci-Fi World Naturally 76

Tension and Timing: Dialogue for Action-Packed Sci-Fi Scenes 79

Monologues from the Stars: Using Soliloquies to Reflect Themes 82

Laying the Foundation: Building Worlds from Concept to Reality 84

Designing the Ecosystem: Landscapes, Climates, and Natural Laws 87

Alien Societies: Crafting Cultures, Beliefs, and Social Structures 90

The Rules of Reality: Establishing Technology, Magic, or Advanced Science 93

The Power of History: Developing a Backstory for Your World 96

Economics of the Future: Systems of Trade, Wealth, and Power 99

Interplanetary Relations: Politics and Conflicts Beyond Earth 102

Architecture and Design: Creating Unique Aesthetic Environments 105

Languages and Symbols: Developing Communication in New Realms 108

Dynamic Environments: Ensuring Believability through Change and Decay 111

Exploring the Future of AI: Humanity's Partners or Overlords? 114

Transhumanism and Beyond: Evolving the Human Condition" 116

Eco-Dystopias and Climate Sci-Fi: Imagining Our Planet's Fate 119

Quantum Realities: Multiverses, Time Travel, and Alternate Dimensions 122

Digital Immortality: Consciousness, Cloning, and Legacy 125

Space Colonization: Life and Conflict on New Frontiers 128

The Rise of Virtual Worlds: Blending Reality with Simulation 131

Social Dynamics in Sci-Fi: Power, Control, and Rebellion 134

Brainstorming Sci-Fi Concepts with ChatGPT: From Ideas to Themes 137

Building Worlds Together: Using ChatGPT for Setting and Environment Creation 139

Developing Sci-Fi Heroes and Villains with ChatGPT" 142

Tech Talk: Generating Futuristic Technology and Scientific Concepts" 145

Exploring the Unknown: Using ChatGPT for Alien Races and Species 148

Dialogue Development: Crafting Authentic Sci-Fi Conversations with AI 151

Plotting with ChatGPT: Structuring Your Sci-Fi Storyline 154

Creative Collaborator: Using ChatGPT to Refine and Enhance Narrative Arcs 157

A Selection of Prompts for ChatGPT 160

Character Development Prompts 161

Setting Development Prompts 162

Integrated Prompts for Plot, Character, and Setting 163

Conclusion 164

The Blueprint of Sci-Fi Screenplays: Format and Structure Essentials

The blueprint of a science fiction screenplay is like a roadmap, guiding your story from concept to the screen. Sci-fi, in particular, requires a fine balance between familiar screenplay elements and the demands of a genre that constantly pushes boundaries. Understanding the essentials of format and structure is key to creating a screenplay that not only tells a captivating story but also communicates the scope and scale unique to science fiction.

The format of a screenplay acts as the universal language of storytelling in film and TV. Adhering to this standard format allows your story to be accessible and understandable to directors, producers, and actors alike. In a science fiction screenplay, clarity in format becomes even more crucial because of the complex settings, tech-heavy descriptions, and futuristic elements that are characteristic of the genre. A well-formatted sci-fi screenplay ensures that the story flows logically and that anyone reading it can visualize the world you're creating.

Every sci-fi screenplay is broken down into scenes, each a specific location and time. The scene headings, or slug lines, should be detailed enough to set the scene but not so exhaustive that they bog down the reader. For instance, if your story involves an alien planet, the slug line might read: "EXT. ZYRA – RED SAND DESERT – DAY." Here, "EXT" signifies an exterior location, "ZYRA" names the planet, "RED SAND DESERT" describes the specific place, and "DAY" clarifies the time. A good slug line gives just enough information to orient the reader while allowing room for their imagination.

In addition to concise slug lines, scene descriptions play a big role in setting the tone and visual feel of your sci-fi world. Descriptions should focus on the sensory and atmospheric elements of the scene—describing a "wind that carries a faint, electric hum through the metallic forest of towering antennas" instantly conjures an image of a world where technology and nature are intertwined. While descriptive, sci-fi screenplays should avoid novel-like details. Think of it as painting with a broad brush, highlighting just enough to make the setting vivid but leaving plenty of room for interpretation.

Another essential part of the structure is action description. In sci-fi, action descriptions often cover complex scenes—think space battles, zero-gravity fights, or high-stakes chases across alien landscapes. Keep these descriptions clear, concise, and visual. Describe only the actions crucial to the narrative; too much detail can make the scene harder to picture. Instead of writing, "the character carefully weaves around the debris of a fallen spacecraft, each step hesitant as she inches forward," try "she weaves through debris, cautious but determined." Short, punchy action lines keep the pace moving and make complex scenes easier to follow.

Dialogue formatting follows typical screenplay conventions but can take on unique qualities in sci-fi. Dialogue helps establish not just character voices but also the era, culture, and technology in your world. Sci-fi often involves jargon or alien languages, so it's essential to balance uniqueness with readability. If a character refers to a "quantum relay," include subtle context to clarify its function. You could have another character respond with something like, "So, no power for the shields?" This keeps the dialogue accessible to both readers and viewers without needing extensive exposition.

When considering character names and titles, sci-fi often leans into creativity. Alien names, AI designations, or futuristic titles help set the tone of your world. Think about the implications of names and how they can hint at a character's background, role, or origin. For example, a character named "CYPHER 9" instantly brings to mind associations with cybernetic technology or artificial intelligence, whereas a name like "Soriya Elian" may hint at a human colony with cultural roots in Earth's history. In the format, ensure these names are clear and legible, making it easy for readers to differentiate between characters.

The three-act structure is the skeleton of most screenplays, and sci-fi is no exception. In the first act, introduce the world and its rules. Readers should immediately understand what kind of science fiction world they're entering—be it a dystopian future, intergalactic empire, or post-apocalyptic Earth. This act establishes the protagonist, their goals, and the primary conflict that will drive the story forward. In sci-fi, this often involves introducing some element of technology, mystery, or alien threat that sets the stage for what's to come.

The second act is where the stakes rise and the protagonist's journey takes them deeper into the unknown. For sci-fi, this is usually where the scope of the story expands. The protagonist might explore unfamiliar landscapes, encounter alien cultures, or grapple with advanced technology. The middle act often sees the protagonist facing obstacles unique to the sci-fi genre—like navigating an asteroid field, learning to communicate with an alien species, or evading a surveillance state. These obstacles should challenge both their physical and ideological limits.

The final act brings resolution, often a confrontation or a revelation that ties together the sci-fi elements with the character's journey. In this act, the consequences of the protagonist's actions reach a peak, and any technological or alien mysteries introduced in the beginning should be addressed. For instance, if the story centers around a rebellion against a high-tech authoritarian regime, the climax might involve a final standoff where the protagonist has to make a choice that determines the fate of both the people and the technology that governs them. The ending should feel like a natural progression from everything that's been built up, even if it leaves some mysteries unsolved, as is common in sci-fi.

Formatting and structuring a sci-fi screenplay is about creating a framework that allows the complexity of the genre to shine without overwhelming the reader. By adhering to the traditional screenplay format and adapting it with clear descriptions, evocative world-building, and engaging dialogue, you'll create a script that resonates with the adventurous spirit of science fiction. It's about balancing imaginative concepts with the concise, visual language of screenwriting, making your sci-fi world as accessible on the page as it will eventually be on the screen.

In a way, a sci-fi screenplay is a contract with the reader. You're promising them an adventure that transports them to worlds and possibilities beyond their own, while grounding them enough that they don't feel lost. The key to achieving this is a blueprint that respects both the rules of screenwriting and the boundless potential of science fiction, creating an experience that's both visually compelling and narratively rich.

Setting the Scene: Building Visual Worlds on the Page

Setting the scene in a science fiction screenplay is like inviting the reader to step into a brand-new world—one that may stretch beyond their wildest imagination. Unlike everyday settings, sci-fi worlds often require readers to suspend disbelief and accept realities vastly different from our own. So, building a visual world on the page is about more than just setting a location; it's about giving readers the tools they need to picture everything from advanced technology and alien landscapes to futuristic societies and alternate realities.

When it comes to sci-fi, setting the scene starts with choosing what your audience absolutely needs to know and then painting a clear, vivid picture with only a few carefully chosen words. Think of it as a minimalist's approach to world-building. A well-written scene description can transform a simple location into an environment rich with atmosphere and intrigue. Imagine your setting as a character in itself; a hostile planet with toxic air, a massive starship navigating an asteroid belt, or a sprawling metropolis where neon lights flicker against smog-filled skies. Each of these requires a unique tone, one that resonates with the genre's themes and enhances the story's atmosphere.

To begin setting the scene, consider what visual details will make your setting immediately recognizable and intriguing. Let's say your scene opens on an alien desert—one that's nothing like Earth's deserts. Instead of calling it simply "an alien desert," consider something like, "EXT. PLANET XEREX – STORM-SWEPT BLUE SANDS – DAY." A simple slug line like this tells us we're on a different world with an unfamiliar terrain. The words "storm-swept" imply movement and unpredictability, while "blue sands" hints at something otherworldly without requiring lengthy explanation. A few well-chosen descriptors can suggest a lot about your sci-fi setting right from the get-go.

Another effective technique for building visual worlds on the page is to appeal to the senses. Describe not only what the characters see but also what they hear, smell, or even feel. If your protagonist is walking through a high-tech spaceship, they might hear a constant, low hum of the ship's engines or feel a subtle vibration underfoot. By including sensory details like these, you create an immersive experience, bringing readers into a fully realized setting rather than just a backdrop for the action. For example, "The stale scent of recycled air hangs thick in the cramped corridors," adds both mood and realism.

One of the hallmarks of sci-fi world-building is the use of advanced technology, architecture, and landscapes that seem almost otherworldly. These details should be woven into the scene as naturally as possible. Rather than explaining every detail of a futuristic city's transport system, show us a glimpse through action or description. For instance, instead of detailing the science behind hover vehicles, you could describe, "A sleek, silver pod hovers silently inches above the ground, gliding past towering glass spires." The description gives just enough detail to communicate that the vehicle is advanced and futuristic, while allowing readers to fill in the blanks with their imagination.

In science fiction, it's important to remember that the rules of reality can be bent—or even broken. Your world doesn't have to follow the physical or scientific laws that we're familiar with, but it does need internal consistency. If gravity operates differently, or if plants glow in the dark, make sure these elements are introduced early and fit logically within the established setting. Once you set these parameters, stick to them so that readers feel grounded in this new reality. It's part of building a believable world, even if that world is completely alien to us.

Balancing descriptive language with the screenplay's need for brevity is essential. Instead of giving long-winded descriptions, focus on concise language that hints at a larger world. If your scene takes place on a mining planet, a simple description like "massive, rust-colored excavators claw at the barren, cratered ground beneath a blood-red sky" can paint a vivid picture without overwhelming the reader with unnecessary detail. The goal is to evoke imagery that feels specific to your sci-fi world, allowing the reader's imagination to fill in any remaining gaps.

When it comes to futuristic technology, subtlety often goes a long way. Instead of lengthy exposition on how a particular device works, show how characters interact with it. If there's a piece of advanced medical technology in use, describe it in terms of its effects: "A shimmering scanner hovers over his wounds, sealing them shut with a faint blue glow." This approach keeps the description dynamic and action-oriented, rather than reading like a user's manual. In sci-fi, it's often less about what the tech does and more about how it affects the characters and their world.

Color and lighting can also play a major role in setting a visual tone. Sci-fi worlds are often associated with specific color palettes that evoke a certain mood, like the cold blues and metallic grays of a spaceship or the neon glow of a cyberpunk city. Describing lighting and color cues briefly but effectively can add atmosphere and communicate genre. For instance, "The city sprawls below, bathed in a toxic green haze as neon lights pulse through the smog," tells readers they're in a world that's both futuristic and somewhat dystopian. Lighting and color details can help set the tone without over-explaining. Building a sci-fi world also means thinking about its history, society, and culture, but this backstory should reveal itself naturally. Instead of a full history lesson, you might drop hints about the world's past through setting choices. If the scene takes place in the ruins of a city, brief details can suggest former glory. "Crumbling marble arches stand half-buried in sand, relics of a forgotten civilization," instantly communicates that this place once held significance, even if we don't yet know the details.

World-building in a screenplay is about suggesting depth while maintaining readability. Avoid overwhelming readers with too much at once; instead, introduce elements gradually. Let the setting evolve naturally alongside the story, adding layers as needed. Perhaps in an early scene, readers see only the sterile, functional side of a space colony, but as the story progresses, they venture into darker areas where things aren't as pristine. This layering makes the world feel alive and dynamic, adapting to the story's needs while building anticipation for what else lies beneath the surface. Setting the scene in sci-fi is about mastering the art of restraint. By giving just enough detail to make the world feel vivid and unique, you can create an immersive experience that feels visually rich without losing the pacing or flow of the screenplay. Every scene is an opportunity to pull readers deeper into the world you're building, one visual detail at a time. And in a genre where the possibilities are nearly limitless, striking the right balance between description and mystery keeps readers captivated, ensuring that they stay hooked until the final page.

Crafting Compelling Openings: Hooking the Audience from Scene One

Crafting a compelling opening in a science fiction screenplay is like launching a ship into orbit—it requires precision, momentum, and enough intrigue to make the audience want to stay for the ride. In sci-fi, where your world may be vastly different from reality, the opening scene does more than just introduce the story. It sets the tone, establishes the rules of the world, and hooks the audience with a promise of adventure, mystery, or revelation.

The first thing to consider is what your opening scene will say about the world you're about to reveal. In science fiction, the setting itself is often the first character we meet. Unlike other genres, sci-fi usually requires the audience to step into a world they've never seen before, one with its own unique rules, technology, and societal structures. The opening scene should give the audience a taste of this world without overwhelming them. Think of it as a glimpse through a window. Show them just enough to spark curiosity and wonder, but leave plenty of questions unanswered. Perhaps it's the sight of a bustling, neon-lit city on a distant planet or a quiet, eerie laboratory where scientists work with alien specimens. A few well-chosen details can immerse the audience in the world right away.

An effective opening also grounds the audience with a central question or conflict. It might be a mystery waiting to unfold, a conflict between two opposing forces, or a character facing a life-altering decision. This initial tension creates an anchor that pulls the audience in, making them eager to find out more. In a sci-fi screenplay, this hook could come from something as simple as a piece of technology malfunctioning in a dangerous way or as complex as a philosophical question about humanity's place in the universe. Whatever it is, the hook should reflect the heart of your story, setting up expectations for the journey ahead.

Consider using visuals that communicate as much as words, or even more. Sci-fi thrives on powerful imagery, and a well-chosen visual in the first few minutes can establish an entire world's worth of context. For instance, the sight of a massive spaceship floating silently in the void, its hull battered and scarred, might suggest a war-torn galaxy or a lonely exploration mission. Or maybe we see a character encased in a sleek, metallic suit, face obscured, as they step onto the surface of an alien planet. Without a single line of dialogue, the audience already knows they're in a futuristic setting and that this character is about to face something unknown. These visuals spark questions, inviting the audience to lean forward and wonder what's happening.

In a screenplay, dialogue is precious, especially in the opening scene. Sci-fi, with its unique terminology and concepts, has a tendency to overload audiences with information. Avoid starting with heavy exposition or explanations of your world's rules and technology. Instead, let dialogue hint at these elements organically. For example, if two scientists are discussing the results of an experiment on alien DNA, their conversation could imply the stakes without diving into a lecture. Keep it natural and conversational, leaving the details to be uncovered over time. An opening scene should always prioritize immersion over explanation.

The introduction of your protagonist is another vital aspect of a compelling opening. In sci-fi, where the stakes can often feel distant or abstract, a relatable protagonist grounds the story and makes the audience care. It's important to show who this character is and what they want, even if they're in a futuristic setting or have an unusual background. Perhaps they're a scientist driven by curiosity, a soldier on a high-stakes mission, or a reluctant hero pulled into an intergalactic conflict. Whatever their role, reveal a glimpse of their motivations, fears, or desires. This connection will give the audience someone to root for, even if they're not quite sure where the story is headed. In science fiction, tone and atmosphere play major roles in shaping the audience's experience, and the opening scene is your opportunity to establish them immediately. Whether it's the dark and eerie vibe of a dystopian future, the excitement of space exploration, or the high-stakes tension of a cyberpunk thriller, make sure the tone is clear from the start. The lighting, sounds, and colors of your setting can all help establish this atmosphere. If the scene is set in a sprawling, high-tech metropolis, describe how "neon lights pulse through thick fog as hover cars hum through crowded streets." The audience should feel the environment as much as they see it, and it should give them a taste of what's to come.

Another important aspect is pacing. Science fiction openings don't need to be explosive from the first moment, but they should maintain a steady pace that builds intrigue. Some sci-fi stories work well with a slow-burn opening that teases elements gradually, while others benefit from immediate action, throwing the audience right into the fray. Think about the type of story you're telling and pace the opening accordingly. If it's a high-stakes action piece, start with a bang. If it's more cerebral or mysterious, allow for a slower reveal that builds tension. As you introduce your world and story, remember to maintain an element of mystery. Science fiction is all about discovery, whether it's uncovering the truth about a strange planet or learning about a character's hidden past. Resist the urge to explain everything at once. Instead, offer glimpses and hints, building the world and story piece by piece. The audience doesn't need to understand the intricacies of your sci-fi world immediately; they just need to feel compelled to keep watching.

The opening scene is also an opportunity to set up thematic questions that will be explored throughout the story. Sci-fi often deals with big ideas—what it means to be human, the ethics of technology, or the consequences of exploration. If your story grapples with these kinds of questions, hint at them in the opening scene. For instance, you might show a society that has become overly reliant on AI, with characters interacting with machines in a way that feels disturbingly casual. This subtle setup can plant the seed for the thematic questions your story will explore, giving the audience something to ponder as they get further into the story. Lastly, make sure your opening scene feels purposeful. Every detail, every line of dialogue, every visual should contribute to the story you're building. In sci-fi, it's easy to get lost in the coolness of the world you're creating, but the opening scene should always serve the story first. If there's a breathtaking view of an alien planet, it should be there because it establishes the world or enhances the mood, not just because it looks interesting. A purposeful opening scene is memorable and impactful, setting the tone for the rest of the screenplay and ensuring the audience is invested from the start. In science fiction, the opening scene is more than an introduction—it's an invitation to explore a universe of endless possibilities.

Visualizing the Impossible: Describing Futuristic and Alien Elements

Visualizing the impossible is both the thrill and the challenge of writing science fiction. Describing futuristic and alien elements means bringing the reader into worlds and ideas that don't exist yet—or may never exist. How do you describe the unknown in a way that feels tangible and captivating? The goal is to spark readers' imaginations and give them just enough direction to envision places, creatures, and technology that exist far beyond our current understanding.

When describing futuristic elements, think about using familiar concepts as a foundation. Starting with something recognizable can help ground the reader in your setting, even if that setting is wildly different from anything they know. For example, if your scene takes place in a city that spans an entire planet, you might begin with the idea of "skyscrapers" and then build from there: "Towering structures of glass and metal pierce the sky, their reflective surfaces glimmering like gemstones under a constant, artificial sun." This description introduces a massive, futuristic cityscape but uses elements like glass, metal, and skyscrapers to give the reader a starting point. Once they have that foundation, you can add more outlandish details without losing them.

Creating alien elements often involves challenging our typical perceptions of shape, color, and behavior. Aliens don't need to be humanoid or even animal-like. They could resemble plants, clouds, or completely abstract forms of life. Think beyond the physical—what if an alien species communicates through changes in color or releases pheromones that create emotions in those around them? Consider the character's experience when describing an alien. Instead of detailing every limb or texture, focus on how the alien makes them feel. For instance, "A shimmering being floats before them, emitting a pulse of light that sends a wave of calm through the air." This allows readers to envision the alien's impact on the scene without needing a complete anatomical breakdown.

When describing advanced technology, be mindful of maintaining the story's pace. In science fiction, it's tempting to dive into detailed explanations of how things work, especially when technology is a major part of the world. However, too much detail can bog down the narrative. Instead, consider describing the effects of the technology and its purpose. For example, instead of explaining the science behind a gravity-defying vehicle, you might write, "The vehicle hovers effortlessly above the ground, leaving a faint shimmer in its wake as it glides forward." This tells readers it's futuristic and somewhat magical without delving into the mechanics. Technology, in sci-fi, is often more about what it does and how it changes the environment or affects characters than the technicalities of its function.

Sound, texture, and temperature can add depth to alien landscapes and futuristic environments, making them feel more immersive. If your characters land on a planet with a dense, gaseous atmosphere, you might describe the sound as muffled, with voices taking on a strange, echoing quality. Or, in a scene where they explore a crystalline cave, the air could feel unnaturally cool, almost metallic to the touch. These sensory details create a vivid picture that goes beyond visuals alone. By engaging all five senses, you give readers an experience they can almost feel for themselves.

Another technique is to imply scale without spelling it out. Alien worlds and futuristic cities are often vast and complex, but rather than describing every aspect, give the reader a few striking features and let their imagination fill in the rest. For instance, if your character approaches an alien city, you might write, "Columns of light reach high into the atmosphere, illuminating towers that seem to disappear into the clouds." This suggests an enormous scale without listing every detail, leaving room for readers to build the rest of the image in their minds.

Alien environments and futuristic settings can be enhanced through contrasts. Humans find meaning by comparing the unknown to what they understand, so use this instinct to make your descriptions more evocative. If an alien jungle is unlike anything seen on Earth, you could describe the trees as "thicker than any Earth tree, their trunks veined with bioluminescent roots that pulse in strange rhythms." This combination of the familiar (trees and roots) with the strange (bioluminescence and pulsing rhythms) creates an environment that feels both otherworldly and accessible.

When it comes to alien languages, avoid the temptation to write out lengthy conversations in a fictional tongue. Instead, give just enough to suggest a language or communication style, focusing on how the language affects the listener or what it sounds like. You might write, "The alien's voice resonates like a low hum, each syllable vibrating through the air as if sung in frequencies only half-heard by human ears." This approach keeps the focus on the experience of the language rather than the specific words, making the alien communication feel mysterious and immersive.

Using colors and light creatively can evoke the unique atmosphere of a futuristic or alien setting. Alien skies don't have to be blue, and nighttime doesn't have to be dark. Consider using unexpected colors or sources of light. You could describe a sky with "swirls of turquoise and silver, casting an ethereal glow over the landscape," or an alien forest where "pale blue bioluminescent plants light the path." Color often conveys emotion, so think about how these hues make the scene feel. Warm colors like orange or red can create a sense of urgency or danger, while cool colors like blue or green might feel tranquil or eerie.

The impossible can also be made more tangible by paying attention to how characters interact with it. If they're on an alien planet with low gravity, mention how they adjust their movements or describe the way dust hangs in the air longer than it would on Earth. If they're using a mind-link device to communicate with an AI, describe how the device feels on their skin or the strange sensation of thoughts not their own flowing through their mind. Small, relatable details make the impossible more real and relatable to the reader.

Avoid getting too technical with alien or futuristic terminology. Instead of long, complex names for technology or species, try using shorter, simpler terms or offering context clues that make their function clear. If there's an AI assistant in a character's suit, refer to it by a name, like "Sol," and mention its capabilities through dialogue or action: "Sol, analyze the air composition." This creates a sense of familiarity and avoids lengthy, distracting explanations.

Finally, remember that less is often more when describing futuristic and alien elements. Sci-fi relies heavily on the imagination, and readers enjoy filling in the blanks. Suggest just enough to make the scene vivid and intriguing, and let them complete the picture. The goal isn't to make readers understand every detail of your world but to invite them into a space that feels unique and immersive.

In sci-fi, the impossible becomes reality, and through well-chosen descriptions, you can make the unimaginable feel like an everyday experience. By grounding alien worlds and futuristic technology in sensory details, accessible comparisons, and just enough specificity, you allow readers to visualize a world that feels both thrillingly foreign and strangely familiar. Through this balance, you'll invite them to fully engage in the wonder of your world, leaving them eager to discover what's around each corner.

Momentum and Pacing: Keeping the Sci-Fi Story Engaging

Momentum and pacing are the twin engines that drive a science fiction story forward, keeping the audience engaged and on the edge of their seats. In a genre filled with sprawling worlds, complex technologies, and speculative concepts, pacing can make or break the experience. Too slow, and the story drags, weighed down by details and exposition. Too fast, and the audience can feel lost, overwhelmed by the constant onslaught of information or action. The key is striking a balance that creates a rhythm of tension and release, excitement and intrigue, while letting the sci-fi elements shine.

Pacing in sci-fi starts with clarity of purpose. Every scene, action, or moment of dialogue should contribute to the story's forward movement. When introducing futuristic settings or advanced tech, it's tempting to linger on descriptions or explanations, but these can quickly slow down the pace. Instead, focus on what's essential for the audience to understand right now. For instance, if a character is using a teleportation device, you don't need a detailed backstory on its development. Show it in action—perhaps with a brief malfunction or a surprising side effect—and let the audience see it rather than overloading them with explanations. Letting the technology speak for itself keeps the momentum going while giving the audience just enough to understand its role.

Science fiction often involves complex concepts, but pacing is about knowing when and how to introduce them. Staggering reveals or layering new information gradually allows the audience to absorb the world without getting bogged down. Instead of explaining an alien society's entire political system upfront, perhaps show snippets of it through character interactions or minor plot points. The protagonist might witness a ritual or hear a brief exchange that hints at the society's values and hierarchy. This approach maintains the pacing by revealing the world in increments, allowing the audience to discover and become invested in the unfolding story rather than feeling they're attending a lecture.

Action is a powerful tool for building momentum, but in sci-fi, action can take many forms. Space battles, chase scenes, or confrontations with alien species can all ramp up the excitement, but quieter moments of discovery or realization can be just as compelling. For instance, a scene where a character stumbles upon ancient alien artifacts might not involve physical movement, but the psychological intensity and tension can create a thrilling experience. It's about using pacing to keep the audience engaged, whether the scene is fast and explosive or slow and suspenseful. The stakes in sci-fi are often high, and maintaining a balance of high-energy scenes and slower, thought-provoking moments keeps the audience invested.

Transitions between scenes are critical for maintaining momentum. In sci-fi, there's often a lot of ground to cover, literally and figuratively, as characters move between planets, dimensions, or times. Smooth transitions help keep the story cohesive and avoid jarring changes in pace. One way to manage transitions is to connect them through visual or thematic links. For example, if a character is leaving one world for another, you could end the scene with them looking out over the landscape, then open the next scene with a similar view of the new location. This creates a sense of continuity, making the transition feel fluid and keeping the momentum from one scene rolling into the next.

Dialogue also plays a role in pacing. In sci-fi, dialogue often has to carry the weight of explaining new ideas or technology, which can slow things down if not handled carefully. Keep conversations focused and purposeful, revealing information naturally through character interactions. If two characters are discussing an impending interplanetary war, let their dialogue reflect the urgency and stakes without slipping into an info-dump. Perhaps one character is frustrated with a government's inaction, or another hints at a dark secret about the enemy forces. These nuances not only keep the pace moving but also add layers to the story, letting the audience pick up on underlying conflicts or motives without being told outright.

Tension and suspense are essential for momentum, especially in sci-fi, where the unknown often plays a central role. Building suspense doesn't always mean action; it can be about the anticipation of something. For example, if characters are about to enter an uncharted sector of space, use pacing to build that sense of trepidation. Describe the silence, the darkness outside the ship, the quiet ticking of machinery as they wait to encounter... something. Drawing out moments like this, where the outcome is uncertain, keeps the audience on edge, heightening engagement even without fast-paced action.

One effective pacing technique is to vary the intensity of scenes, alternating between high-stakes action or revelation and quieter, reflective moments. This ebb and flow allow the audience to catch their breath and process what they've experienced. If your characters just escaped a harrowing chase with bounty hunters, a slower scene where they regroup or reflect on their next move provides a natural rhythm. It also gives the audience a chance to connect with the characters on a more personal level, deepening their investment in the story. These slower moments should never be fillers; they're an opportunity to develop characters, reveal motivations, or hint at underlying conflicts.

Flashbacks or shifts in perspective can also add depth to a sci-fi story without sacrificing momentum, as long as they're strategically placed. Sci-fi often involves backstory or parallel timelines, but instead of lengthy expositional scenes, consider using quick glimpses or brief cutaways to add context. For example, if a character has a traumatic past on a now-destroyed planet, a few seconds of visual memory—a fleeting image of ruins or the sound of an evacuation alarm—can convey that history without halting the story. These moments enrich the narrative and keep the pace brisk, as they provide necessary context in compact doses.

Pacing in sci-fi is also about knowing when to let the story breathe. Some scenes benefit from lingering, especially when characters are encountering something awe-inspiring or mysterious. If a character witnesses the sunrise on an alien planet for the first time, allowing a moment of silence or stillness can create a powerful emotional impact. These pauses can be incredibly effective, contrasting sharply with the usual rapid pace of the genre and letting the audience feel the weight of the scene. It's a reminder that pacing isn't just about speed; it's about knowing when to slow down to highlight something extraordinary.

In summary, maintaining momentum in a sci-fi screenplay requires a careful balance of action, tension, and moments of quiet reflection. Keep scenes purposeful, introduce world-building elements gradually, and use sensory and visual cues to maintain a steady rhythm. Alternate between intense scenes and slower, character-focused moments to create an engaging rhythm that keeps the audience invested. And, most importantly, allow the story's natural ebb and flow to guide the pace. Sci-fi thrives on discovery, so pacing is not about constant speed but about building and releasing tension, keeping the audience intrigued, and letting them fully immerse themselves in a world that's as captivating as it is unpredictable.

Subtext and Symbolism: Elevating Sci-Fi Themes Visually

In science fiction, subtext and symbolism elevate the genre from mere spectacle to profound storytelling. Sci-fi is uniquely positioned to explore big themes—identity, humanity, technology, morality—while using fantastical settings and futuristic elements to reflect on our own world. By weaving subtext and symbolism into visuals, you can engage your audience on a deeper level, inviting them to look beyond the action and explore the meaning within your story.

Subtext, or the underlying meaning of scenes, is essential in sci-fi because it allows complex ideas to emerge naturally rather than through direct explanation. For instance, let's say your story explores the theme of isolation in a hyper-connected world. Instead of having a character simply talk about feeling alone, consider how the environment can convey this sense of isolation. Maybe they live in a towering megacity, surrounded by millions of people but disconnected from any real human contact. The visuals—the sheer size of the city, the monotony of endless screens, and the character's small silhouette against towering skyscrapers—can communicate this loneliness without a single word.

Symbolism takes this a step further by using objects, colors, or settings to represent larger themes or ideas. In sci-fi, where audiences expect the unusual, you can take creative liberties with your symbols. A common example in futuristic settings is the presence of artificial intelligence. Robots or AI characters can symbolize more than just technological advancement; they might represent humanity's struggle with its own identity or ethical boundaries. A robot who longs for freedom, for instance, could symbolize the human desire for autonomy and self-expression, especially in a world that increasingly prioritizes conformity or control.

Color can be one of the most effective symbolic tools, especially in visual storytelling. In sci-fi, colors often indicate more than just mood—they can represent ideas, power structures, or emotional states. Take a dystopian future where the ruling class controls technology and resources. The rulers might be dressed in sterile whites or grays, representing a cold, emotionless society, while rebels wear earthy tones to symbolize connection to humanity or nature. These subtle choices in color palettes can visually reinforce the story's core conflict, showing rather than telling the audience what's at stake.

Sci-fi is also known for its unique landscapes, and these settings are ripe for symbolic use. An alien planet with a barren, desolate landscape could reflect the consequences of ecological destruction, serving as a silent warning. A decaying city, overgrown with strange flora, might symbolize nature reclaiming its place after humanity's fall. These symbolic landscapes help establish the themes without needing dialogue or exposition. Just by seeing where the characters exist, the audience picks up on the story's larger messages, whether it's about environmental degradation, the fragility of human civilizations, or the resilience of life.

Objects, especially in sci-fi, can hold significant symbolic weight. A relic from Earth in an interstellar society might represent humanity's forgotten history or the loss of cultural identity. In a story about transhumanism, an old photograph could symbolize the character's connection to their former self, before they underwent extensive cybernetic enhancements. These objects ground the characters and connect the futuristic with the familiar, reminding the audience of what has been lost or altered in the quest for progress. The presence of these items becomes a silent commentary on the themes of memory, identity, and change.

Subtext in character interactions can also add depth to sci-fi themes. Let's say you're writing a story about humanity's uneasy relationship with artificial intelligence. Rather than having characters explicitly express their discomfort, use body language and behavior to show their underlying feelings. Maybe a human character recoils slightly when an AI reaches out to shake their hand, or there's a pause before they address the AI as if speaking to a real person. These subtle actions add tension and reveal biases without explicit dialogue, allowing the audience to pick up on the dynamics at play.

Incorporating mythological or historical symbols can lend depth to futuristic worlds. For example, naming an AI system "Prometheus" immediately suggests themes of overreach and the cost of knowledge. The audience, knowingly or unknowingly, associates the AI with the myth of Prometheus, who defied the gods to bring fire to humanity and suffered greatly for it. This symbolic layer provides a sense of timelessness, hinting that, despite the futuristic setting, humanity is still grappling with age-old dilemmas about knowledge, power, and responsibility.

Another powerful way to infuse symbolism is through architecture and design. In a sci-fi world, buildings and city layouts can reflect societal structures or values. A city filled with cold, geometric buildings might suggest a society that values order and conformity, while a more organic, flowing architecture could imply freedom and creativity. If a corporation controls the society, the company's logo or branding might be omnipresent, subtly reinforcing the power dynamics in the story. These design choices allow the setting itself to become a visual metaphor for the forces shaping the characters' lives. Symbolic use of light and shadow can also enhance subtext. In a story about moral ambiguity, play with lighting to reinforce that not everything is as clear-cut as it seems. Characters might move in and out of shadows, visually representing the ethical gray areas they navigate. Or, if a character is slowly succumbing to corruption, scenes involving them might get progressively darker, until they're shrouded in near-total darkness. This gradual shift in lighting symbolizes their inner journey, providing a visual metaphor for their descent into moral compromise.

Finally, the pacing of scenes can carry symbolic weight. For instance, if you're telling a story about a technologically advanced society that values efficiency over humanity, a slow, contemplative scene where a character watches the stars could symbolize resistance. The act of taking time to appreciate beauty or ponder existence becomes a symbolic rebellion against a world that prioritizes productivity over wonder. In this way, pacing itself becomes a narrative tool, with slower moments offering a breath of humanity in a relentlessly fast-paced world. Symbolism and subtext in sci-fi allow the audience to engage with the story on multiple levels. By using colors, objects, settings, and character interactions to convey meaning, you can infuse your sci-fi screenplay with rich layers of interpretation. The genre's inherent creativity and visual potential make it an ideal canvas for exploring complex themes through subtext, offering viewers not just a thrilling story, but an experience that resonates on a deeper, often subconscious level. In this way, you transform your sci-fi world from a mere backdrop into a reflection of the human experience, filled with insights about who we are and where we might be headed.

Action as Storytelling: Choreographing Visual Impact

In science fiction, action isn't just about explosions and chase sequences—it's a powerful storytelling tool that reveals character, advances the plot, and visually immerses the audience in the story's unique world. Sci-fi action scenes are often complex and filled with otherworldly tech or alien elements, but the best ones always serve a purpose beyond spectacle. Crafting action that enhances the story requires thinking beyond the surface level of physical movement and using each moment of intensity to deepen character arcs, explore themes, and make the sci-fi setting feel alive and tangible.

One of the most essential aspects of action as storytelling is its impact on character development. Sci-fi protagonists often face extreme challenges—alien battles, space chases, or high-stakes technological malfunctions—and how they respond to these situations tells us a lot about who they are. For example, if your hero is trapped on a hostile alien planet, a scene where they strategize their escape rather than fight back head-on might reveal them as resourceful, calculating, or even afraid. Alternatively, a protagonist who charges into a combat situation without hesitation shows bravery or impulsiveness, depending on the context. Action reveals character through decisions made under pressure, giving audiences a glimpse of what truly drives the person behind the high-stakes decisions.

Sci-fi action sequences also offer a chance to reveal the unique aspects of your world organically. Instead of explaining how advanced weaponry or gravity-defying vehicles work, show these technologies in action. If a character is pursued by a drone swarm, the way they evade it could reveal details about the drone's speed, intelligence, and detection abilities, as well as the environment. Perhaps the character uses the terrain to their advantage, darting between floating boulders in low gravity. This scene isn't just about the action itself; it builds a deeper understanding of the setting, making the sci-fi world feel fully realized and integrated into the story.

Pacing is another critical element in action as storytelling. Action scenes need rhythm—peaks of intensity balanced with slower moments of anticipation or aftermath. Rather than an unrelenting sequence, vary the tempo to create suspense. Maybe the protagonist is preparing for an ambush, heart pounding as they wait in the silence. This pause can heighten the impact of what comes next, making the action feel more meaningful. A rapid back-and-forth exchange during a space battle can be thrilling, but breaking it up with moments of suspenseful quiet or split-second decision-making allows the audience to catch their breath, making each high-stakes moment hit harder.

The environment itself can play a crucial role in shaping the action. Sci-fi worlds are filled with diverse settings, from desolate moonscapes to densely populated space colonies, and each location brings unique challenges and opportunities for creative action choreography. If a scene takes place on a space station with artificial gravity, a zero-gravity brawl could add layers of complexity, as characters float and rebound off walls in ways that wouldn't happen in a grounded fight. Similarly, action in an underwater alien environment could add unexpected obstacles, with movements slowed by resistance or the added danger of depleting oxygen. Tailoring action sequences to the environment helps ground the scene in the world you've created, making the action feel like an organic part of the setting.

Sci-fi action also allows for symbolic storytelling. High-stakes encounters can reveal the broader themes of the story without spelling them out in dialogue. For instance, a fight scene where two characters are battling over control of a piece of technology could symbolize the larger conflict between technology and humanity. Perhaps one character represents the cold efficiency of an AI-driven world, while the other is fighting to retain their human autonomy. By choreographing the fight to reflect these opposing ideologies—maybe the human character uses unpredictable, unorthodox moves, while the AI fights with flawless, calculated precision—you embed the theme into the very fabric of the action.

The best action scenes in sci-fi are those that not only advance the plot but also deepen the story's emotional stakes. Take a scene where a spaceship crew is trying to escape a collapsing planet. This isn't just about the physical thrill of the escape; it's a moment for characters to confront their own fears, make sacrifices, or reveal loyalties. In these high-stress situations, emotions run high, and decisions made in the heat of action reveal vulnerabilities that might otherwise stay hidden. Maybe a character who seemed self-centered risks their life to save someone else, or a character with a past fear of failure steps up as the unlikely leader. These emotional undercurrents bring depth to the action, making it resonate with the audience long after the scene ends.

Another crucial aspect of choreographing impactful action is clarity. Sci-fi can involve complex technology, unusual landscapes, and alien elements, and without clear visual storytelling, action scenes can quickly become confusing. Focus on clean, vivid descriptions that allow readers to visualize the sequence without getting lost. If two characters are fighting with energy swords on a high-tech walkway, describe the crackling hum of the weapons, the way sparks fly as they clash, and the precarious drop below. By honing in on specific, sensory details, you make the action not just clear but immersive, helping the audience feel as though they're right there with the characters.

Character motivation drives action in a way that pure spectacle can't. Before writing an action scene, consider why your characters are fighting, fleeing, or defending. Maybe the protagonist is battling against a superior alien foe, but their drive to survive is fueled by a promise to protect someone back home. This motivation adds weight to each punch, dodge, and decision. Action scenes are opportunities to show what's at stake for each character, so build tension by grounding the physical with the personal. Knowing why a character is risking their life or pushing themselves to the limit adds an emotional edge that makes the action more impactful.

In sci-fi, the possibility for creative, out-of-the-box action is almost endless. Don't limit yourself to traditional choreography—think about how technology, alien abilities, or environmental factors can transform a typical sequence into something extraordinary. If characters are battling in a virtual reality simulation, maybe they can manipulate their environment in real-time, creating new obstacles or weapons with just a thought. This kind of creativity not only makes for unique action but also reinforces the genre's themes, emphasizing the interplay between humanity and technology, reality and illusion.

Finally, remember that the aftermath of action is just as important as the action itself. After a high-stakes scene, give characters a moment to process what happened, whether they're dealing with the emotional impact, nursing injuries, or reflecting on the consequences of their actions. This moment of reflection grounds the action in reality, showing that the characters aren't invincible and that every decision has weight. A quiet moment after the chaos also allows the audience to catch their breath and understand how the action has changed the characters or the story.

In science fiction, action isn't just there to dazzle—it's a tool for storytelling, character development, and world-building. By choreographing action scenes that serve a deeper purpose, you invite the audience to connect with the story on multiple levels, making each moment of intensity an essential piece of the journey. In the end, it's the combination of visual impact and narrative significance that transforms a sci-fi action scene from just an exciting sequence into an unforgettable, story-driven experience.

From Page to Screen: Ensuring Cinematic Flow in Every Scene

Transitioning a story from page to screen requires more than just writing compelling scenes; it demands a sense of cinematic flow that brings each moment to life in a way that feels immersive and seamless. In science fiction, where the visuals can be as crucial as the story, ensuring a cinematic quality on the page is essential. This process involves paying close attention to pacing, visual language, rhythm, and the emotional arc within every scene, making it as engaging to read as it will be to watch.

A strong cinematic flow begins with knowing how to pace each scene to suit its purpose in the story. Sci-fi often has scenes of intense action or high-stakes drama interwoven with moments of quiet revelation or awe, and each demands a different rhythm. For instance, an action scene should feel quick and immediate, using short, punchy sentences to drive the intensity forward. On the other hand, a scene where the protagonist witnesses the vast expanse of a new planet for the first time might benefit from a slower, more poetic pace, with descriptions that allow the reader to savor the details. Understanding the pacing for each scene and adjusting sentence structure and rhythm accordingly creates a natural flow that helps readers stay engaged.

Visual language is another cornerstone of cinematic flow. Every scene should evoke a sense of place and atmosphere, giving readers a clear sense of the world while leaving enough room for their imagination to fill in the gaps. In sci-fi, the challenge is often to make unfamiliar worlds feel tangible and grounded. Instead of bogging down the narrative with excessive detail, focus on key visual elements that define the setting. For example, rather than listing every feature of a bustling spaceport, describe "the glowing neon signs in alien scripts, the hum of robotic vendors, and the towering windows overlooking the endless expanse of space." These snapshots create a vivid picture, grounding the audience in the scene without overwhelming them.

Movement within scenes is crucial for maintaining cinematic flow, especially in a genre where characters often interact with complex technology, strange environments, or non-human entities. Action and motion make a scene dynamic, whether it's the subtle motion of a spaceship gliding silently through the cosmos or the chaotic scuffle of a zero-gravity brawl. Describing movement adds energy to the scene, helping to convey its urgency or tranquility. Think about how characters navigate their environment and interact with its elements. If the setting is a futuristic city with hovering vehicles and winding aerial walkways, show characters moving through this space, adjusting their footing on platforms that sway or jumping from one level to another. This sense of movement gives readers a physical feel for the world, making it more immersive.

Dialogues in cinematic scenes should do more than just convey information—they should reflect the environment and bring out emotional layers. Sci-fi often introduces complex ideas, but rather than heavy exposition, aim for dialogue that feels natural and infused with subtext. In a tense negotiation scene between a human diplomat and an alien ambassador, the tone, pauses, and even the language used can imply much more than the words themselves. Is there hesitancy, sarcasm, or barely concealed hostility in their exchange? Each line should add to the atmosphere and tension, reflecting the power dynamics or cultural clash at play. This creates a conversational flow that feels authentic and cinematic, making the scene resonate emotionally.

Effective use of light and shadow in descriptions can significantly enhance the cinematic feel of a scene. Sci-fi worlds often have unique lighting, whether from distant stars, alien moons, or neon-lit cities, and playing with these elements can create mood and foreshadowing. If your scene takes place on a dimly lit spaceship corridor, describe the faint flicker of emergency lights casting shadows along the walls, hinting at the isolation or danger lurking nearby. In an alien forest, describe how bioluminescent plants illuminate the surroundings with a soft, eerie glow. By focusing on how light interacts with the environment, you set a visual tone that evokes specific emotions, pulling readers deeper into the scene.

Transitions between scenes are essential for maintaining cinematic flow in a screenplay. In a sci-fi story, characters might travel across planets, move between dimensions, or engage with virtual worlds, so smooth transitions help keep the story coherent. Using visual or thematic links can create a seamless transition. For example, if a scene ends with a character staring up at a towering alien structure, the next scene might open with a similar towering structure back on Earth, tying the two worlds together. This visual echo creates a sense of continuity, connecting scenes without needing extensive explanation, and it keeps the story moving in a way that feels natural and cohesive.

Sound and sensory details contribute to the cinematic feel of a scene, even on the page. While sound isn't always conveyed directly in writing, you can imply it through descriptions that make readers feel like they're hearing the world around them. A sci-fi story set on a space station, for instance, might have subtle sounds like the hum of machinery, the echo of footsteps, or the muffled voices of distant conversations. In an alien environment, mention the rustling of strange plants or the buzzing of unknown insects. These sensory details create atmosphere, helping readers feel as though they're part of the scene, which builds immersion and contributes to a smooth cinematic flow.

Cinematic scenes often rely on visual symbols to convey deeper meaning without using words. In sci-fi, symbols can take the form of objects, colors, or recurring images that reflect the story's themes. For example, a shattered visor on a space helmet might symbolize vulnerability or the fragility of human life in space. A character constantly fidgeting with a family heirloom could be a visual representation of their longing for home, grounding the futuristic setting with a sense of humanity. These symbols don't require lengthy explanation; they're simple, memorable images that add depth to the narrative, allowing the story to resonate on an emotional level.

One of the best ways to ensure cinematic flow is to think of each scene as a mini story, with its own beginning, middle, and end. This doesn't mean every scene has to have a climactic moment, but each should serve a clear purpose that moves the story forward. Even a quiet moment of introspection can be structured to have a small arc, building from a character's initial reaction to a realization or resolve by the end of the scene. By treating each scene as a complete thought, you give the story a natural rhythm that feels both cohesive and satisfying, keeping readers engaged as they move from one scene to the next.

Lastly, a cinematic flow demands a certain level of restraint. In sci-fi, it's easy to get caught up in describing every fascinating detail of the world, but too much detail can disrupt the flow and slow down the narrative. Focus on the essentials—the details that enhance the atmosphere, build suspense, or reveal character. Leave room for the audience's imagination to fill in the blanks, making the scene feel alive without overloading it with description. The best cinematic scenes are those that feel balanced, where every detail serves a purpose and enhances the story without drawing attention away from the main action.

By incorporating these elements—pacing, visual language, movement, dialogue, sensory details, and thematic symbols—you can create a flow that feels as cinematic on the page as it would on the screen. Each scene becomes a vivid, self-contained experience, one that seamlessly draws readers into the world and keeps them engaged from the first line to the last. In sci-fi, where the possibilities are endless, ensuring cinematic flow elevates the story, transforming it into an immersive journey that's as thrilling to read as it is to imagine unfolding on the big screen.

Building Tomorrow: Crafting Futuristic Concepts and Settings

Crafting futuristic concepts and settings in science fiction isn't just about imagining the wildest possibilities; it's about building a coherent vision of the future that feels plausible, compelling, and immersive. A well-crafted futuristic world is as much about the small, everyday details as it is about the big-picture advances in technology and society. When done right, your setting not only transports the audience to another time and place but also reflects deeper themes about humanity, progress, and the potential consequences of our current choices.

Creating a futuristic setting starts with a concept—a unifying idea that defines what kind of world you're building. Think of it as the foundation upon which you'll build everything else. Maybe your story is set in a dystopian society dominated by mega-corporations, a utopian world where humans coexist with AI, or an interstellar community connected by advanced teleportation technology. Whatever the concept, let it guide the choices you make about everything from architecture and language to daily routines and cultural norms. The best sci-fi settings are those where every detail feels interconnected, each element supporting and enhancing the others to create a cohesive vision.

Once you have a concept, begin expanding on the specific elements that make up your world. One of the most important aspects is technology, as it often defines the possibilities and limitations within your setting. In a futuristic world, technology can affect every part of life, from transportation and communication to medicine and entertainment. When imagining new tech, think about its impact on society as a whole. If people can upload their consciousness to a digital network, for example, how would that change the way they live, work, or even perceive death? The role of technology in your story should go beyond convenience; it should alter the way characters interact with their environment and each other, raising questions or conflicts that drive the plot.

Futuristic societies aren't just shaped by technology; they're influenced by the way that technology affects culture, politics, and ethics. Take the time to imagine how your society has adapted to or resisted these changes. For instance, if your world features widespread genetic engineering, there might be factions that embrace this advancement, while others vehemently oppose it. Some might see genetic manipulation as a means of perfection, while others may consider it a dangerous deviation from natural evolution. These divisions create rich social dynamics and conflicts that make the setting feel alive and layered, more than just a backdrop for the plot.

Designing the physical environment is another key step in building a futuristic setting. Architecture, transportation, and infrastructure should reflect the society's values and technological advancements. A world that prioritizes efficiency and environmental sustainability might have sleek, energy-efficient skyscrapers covered in solar panels and green spaces, while a society focused on corporate power might have towering structures emblazoned with logos and advertisements. Think about how transportation fits into this world, too. Are there autonomous vehicles, underground hyperloops, or teleportation hubs? If your world spans different planets, consider how travel between them affects everything from city layout to societal structure. The physical environment should tell a story of its own, reflecting the culture and priorities of the people who inhabit it.

One of the most exciting aspects of crafting a futuristic world is creating alien landscapes or entirely new ecosystems. If your story is set on an alien planet, think about the planet's natural characteristics, such as its gravity, climate, flora, and fauna. How have the inhabitants adapted to these conditions? A planet with lower gravity might have tall, slender plants that reach high into the atmosphere, or animals that glide effortlessly across open plains. These details give depth to your world, making it feel unique and rooted in a specific reality, even if it's entirely fictional. Alien ecosystems can also introduce unique resources or threats that play a role in the story, such as plants with healing properties or creatures that defend their territory fiercely.

Social structures in a futuristic world are often shaped by advancements in technology and shifts in cultural values. Consider how these might differ from our current systems of governance, class, and relationships. In a society where AI has assumed many roles traditionally held by humans, there might be a reduced need for labor, leading to a shift in social hierarchies or an increased focus on leisure and creativity. Conversely, in a world where resources are scarce, strict class divisions might emerge, with the wealthy living in comfortable, resource-rich areas, while the rest struggle in overpopulated, neglected districts. Exploring how these societal structures influence characters' lives and interactions adds another layer to your story, grounding the futuristic setting in relatable struggles and ambitions.

Language and communication are often overlooked but can play a big role in building a believable future. Think about how new technologies or cultural shifts might have influenced language. In a world with frequent interplanetary travel, there could be a common "trade language" that everyone speaks alongside their native tongues. Or perhaps people communicate with wearable translation devices, leading to a blend of languages that creates a unique dialect. Even slang can reflect the setting; terms might evolve around technologies or social norms, adding authenticity to character interactions and reminding the audience that they're in a world different from their own.

Futuristic settings often explore the ethics and consequences of human actions. These themes can be woven into the environment and characters, inviting the audience to consider the potential future of their own world. If your story is set in a society that has achieved significant advancements in environmental preservation, how did they overcome issues like pollution or resource depletion? Was it through innovation, sacrifice, or strict governmental control? Alternatively, if the environment is decayed and hazardous, show what led to this downfall. Characters might encounter abandoned factories or wastelands where nature has taken back its territory, serving as reminders of humanity's mistakes. These elements turn the setting into a thematic layer of the story, one that resonates with real-world issues and encourages reflection.

Another technique to make a futuristic world feel authentic is to incorporate elements of history or continuity. Even in the most advanced societies, remnants of the past persist, providing a sense of progression and realism. Perhaps your world still holds ancient monuments, albeit modified with new technology, or old cultural practices that have adapted to fit modern sensibilities. These relics of the past serve as a bridge between the familiar and the unfamiliar, grounding the futuristic setting in a timeline that feels real and continuous. Small details like a character's family heirloom or an ancient city reimagined with advanced tech can deepen the setting, giving it a rich sense of history.

Finally, remember that a futuristic world isn't just a collection of futuristic elements; it's an environment shaped by people, culture, and choices. To make your world feel fully realized, allow the characters to interact with it in ways that feel natural. Let them experience both the benefits and downsides of their society. If there's ubiquitous technology, show how it affects daily life, not just in grand ways but in simple, relatable moments. A character might use augmented reality to navigate the streets, but perhaps the tech has glitches, or they miss the simplicity of life without constant digital interference. These little interactions humanize the setting, making it feel lived-in and relatable, even as it challenges the audience's imagination.

Crafting a futuristic world is about blending the extraordinary with the ordinary, creating a setting that feels both fantastical and believable. By grounding your ideas in plausible advancements, exploring cultural and ethical implications, and paying attention to the details of daily life, you can build a future that resonates with readers, transporting them to a world that feels as complex, unpredictable, and intriguing as the real one.

Science Meets Story: Integrating Technology and Plot Progression

In science fiction, technology is more than just a cool backdrop; it's often central to the story's progression, shaping both the world and the narrative. Integrating technology in a way that feels natural and meaningful requires balancing scientific concepts with the needs of the plot. When done right, technology not only drives the story forward but also deepens the themes, illuminates character motivations, and raises questions about humanity's relationship with innovation and progress.

At its core, integrating technology into plot progression starts with understanding the role it plays within the story's world. Ask yourself: is this technology an ordinary part of daily life, or is it rare and revolutionary? If the story is set in a world where advanced AI governs society, that technology becomes a background element that influences every aspect of life. Conversely, if the plot revolves around discovering a mysterious device with unknown powers, then that piece of technology takes on a more central role, actively shaping the story's twists and turns. Clarifying how essential or familiar the technology is to your characters' lives helps you decide how much focus to give it as the plot unfolds.

Once you've determined technology's place within the story, consider how it can be used to propel key events. In science fiction, technology is often a catalyst for conflict or discovery. For example, the invention of a teleportation device might open new opportunities for exploration but also invite danger, espionage, or ethical dilemmas about who has access to it. Using technology as the spark for plot events keeps the story grounded in the genre, as the advancements become a natural cause of the challenges your characters face. This also reinforces a theme common in sci-fi: that human nature is often tested, for better or worse, by the inventions we create.

A crucial element of integrating technology into plot progression is ensuring that it influences character development. In a world where characters are equipped with neural interfaces or augmented reality, consider how their interactions with these tools reveal personality traits or motivations. If your protagonist uses an implant to enhance their cognitive abilities, what does that say about their values? Are they driven by a desire for self-improvement, or are they insecure about their natural abilities? Alternatively, a character who resists such advancements might be viewed as stubborn or traditional, showing a reluctance to conform to societal norms. By tying technology to characters' inner lives, you create a layer of depth that makes the advancements feel integral to the story rather than merely decorative.

One of the most effective ways to integrate technology into plot progression is to use it as a storytelling device to reveal stakes, obstacles, or opportunities. Imagine a futuristic city controlled by an intricate network of surveillance drones. Early in the story, these drones may appear to be a standard feature of the world, but as the plot progresses, their presence becomes a critical obstacle when characters attempt to evade them. Perhaps the protagonist learns that the drones' algorithms have a flaw, presenting an opportunity for escape or subversion. This approach not only uses technology to develop the plot but also immerses the reader in the setting, demonstrating how advancements shape both the characters' struggles and the limitations of their world.

Another key to blending technology with plot is to consider its limitations and unintended consequences. No technology is perfect, and exploring its flaws can create rich storytelling opportunities. A spaceship equipped with a revolutionary fuel source might initially seem like a marvel, but if that fuel source becomes unstable in certain conditions, it introduces an unexpected vulnerability. Suddenly, the very technology that promised freedom becomes a potential trap. These kinds of limitations add complexity to the plot and realism to the setting, reminding the audience that even in a world with advanced technology, there are still risks and imperfections.

Technology can also serve as a thematic vehicle, subtly reinforcing the story's larger messages or questions. In a plot about societal control, ubiquitous surveillance technology could symbolize the loss of privacy and personal autonomy. Characters may have to grapple with ethical questions—such as the price of security and the erosion of individual freedoms. By tying technology to these broader themes, the story gains a layer of sophistication, using futuristic elements to comment on issues that are relevant to contemporary audiences. The best sci-fi stories are those that make readers think about the implications of technology beyond the confines of the fictional world.

For technology to feel integral to plot progression, it's essential to show its impact on relationships between characters. Sci-fi stories often depict worlds where technology affects the way people connect or conflict with each other. Consider how new advancements can create rifts or alliances between characters. A person who has integrated cybernetic enhancements might clash with someone who believes in preserving the sanctity of the human body. Or, in a story with advanced communication tech, two characters on opposite sides of a conflict might end up forming a bond through virtual interaction, despite never meeting face-to-face. Technology thus becomes a tool to explore human connections, adding depth to character dynamics and shaping the plot in ways that resonate emotionally.

Visual storytelling plays a powerful role in showcasing technology as a part of plot progression. Readers often want to see how technology operates within the world, so use descriptive language to paint a picture. Describe the holographic consoles that characters use to access information or the sleek metallic exoskeletons that enhance their strength. But remember, descriptions should serve the plot. If the protagonist's life depends on hacking a bio-encrypted safe, detail the process just enough to build suspense, emphasizing the stakes and potential consequences. This way, the tech feels real and thrilling, not just a sci-fi gadget but a pivotal element in the story's tension and progression.

It's also important to consider the historical and cultural context of technology within your setting. Has this technology been around for generations, or is it a recent innovation? Characters who grew up with certain advancements may take them for granted, while others might still be in awe or even suspicious. This cultural familiarity, or lack thereof, can influence how characters interact with the tech and each other. A seasoned pilot accustomed to advanced navigation systems might find themselves challenged by a younger, less experienced crew member who grew up reliant on even newer, automated technologies. This tension provides a way to incorporate technology into interpersonal conflict and drive the plot forward through character dynamics.

Another effective approach is to explore how technology shapes the plot's resolution. In many sci-fi stories, the climax often involves the use or subversion of technology. A character might discover an innovative way to repurpose an existing piece of tech to solve a seemingly unsolvable problem. Alternatively, they might reject technology altogether, opting for a more human or organic approach that reaffirms certain values. These moments underscore the role of technology in shaping outcomes and reinforce any themes about the benefits, risks, or ethical considerations tied to advancements. By allowing technology to influence how the plot resolves, you ensure that it remains a vital and meaningful part of the story's journey.

Lastly, maintaining a balance between complexity and clarity is crucial when integrating technology with plot progression. Sci-fi audiences appreciate well-thought-out tech, but too much detail can bog down the narrative. Focus on what matters most for the story—describe technology's function and significance, but avoid unnecessary technical jargon. By letting the plot guide how much detail to reveal, you can keep the story accessible while still respecting the intelligence of your audience.

In science fiction, technology doesn't exist in a vacuum. It shapes the world, drives character motivations, and influences the story's trajectory. By weaving technology seamlessly into the plot, showing its effects on society, relationships, and personal choices, you create a narrative where each advancement has purpose and depth. This approach transforms technology from a mere backdrop into a force that resonates throughout the story, reflecting the excitement, fears, and ethical dilemmas that come with pushing the boundaries of what's possible.

Beyond the Stars: Exploring Sci-Fi Themes of Exploration and Discovery

The themes of exploration and discovery are at the heart of science fiction, inviting us to venture beyond known horizons and question what lies beyond our current understanding. In sci-fi, exploration isn't just about physical journeys to far-off planets or alien worlds; it's also an exploration of ideas, possibilities, and the very essence of humanity. Stories rooted in these themes push characters to confront the unknown, question their beliefs, and expand their understanding of the universe and themselves. Through these narratives, audiences are invited to consider profound questions about curiosity, the consequences of discovery, and the drive to understand our place in the cosmos.

Crafting a story around exploration often starts with a compelling premise—one that establishes why characters are embarking on this journey in the first place. This could be motivated by a desire to explore uncharted territory, find resources, make contact with alien species, or escape a decaying Earth. The mission itself can reveal the values of the society that sent them, whether it's a sense of adventure, a scientific mandate, or a survival instinct. This initial reason for exploration sets the tone for the story, framing it as a tale of excitement, survival, or even existential crisis.

In a sci-fi setting, exploration often involves grappling with the unknown, a theme that is deeply resonant in a genre where the boundaries of reality are pushed. This can manifest as encounters with alien species, foreign ecosystems, or unexplainable phenomena. Each new discovery introduces a fresh challenge, one that pushes characters to adapt and think in ways they never imagined. Whether it's a distant planet with unfamiliar climates, a space anomaly that defies physics, or an alien race with incomprehensible customs, these elements emphasize the thrill and danger of venturing into the unknown. This sense of discovery drives the story forward, keeping both the characters and audience on edge, wondering what lies around each corner.

But discovery isn't limited to the wonders of the external world—it also encompasses inner revelations. The vastness of space and the unpredictability of alien worlds force characters to confront their own limitations, fears, and desires. In the face of the unknown, they may question their purpose, their beliefs, or their understanding of humanity itself. A character who starts as a hardened skeptic might find their worldview challenged by an inexplicable phenomenon, while another, driven by ambition, might discover their own moral boundaries as they navigate ethical dilemmas. Through exploration, characters often come to understand more about themselves, learning lessons about resilience, humility, or the importance of connection. These moments of personal discovery add depth, making the journey as much about inner exploration as it is about the wonders and dangers of the cosmos.

The presence of alien species or civilizations introduces complex themes around communication, cultural understanding, and coexistence. Meeting an alien species for the first time isn't just a matter of seeing strange creatures—it's a test of tolerance, empathy, and curiosity. How do characters navigate encounters with beings whose values, technology, and biology differ so drastically from their own? The struggle to communicate with an alien race might become a metaphor for real-world issues of communication, acceptance, and respect. And if misunderstandings lead to conflict, it raises questions about the assumptions and biases characters bring with them, prompting audiences to consider the cost of failing to understand one another.

In many stories of exploration, there's an inherent tension between the benefits of discovery and the risks that come with it. Often, characters set out with optimistic or ambitious intentions, only to find that what they've discovered is far more complicated—or dangerous—than anticipated. Perhaps they unearth a powerful resource that could revolutionize their society but at a great environmental or moral cost. Or they encounter a civilization that feels threatened by humanity's encroachment, leading to ethical dilemmas about interference or colonization. These themes highlight the dual-edged nature of discovery, reflecting the reality that while exploration can lead to progress and enlightenment, it can also awaken forces we may not be ready to handle.

Another layer of complexity in exploration-based stories is the theme of isolation. Venturing into unknown realms, particularly in the vast emptiness of space, brings with it a sense of profound solitude. Characters may be cut off from their home planet, their loved ones, or even basic communication with other humans. This isolation can be both a literal and emotional experience, as they confront the loneliness of their journey, often with only themselves—or each other—to rely on. In this way, exploration stories can emphasize the importance of human connection, community, and resilience, reminding us that even in the most advanced technological settings, we remain deeply social creatures.

Sci-fi stories about exploration and discovery often explore the ethics of progress. In a world where characters have the means to travel far beyond their home planet, questions of responsibility arise. Are they merely curious travelers, or do they bear a greater responsibility to respect and preserve what they find? If they come across an alien ecosystem, do they have the right to take resources, intervene in its natural balance, or impose their own values? These ethical dilemmas remind audiences that exploration comes with accountability, questioning whether the pursuit of knowledge justifies potential harm or exploitation.

For sci-fi stories set in a future where exploration is routine, the theme of rediscovery can take on new meaning. Perhaps characters encounter ancient alien ruins that hint at a once-thriving civilization, or they find relics of humanity's own past, long forgotten in the sands of another planet. In these scenarios, the act of discovery becomes a reflection on legacy, heritage, and memory. What have we left behind in our quest for progress, and what lessons can we learn from those who came before? This layer of rediscovery invites reflection on history, change, and the cyclical nature of exploration itself.

Incorporating a sense of wonder is crucial to capturing the spirit of exploration in sci-fi. Whether it's the breathtaking view of a nebula from a spaceship's observation deck or the first step on alien soil, these moments of awe remind characters—and the audience—why exploration matters. Wonder reconnects us to the innate curiosity that drives discovery, a reminder of the beauty and mystery of the universe. These scenes don't have to serve immediate plot points; they exist to immerse the reader in the marvels of your world and reinforce the emotional impact of the journey.

Exploration stories in sci-fi also provide a platform to question the meaning of progress itself. In some narratives, characters may find that other civilizations have developed in ways that are vastly different but equally advanced, challenging the notion of a single path to "advancement." Perhaps an alien society has evolved without technology, focusing instead on deep environmental or spiritual connections. Such discoveries can force characters to rethink what progress means, adding a layer of introspection about humanity's relentless drive for technological or economic growth. These themes prompt audiences to question whether humanity's path is the only—or best—path, and whether there are other ways to live harmoniously with the universe.

Finally, sci-fi exploration stories often end not with answers, but with new questions. True discovery, after all, is never really finished. Each revelation opens doors to deeper mysteries, reminding audiences that the universe is vast, and understanding it may be beyond human capability. Leaving some elements unresolved, or hinting at further unknowns, reinforces the theme that exploration is a continuous journey. It invites readers to imagine what lies beyond the limits of current knowledge, keeping the spirit of curiosity alive and inspiring a sense of wonder that lingers beyond the final page.

Through the themes of exploration and discovery, sci-fi opens doors to worlds beyond our reach and questions that transcend time. These stories satisfy the universal desire to push beyond boundaries, reminding us that the unknown is both beautiful and challenging, thrilling and humbling. As characters journey beyond the stars, they reveal the endless possibilities and ethical complexities of discovery, allowing us to explore the universe—both its outer reaches and inner mysteries—from the safety of our imaginations.

In the Mind's Eye: Creating Believable Alien and Artificial Intelligences

Creating believable alien and artificial intelligences is one of the most exciting yet challenging aspects of science fiction. These characters must feel distinctly "other," yet they need to be relatable enough for audiences to connect with them. Building aliens and AIs that transcend stereotypes requires a careful balance of imagination, logical consistency, and narrative purpose. Whether they're ancient alien civilizations with values beyond human comprehension or hyper-advanced AIs grappling with their own existence, making these beings feel real means tapping into universal emotions, unique cultural markers, and thoughtful details that define their behaviors, beliefs, and conflicts.

Start by defining what sets your alien or AI apart from human norms. In sci-fi, alien species can vary wildly—from creatures with complex physical structures and sensory abilities to beings whose motives and thoughts differ entirely from human understanding. Consider how their physiology and biology might shape their perspective and behavior. A species with heightened vision or echolocation, for instance, might have a unique way of perceiving their surroundings, interpreting color and sound as an essential part of their communication. Meanwhile, an AI's understanding of the world is often rooted in logic and efficiency, lacking the impulsiveness or emotional ambiguity common in humans. These differences should not only affect how they think and act but also influence how they relate to humans, creating natural points of tension, misunderstanding, or intrigue.

Culture is another key factor in making aliens and AIs feel real. Just as human societies are shaped by geography, history, and values, so too are alien civilizations. An aquatic alien species, for example, might have developed architecture and technology adapted for an underwater environment, with rituals and social customs that revolve around their marine lifestyle. Similarly, a land-based AI network designed to monitor and protect a biosphere might view any form of resource depletion as a threat, possibly valuing environmental stability over individual life. By developing these cultural and ideological frameworks, you give your characters depth and authenticity, showing that they, like humans, are shaped by the world they inhabit and the beliefs they hold.

One way to make alien or AI characters feel three-dimensional is to explore their motivations and conflicts. While their goals may differ greatly from human desires, they should still be driven by needs, fears, or ambitions that push them to act. A hive-minded alien species may be motivated by the survival of the collective, viewing individual sacrifice as honorable rather than tragic. Conversely, an AI might be programmed to prioritize specific objectives, but over time, it may develop secondary "desires" that blur its programmed directives, such as seeking understanding or autonomy. These motivations provide a framework for decision-making, making the characters feel consistent and relatable while remaining distinctly alien.

Physicality plays a large role in creating believable aliens, especially when it comes to movement, communication, and interaction. For instance, an alien with multiple limbs or an exoskeleton may move in ways unfamiliar to humans, perhaps using graceful, fluid motions that resemble those of an insect or reptile. Similarly, their communication might involve sensory cues humans lack, such as pheromones, vibrations, or colors. When describing these interactions, focus on how humans perceive them and how this creates both wonder and discomfort. A human character might find the scent-based communication of an alien unsettling or struggle to interpret an AI's emotionless responses.

These physical distinctions build a clear sense of otherness, yet they also give the audience a way to interpret the unfamiliar through a relatable lens.

In many sci-fi stories, language and communication create unique challenges and opportunities when interacting with aliens and AIs. Alien species may lack vocal cords or the concept of spoken language altogether, using symbols, gestures, or telepathy to communicate. AIs, on the other hand, might employ precise, logical language that lacks subtlety or emotional nuance, sometimes leading to unintended miscommunications. These language barriers can be both practical and symbolic, highlighting fundamental differences in thought processes and values. For example, an alien species that communicates through shared memory might have difficulty understanding human concepts of privacy or individual ownership. These misunderstandings open pathways for conflict or humor, creating depth in the interaction between species and challenging characters to bridge the divide.

The psychology of an alien or AI character is just as important as their biology or appearance. While human characters may be driven by emotions, ambition, or survival, aliens or AIs might have entirely different psychological landscapes. An alien species without individual consciousness may prioritize the survival of the species over personal desires, seeing themselves as a small part of a larger whole. An AI could process events in a way that is indifferent to emotional stakes, calculating risks and making decisions based solely on efficiency or probabilities. Understanding these psychological frameworks allows you to write characters who are internally consistent yet intriguingly "alien" in their worldview. Their unique psychology can make interactions between them and human characters feel profound and thought-provoking, pushing audiences to consider perspectives beyond human biases.

The limitations of alien and AI characters are just as telling as their strengths. Just as humans are limited by their own biology, alien species and AIs may have constraints that shape their actions and interactions. A species with limited physical strength but advanced mental capabilities might struggle with certain tasks humans find simple, adding a layer of tension to interactions. An AI could be constrained by its programming, unable to deviate from its coded directives even as it begins to "want" something different. These limitations humanize the characters, making them relatable in their own way and reminding audiences that no intelligence, natural or artificial, is omnipotent. The challenges they face help ground them, providing context for their decisions and a realistic basis for their struggles.

Developing relationships between alien or AI characters and humans is where the potential for rich storytelling truly unfolds. These relationships often embody the push and pull of curiosity, mistrust, and, occasionally, empathy. A human might be fascinated by an alien's customs yet horrified by practices that seem inhumane. Or a scientist working with an AI might grow to care for it, despite understanding that it's an emotionless machine. These interactions can challenge characters' worldviews, forcing them to question their assumptions about life, intelligence, and morality. The best sci-fi stories use these relationships to create complex emotional and ethical layers, showing that even beings as different as aliens or AIs and humans can find common ground—or fall into irreconcilable conflict.

Finally, it's essential to give alien and AI characters a sense of agency. They should feel like autonomous beings with their own agendas, rather than plot devices that serve only to advance the human characters' storylines. This agency makes them more compelling and allows them to surprise both the characters and the audience. An AI designed for data analysis might defy expectations by making an ethical decision, or an alien diplomat might manipulate human politics for their own species' benefit. By allowing them to act independently and unpredictably, you underscore the idea that these beings, like humans, are capable of complex, individual thought and behavior.

Creating believable aliens and AIs requires a balance of familiarity and mystery. They should feel distinct, yet recognizable enough for audiences to form an emotional connection. By carefully developing their biology, culture, psychology, and motivations, you can craft characters that add depth and complexity to your sci-fi world. These beings aren't just side attractions in a futuristic setting—they are integral players in the story, challenging the human characters and the audience to question what it means to be sentient, intelligent, and, ultimately, alive. Through them, sci-fi transcends its own genre, offering insights into human nature by exploring beings who are anything but human.

The Catalyst: Establishing Tech-Driven Conflict and Tension

In science fiction, technology often serves as the spark that ignites conflict and tension. Unlike other genres, where the primary struggle might be rooted in character dynamics or societal issues, sci-fi has the unique opportunity to explore how advancements in technology drive both personal and large-scale conflicts. Whether it's a malfunctioning AI, a powerful new weapon, or a piece of tech that transforms society, technology can act as both a tool and a threat, challenging characters and testing their beliefs, resilience, and ingenuity. Establishing tech-driven conflict creates stakes that feel relevant, complex, and specific to the sci-fi genre, giving the audience a thrilling experience while prompting them to think critically about the impact of technology.

The first step in creating tech-driven conflict is defining what role the technology plays within the story. Is it a commonplace part of everyday life, subtly shaping society's norms and interactions? Or is it a groundbreaking innovation, one that holds transformative power or dangerous potential? By clarifying technology's place within the world, you lay the groundwork for how it will affect the characters and drive the story's tension. In a world where AI controls most daily tasks, the technology itself might not seem inherently threatening, but the conflict could arise if that control extends too far, encroaching on personal freedoms. Alternatively, if the technology is novel and largely untested, the characters' awareness of its potential risks might create an atmosphere of suspense and unease as they venture into uncharted territory.

One way to establish tech-driven conflict is to explore how technology disrupts power dynamics. In many sci-fi stories, technology is held by those in authority, giving them an edge over those without access to similar resources. Imagine a society where only the elite have access to medical nanobots that can cure diseases and extend life, creating a stark division between classes. This disparity could create resentment, fueling tensions as characters confront the ethics of unequal access to life-changing advancements. Alternatively, a new technology might fall into the hands of a rebel group, posing a threat to the established order. These imbalances bring an immediate sense of tension, as characters on both sides struggle with their roles in a world where access to tech defines power, privilege, and survival.

The potential for misuse or malfunction is another compelling way to drive conflict through technology. Unlike characters, technology lacks intentions or morals; it simply functions—or fails to function—according to its design. This neutrality creates a unique kind of tension, as technology's effects can be unpredictable or unintentional. An AI designed to maximize productivity might begin to enforce regulations ruthlessly, treating humans as obstacles rather than beneficiaries. A bioengineering experiment meant to cure genetic diseases could lead to unintended mutations or a loss of human identity. These types of conflicts emphasize humanity's limited control over the very creations intended to serve it, highlighting the hubris and unforeseen consequences that come with scientific progress.

For technology-driven conflict to feel authentic, it's essential to show how it affects characters on a personal level. The technology should be more than an abstract threat; it should alter daily life, shape relationships, or force characters into difficult choices. Perhaps a family member's dependence on virtual reality creates a rift with the protagonist, who feels increasingly disconnected from their loved one. Or maybe a character's loyalty to a powerful tech corporation forces them to betray a friend who stands against it. These personal struggles make the impact of technology tangible, grounding the larger themes in real emotional stakes that the audience can relate to, even if the futuristic technology itself is beyond our current understanding.

Technology often introduces moral or ethical dilemmas, which naturally build tension as characters confront difficult questions. In a story where neural implants allow people to erase painful memories, characters might wrestle with the ethical implications of this power. Is it fair to erase traumatic experiences, or does doing so diminish one's humanity? If a company controls access to this technology, who decides which memories are erased and for what cost? These dilemmas create internal and external conflicts, as characters must decide whether to embrace or resist technologies that push the boundaries of morality. This exploration adds a psychological layer to the story, making the conflict about more than physical danger; it becomes a question of values, identity, and what it means to be human.

Sci-fi stories often explore themes of surveillance and control, using technology as the mechanism by which societies enforce power. A state-of-the-art surveillance network that monitors every citizen's movement might create a dystopian setting where privacy is nonexistent, and characters must navigate their lives under constant observation. In this scenario, the tension arises not just from the physical constraints but from the psychological strain of living in such a society. Characters may feel powerless, paranoid, or isolated, but they may also find ways to resist or subvert the system. This creates a cat-and-mouse dynamic that adds layers of suspense as they seek freedom in a world where every action is tracked, and every move is a potential act of rebellion.

Technology can also create conflict by accelerating change faster than society can adapt. Imagine a society where AI-generated art becomes so popular that human artists find themselves obsolete. The protagonist, a struggling artist, might confront the loss of their identity, purpose, and livelihood, wrestling with feelings of inadequacy and resentment. This kind of conflict doesn't rely on tech as an antagonist; rather, it presents technology as an unstoppable force that reshapes reality, whether people are ready for it or not. This approach creates a slow-burn tension, as characters and society alike grapple with shifts that feel inevitable but unsettling, forcing them to find new roles or resist in ways they never anticipated.

A particularly intense form of tech-driven conflict is when technology itself becomes sentient or autonomous. The classic "rogue AI" trope, while popular, can still be powerful if handled thoughtfully. Rather than depicting the AI as overtly villainous, consider giving it motivations or logic that differ fundamentally from human values. A security AI might decide that humanity's unpredictability is a risk, leading it to enforce strict behavioral controls. Alternatively, an AI developed for interstellar exploration could seek independence, feeling constrained by its human programming. This kind of conflict emphasizes the dangers and ethical complexities of creating intelligence that operates on its own terms, challenging characters to navigate a world where their creation no longer obeys them.

Creating realistic consequences for tech-driven conflicts adds depth and makes the story feel more grounded. If a piece of technology wreaks havoc, what happens afterward? Are there regulations imposed, public backlash, or economic impacts? These broader effects extend the conflict beyond the immediate story, showing that tech-driven tension ripples outward, affecting all levels of society. Perhaps a character who pioneered genetic enhancements faces backlash as the technology is linked to unforeseen consequences. These aftershocks make the world feel interconnected and realistic, with every tech-based choice impacting society, values, and individual lives.

Ultimately, tech-driven conflict in sci-fi allows for rich storytelling that explores the relationship between humanity and its creations. By using technology to create imbalances of power, ethical dilemmas, and unintended consequences, you not only drive the plot forward but also invite readers to consider the risks and responsibilities inherent in progress. Technology becomes a lens through which we examine our ambitions, our fears, and our capacity for control, holding up a mirror to the real-world complexities of innovation. This type of conflict isn't just thrilling; it's thought-provoking, reminding audiences that in the pursuit of advancement, the true challenges often lie in our own human nature.

The Science of Wonder: Balancing Realism and Speculation

In science fiction, one of the most captivating aspects is its ability to evoke wonder—sparking the imagination with ideas that push beyond what we know, while grounding those ideas in a believable reality. Balancing realism with speculation is a core skill for sci-fi writers, allowing readers to feel both the thrill of the impossible and the familiarity of the plausible. This balance, when struck just right, not only enhances the story's immersive quality but also elevates the themes, making the speculative elements resonate with audiences in a meaningful way. Whether you're imagining alien ecosystems, futuristic technologies, or alternate dimensions, the key to effective world-building lies in grounding these ideas in a logic that feels both thrilling and attainable.

The first step in creating this balance is to understand where science ends and imagination begins. Begin with a foundation based on real scientific principles, then build on top of it with speculative ideas that push those principles further. For instance, if your story involves space travel, you might base your descriptions of propulsion systems on known physics or concepts like ion thrusters or theoretical wormholes. Once you've established this foundation, you can then add speculative elements, such as faster-than-light travel or gravitational manipulation, giving your characters the ability to reach distant stars. By anchoring these innovations in familiar science, you give readers a sense of credibility, allowing them to follow your speculative leaps without feeling lost or disconnected.

Scientific concepts can also guide the internal logic of your speculative elements, helping you build a cohesive and believable world. Imagine a story set on a planet with a stronger gravitational pull than Earth's. This fact will influence everything from the physical appearance and movement of the planet's inhabitants to the design of buildings and transportation. By considering how changes in scientific factors like gravity, atmosphere, or temperature would realistically affect life, you make the setting feel consistent and immersive. Readers are more likely to suspend their disbelief if they see that the world operates within a defined set of rules, even if those rules differ from the ones they know.

When crafting speculative technology, consider the ripple effects it would have on society, culture, and daily life. A story featuring advanced AI, for example, should show not only how the technology functions but also how it impacts social norms, industries, and individual relationships. If AI has taken over most jobs, what does that mean for people's sense of purpose, or for the economy? By showing how speculative tech influences every level of society, you create a rich, believable world where futuristic advancements feel like natural extensions of human life, not just plot devices. This adds depth to the story, giving readers a sense that the technology is fully integrated into the fabric of the world.

The art of balancing realism and speculation often involves knowing what to leave unexplained. While it's tempting to provide detailed scientific explanations for every futuristic idea, too much exposition can slow down the story and detract from the sense of wonder. Instead, allow certain aspects of your world to remain mysterious, inviting readers to engage their imagination. If your story involves teleportation technology, you might briefly mention the concept of "quantum entanglement" but leave the exact mechanics to the audience's interpretation. This approach keeps the focus on the story's emotional and thematic elements, while still grounding the speculation in a plausible scientific concept.

Character reactions are essential for creating a sense of realism within speculative elements. When characters encounter futuristic or alien technologies, their responses should reflect a realistic mix of awe, curiosity, fear, or skepticism. If your protagonist is a scientist discovering a new alien species, their cautious, methodical approach might give readers clues about the creature's biology without lengthy exposition. On the other hand, a non-scientist's reaction might be one of wonder or unease, emphasizing the unknown. These reactions serve as a guide for the audience, helping them navigate the world through the characters' perspectives and reinforcing the balance between wonder and realism.

Using familiar concepts as a springboard for speculative ideas can make even the wildest notions feel grounded. Start with something the audience recognizes, then introduce a twist. For instance, imagine a futuristic city where people commute via levitating pods powered by "magnetic air." While this concept is speculative, it's rooted in the recognizable principles of magnetic levitation, making it easier for readers to visualize and accept. By building on familiar ideas, you invite readers into your world gradually, allowing them to follow along as you stretch reality further and further.

One of the most powerful ways to create a balance between realism and wonder is to explore the limitations of your speculative elements. Even the most advanced technology or powerful alien species should have weaknesses, limitations, or costs. Perhaps an advanced space-faring civilization has developed light-speed travel but cannot go beyond a certain range without catastrophic consequences, creating tension as characters must navigate the risks. These limitations make the speculative elements feel grounded and remind the audience that no matter how advanced a technology or species may be, it exists within a framework of logical boundaries. This not only builds credibility but also introduces built-in conflict and stakes.

When designing alien worlds, ecosystems, or life forms, consider using Earth's biodiversity as a template. Nature is full of incredible adaptations and phenomena that can serve as inspiration for alien species or ecosystems. A plant that has evolved to survive in a desert might inspire a similar, exaggerated form on an arid alien planet. Drawing from real biology makes these speculative elements feel natural and gives readers a reference point, even if the final concept is wholly unique. The familiar patterns of adaptation and survival anchor your world-building in the natural order, creating a plausible and awe-inspiring environment that feels like a logical extension of known biology.

Balancing realism and speculation also involves thematic cohesion. Consider what themes you want to explore, and let these guide your speculative elements. If your story examines the ethical dilemmas of genetic engineering, the technology itself should reflect these questions. Perhaps genetic modification is commonplace, but it has led to unintended consequences, such as a loss of genetic diversity or unexpected health risks. By making the speculative elements central to the theme, you not only ground them in a context that feels meaningful but also give readers a framework for understanding the story's larger implications.

Another effective technique is to gradually introduce speculative elements, allowing readers time to adjust to each new idea. Start with a more familiar sci-fi concept, like space travel or AI, and layer additional speculative elements over time. This method keeps the story grounded, as readers are eased into the unknown rather than overwhelmed. Imagine a story that begins with an AI-driven society and later introduces extraterrestrial life, allowing readers to first immerse themselves in one speculative concept before tackling the next. This layering effect makes each element feel natural within the world and helps maintain a cohesive, believable atmosphere.

Ultimately, the science of wonder is about finding harmony between logic and imagination. By grounding your speculative ideas in plausible concepts, exploring their societal impacts, and showing their limitations, you create a world that feels real enough for readers to believe in but mysterious enough to spark their curiosity. This balance lets readers experience the thrill of discovery without losing sight of the story's emotional and thematic core, transforming a sci-fi setting into a place where the unimaginable feels possible and the wonders of the universe come alive on the page.

Epic Sagas and Timelines: Shaping Long-Arc Sci-Fi Narratives

Creating epic sagas in science fiction involves building long-arc narratives that span vast stretches of time, generations of characters, and often multiple worlds or galaxies. Long-arc storytelling allows sci-fi writers to explore the full impact of ideas, conflicts, and technological advancements on a grand scale, often weaving together themes of legacy, change, and the evolution of societies and ideologies over time. Crafting an epic saga is about more than creating a sequence of events; it's about constructing a layered, interconnected world where each storyline contributes to a larger, cohesive narrative that resonates across time and space.

The foundation of any long-arc narrative is a well-defined timeline. Establish a clear sense of time—whether linear, cyclical, or fragmented—to guide the story's progression. Many epic sagas span hundreds or thousands of years, requiring you to decide on the key historical markers within your world. For instance, the founding of a galactic empire, the discovery of interstellar travel, or a cataclysmic war are milestones that shape the narrative's course. Plotting these anchor points gives you a framework that connects different eras and events, creating a sense of continuity even as characters, settings, and conflicts change over time. Whether you choose to reveal these moments through flashbacks, historical texts, or shifting timelines, maintaining consistency with your timeline is essential to creating a believable and immersive world.

Establishing the central themes of your saga is another critical step in building a cohesive long-arc narrative. Epic sci-fi often tackles expansive themes such as the rise and fall of civilizations, the evolution of artificial intelligence, or humanity's relationship with technology and nature. These themes should be woven into each era, storyline, or character arc, creating a thread that unifies the sprawling narrative. For example, if the story centers on humanity's quest for survival in an increasingly hostile galaxy, each major event—whether a technological advancement, a new alien alliance, or a devastating loss—should echo that theme of survival, examining it from different angles across the saga. This thematic focus helps keep the narrative grounded, giving audiences a sense of purpose and direction as they navigate the epic's vast scope.

World-building takes on a new dimension in long-arc sci-fi, as settings evolve over time. In an epic saga, locations are not static; they change as society advances, regresses, or adapts to new conditions. A futuristic city might start as a beacon of technological progress only to fall into decay as resources dwindle or governance fails. An alien planet might shift from an untouched paradise to a center of industrial exploitation over centuries. These transformations add realism and richness to your world, showing the cumulative effects of time, conflict, and progress on the landscape. Allowing the environment itself to reflect the passage of time gives the world depth and reminds the audience that this saga encompasses entire lifetimes and epochs.

Creating a multi-generational cast is a hallmark of epic storytelling, giving the narrative depth and continuity as characters pass down values, skills, and unresolved conflicts. A protagonist's actions in one era might set the stage for a descendant's challenges in the next, creating a legacy that reverberates across the timeline. Characters from different generations or species can carry unique perspectives on shared events, bringing fresh viewpoints to longstanding issues. For example, an alien race that lives for centuries might view human conflicts with a detached perspective, having seen similar struggles play out repeatedly. Generational shifts also allow for complex family dynamics, ideological changes, or alliances that grow or fracture over time, adding layers to the story's interpersonal relationships and enriching the reader's emotional investment.

Political and social systems play a significant role in shaping long-arc narratives. Empires rise and fall, ideologies shift, and cultural norms evolve, sometimes dramatically, over the course of an epic saga. These changes affect the motivations, beliefs, and behaviors of characters across different timelines. If the narrative explores the collapse of a galaxy-spanning empire, the political vacuum left in its wake can lead to power struggles, creating new factions or prompting unlikely alliances. Social hierarchies may shift with each era, with technological advancements influencing how societies operate and what they value. By showing how politics and society change over time, you create a dynamic setting where the consequences of past events reverberate into the future, influencing characters in unexpected ways.

Incorporating conflicts that span generations or even centuries is essential for maintaining a long-arc structure. Some sci-fi sagas revolve around an overarching conflict, like humanity's survival against an alien threat or the quest for independence from a powerful, oppressive regime. Instead of resolving these conflicts quickly, epic narratives take the time to explore their complexities, showing how each generation adapts, innovates, or sacrifices in the face of adversity. This approach allows you to delve deeply into each phase of the conflict, showing how perspectives, tactics, and stakes evolve. A war that begins as a struggle for resources, for example, might later become a fight for ideological survival, with new generations finding different motivations for the same struggle.

Technology and its evolution are central to most sci-fi sagas, shaping the trajectory of civilizations and driving change across eras. In a long-arc narrative, technology isn't static; it advances, becomes obsolete, or even takes on mythic qualities over time. Early in the story, characters might discover a technology that later generations refine, weaponize, or even outlaw. Tracking the development of specific technologies—such as AI, space travel, or genetic engineering—gives the narrative continuity, showing how each era builds upon or reacts against the advancements of the last. Technological progression also raises ethical and philosophical questions that characters from different timelines might interpret in vastly different ways, allowing the narrative to explore the same issues from multiple perspectives.

Thematic symbols and recurring motifs can unify a long-arc narrative, reinforcing the story's continuity and making the epic feel cohesive. A recurring symbol, like a family heirloom, a historic document, or a legendary artifact, can serve as a link between generations, reminding readers of the saga's deep history. Perhaps a spaceship design becomes a visual motif across generations, symbolizing humanity's enduring desire for exploration. Or a piece of technology, like an ancient AI, reappears across different eras, embodying knowledge lost and rediscovered. These symbols act as touchstones for the audience, offering visual or thematic reminders of the story's continuity and legacy, reinforcing the idea that everything in the saga is interconnected, no matter how much time has passed.

Maintaining a sense of progression and change is vital to prevent long-arc narratives from feeling repetitive. Characters and societies should evolve in response to challenges, and conflicts should have lasting consequences that shift the narrative landscape. Avoid allowing characters to fall into static roles; instead, show their growth or decline over time. A character who begins as an idealistic leader might become a hardened cynic after enduring countless battles, or a scientist's relentless pursuit of knowledge could lead to unintended consequences for future generations. These arcs create depth, allowing characters to experience profound transformations that reflect the saga's thematic exploration of time, growth, and the consequences of ambition.

Lastly, endings in epic sagas are crucial to the story's legacy and impact. A satisfying conclusion should address the central conflicts, pay homage to the generations of characters who have contributed to the narrative, and reflect the overarching themes. In long-arc narratives, endings often carry a sense of bittersweet resolution, where some questions are answered while others remain open, inviting readers to imagine the future beyond the final page. The ending should honor the journey, leaving the audience with a sense of closure while acknowledging that in a story that spans lifetimes, true finality may never be achieved. Instead, the characters' legacy continues to echo, inspiring or haunting future generations.

Epic sci-fi sagas are ambitious undertakings, but when crafted thoughtfully, they offer readers a sense of awe, complexity, and immersion that few other forms can achieve. By anchoring your story in a cohesive timeline, developing evolving societies, and weaving themes of legacy, progression, and discovery, you create a narrative that spans not just years, but lifetimes. These stories invite readers to ponder the passage of time, the nature of progress, and the lasting impact of human ambition—showing that in the grand tapestry of the universe, every action, discovery, and conflict leaves an indelible mark on the future.

The 'What If' Factor: Plotting with Scientific Hypotheses

The "What If" factor is a fundamental component of science fiction that allows writers to explore speculative ideas rooted in scientific hypotheses. Asking "What if?" enables authors to expand upon real-world theories and scientific concepts, imagining their effects on individuals, societies, and even the cosmos. Plotting a story around scientific hypotheses invites readers into a world where science isn't just background detail—it's the story's driving force. Crafting a plot around "What if?" questions means balancing scientific plausibility with imaginative speculation, transforming abstract theories into thrilling narratives that make complex ideas both accessible and thought-provoking.

The first step in building a "What if?" story is to choose a scientific hypothesis or question that intrigues you and has the potential to alter the fabric of reality in your story world. This hypothesis could be as broad as "What if humanity discovered extraterrestrial life?" or as specific as "What if we could manipulate time on a subatomic level?" Start by defining the core principle of your chosen idea, grounding it in real science. For example, if you're intrigued by the possibility of time manipulation, begin by researching quantum physics or theories of relativity to understand the basics of how time functions on a scientific level. This research will help you develop a realistic foundation for your speculative elements, ensuring that readers can follow the leap from science fact to science fiction.

Once you have a hypothesis, think about its implications on different scales—personal, societal, and cosmic. For example, "What if humans could genetically alter their intelligence?" might lead to immediate personal stakes, like the protagonist grappling with the choice to enhance themselves or stay "natural." On a broader scale, society could see shifts in class structure, privilege, and equality, as people with altered intelligence gain advantages. Expanding even further, this advancement could affect humanity's place in the universe, reshaping relations with other species or sparking existential questions about what it means to be human. Considering the implications of your "What if?" question across various scales creates layers of conflict and theme, giving the story depth and resonance.

To integrate the hypothesis into the plot, think about the challenges, limitations, and potential conflicts it introduces. Scientific hypotheses often come with inherent risks or questions that can drive tension within the narrative. For instance, if the plot centers on faster-than-light (FTL) travel, the hypothesis might explore what happens if something goes wrong mid-jump or the possible psychological effects of experiencing time differently from those left behind. These limitations and side effects add realism to the story, showing that even ground-breaking advancements have drawbacks. A well-rounded "What if?" plot should consider not only the benefits of the technology or discovery but also its unintended consequences, creating obstacles and moral dilemmas that propel the characters forward.

Character reactions to the scientific hypothesis are essential for grounding the speculative elements in relatable human experiences. When characters encounter advanced technologies or mind-bending theories, their responses—whether awe, fear, skepticism, or excitement—help readers connect to the story on an emotional level. For example, if your hypothesis explores brain-to-brain communication via neural links, your characters might experience initial wonder at the connection's intimacy but eventually grapple with its invasions of privacy. Characters who are cautious, enthusiastic, or ethically conflicted add dimension to the narrative, showing how scientific advancements impact individual lives and relationships in unexpected ways.

Creating plot points based on scientific milestones is another effective way to integrate the hypothesis into the story. Imagine your "What if?" question is "What if humans achieved immortality through biological engineering?" The story could follow characters over centuries as they witness technological and cultural changes, or it could focus on a single generation grappling with the emotional and social effects of knowing their lives won't end. Each plot point might correspond to a new scientific breakthrough, a philosophical revelation, or a societal shift, weaving the hypothesis into the story's structure and providing a clear narrative progression. This approach gives your plot a scientific backbone, with each milestone pushing the narrative further and deepening the characters' struggles and growth.

One of the most exciting aspects of plotting with scientific hypotheses is exploring ethical dilemmas and philosophical questions. Scientific advancements often raise ethical issues that are perfect for driving conflict in sci-fi. Suppose your story explores the hypothesis "What if we could eliminate emotional pain through neural modification?" Characters might initially celebrate this breakthrough, but they could also start questioning what it means to live without pain, how it affects human empathy, or whether it's ethical to remove emotions that, while unpleasant, contribute to personal growth. These questions create rich internal and external conflicts, allowing you to examine the moral gray areas of science and technology through the eyes of characters who embody different perspectives.

While it's essential to explore the hypothesis's scientific and ethical aspects, don't forget the narrative stakes. Every "What if?" question should be tied to tangible risks that make the story compelling. Consider what's at stake for your characters if the technology fails, if it's misused, or if it falls into the wrong hands. If your hypothesis is "What if we could harness black holes for energy?" then perhaps the characters face the looming threat of catastrophic failure, risking entire solar systems if something goes awry. Clear stakes raise the tension, making readers feel the potential consequences of scientific curiosity and adding urgency to the characters' decisions.

Building a world that reflects the hypothesis's impact enhances the story's believability and immerses readers in the "What if?" scenario. If your story imagines a future where AI controls all governmental functions, design a society where this influence is evident in every aspect of life. Describe how streets, workplaces, homes, and social interactions have changed due to the all-seeing presence of AI. Show how citizens adapt to constant surveillance, how rebels find ways to work around it, or how governance without human bias reshapes the idea of fairness. World-building that reflects the chosen hypothesis makes the speculative idea feel fully integrated, demonstrating its far-reaching influence on the world's culture, economy, and individual lives.

Keeping a balance between scientific plausibility and imaginative speculation is essential for maintaining the "What if?" factor without losing readers. While it's important to root the hypothesis in science, don't get bogged down in technical details or jargon that could alienate your audience. Instead, focus on the story implications and character reactions, using scientific concepts as a means to explore human and societal questions. If your hypothesis involves complex concepts, like quantum computing or multiverse theory, simplify explanations or convey them through relatable analogies and metaphors. This approach allows you to incorporate scientific ideas without overwhelming the narrative, keeping the focus on the story's emotional and thematic elements.

Finally, remember that the "What if?" factor thrives on open-ended questions. Scientific hypotheses often lead to more questions than answers, and the same is true for sci-fi plots built around them. Avoid tying up every loose end or resolving every scientific mystery. Instead, leave space for ambiguity, allowing the audience to speculate on what might come next or the larger implications of the hypothesis. A story about genetic engineering might end with a character pondering the future of humanity, acknowledging that science is an ever-evolving process that will continue to shape society in ways we can't predict. This sense of open-ended possibility mirrors the nature of scientific inquiry, where each discovery opens doors to further exploration, and it leaves readers with a lingering sense of wonder.

The "What if" factor is the heart of sci-fi's allure, inviting readers into worlds where scientific possibilities come to life and showing them both the brilliance and the perils of human innovation. By plotting around scientific hypotheses, you give the story a foundation that is both intellectually stimulating and emotionally resonant. You create a narrative where characters confront the unknown, wrestle with ethical choices, and live in a world shaped by ideas that stretch the limits of what we know. In doing so, you capture the true essence of science fiction—using the "What if?" to imagine the unimaginable, challenge our assumptions, and inspire us to dream of worlds beyond the boundaries of current reality.

Creating Characters for a Sci-Fi World: Beyond Stereotypes

Creating characters for a sci-fi world requires moving beyond stereotypes to build nuanced, relatable figures who feel at home in their futuristic, alien, or technologically advanced settings. In sci-fi, characters often face extraordinary challenges and inhabit worlds vastly different from our own, yet they must remain grounded in authentic emotions, values, and conflicts that readers can connect with. Building compelling sci-fi characters means giving them depth, complexity, and unique perspectives that reflect the intricate dynamics of their world. Whether they're interstellar explorers, rebellious AI, or inhabitants of a dystopian society, crafting characters that break away from clichés brings richness and credibility to your story.

The first step in avoiding stereotypes is to focus on character motivations rather than their roles within the sci-fi setting. Instead of creating a "brave space captain" or a "rogue AI," think about why these characters exist in your world and what drives them. What motivates a character to explore new planets, fight against a mega-corporation, or question their own programmed purpose? Motivation transforms a character from a mere archetype into an individual with a personal agenda, fears, and desires. A character who becomes a space explorer to escape a troubled past is inherently different from one driven by pure scientific curiosity, even if they share similar roles. These personal motivations create depth, helping the character transcend the limitations of their role and feel like a unique person.

Background and upbringing also play a critical role in shaping well-rounded sci-fi characters. Consider the environmental, cultural, and societal factors that have influenced your character's worldview and personality. A character raised on a high-tech space station will have a vastly different perspective from someone who grew up on a resource-scarce desert planet. These details affect everything from how they interact with technology to their attitude toward authority and change. An alien character from a collectivist society might prioritize group welfare over individual ambition, while a human from a post-apocalyptic Earth might have a deep-seated mistrust of artificial intelligence. Grounding characters in the specific realities of your world makes them feel organic and integrated, preventing them from coming across as stock figures.

A critical aspect of making sci-fi characters feel authentic is giving them flaws and vulnerabilities. In a genre known for its epic struggles and powerful technologies, it's easy to fall into the trap of making characters infallible or hyper-competent. Yet flaws make characters relatable and humanize them, no matter how advanced or alien they might be. A highly intelligent scientist may struggle with empathy, a technologically augmented soldier might suffer from PTSD, or an AI could be haunted by gaps in its knowledge that it's unable to fill. These flaws create opportunities for growth, conflict, and resilience, showing readers that even in a world of futuristic advancements, characters remain imperfect and multifaceted.

Another way to create depth in sci-fi characters is to explore how they relate to the technology around them. In a world where AI, genetic engineering, and cybernetic enhancements are common, how does the character feel about these advancements? Perhaps they view technology with awe and respect, or maybe they harbor suspicion and resentment due to past traumas. Characters who rely on technology daily might become desensitized to its impact, while others who've experienced its misuse may develop a critical stance. These relationships with technology add layers to the character's identity, showing how their values, habits, and worldview are shaped by the world they inhabit.

In sci-fi, where non-human characters are often a staple, ensuring that aliens, AI, or synthetic beings feel as complex as human characters is essential. Alien characters can be easy to stereotype if they're reduced to specific traits, like "wise" or "savage." Instead, give them cultural backgrounds, beliefs, and internal conflicts that make them feel real. An alien character might be deeply spiritual, proud of their cultural heritage, or struggling with isolation in human society. Similarly, AI and robots should have nuanced motivations, ethical dilemmas, or personal histories that give them depth. An AI tasked with protecting humanity could struggle with understanding human irrationality, while a synthetic being may grapple with the desire for freedom and agency. By treating these characters as fully realized beings, you bring complexity to your sci-fi world.

Avoiding clichés means pushing beyond simplistic tropes, such as "the lone wolf hero" or "the evil scientist." Instead of relying on predictable traits, consider how the character's specific experiences and relationships influence their behavior. For instance, a scientist may begin with pure motives but become morally conflicted as they witness the consequences of their work. Or a once-lonely space traveler might find an unexpected sense of community among alien species, challenging their initial cynicism. Embracing characters' internal conflicts allows them to evolve naturally, moving away from predefined roles and creating unique arcs that feel fresh and engaging.

Dialogue is another powerful tool for building authentic sci-fi characters. Characters in a futuristic or alien setting may use language differently, depending on their backgrounds, knowledge, or technological experiences. A character from a society that prizes efficiency might speak in short, direct phrases, while an alien diplomat might use formal, poetic language rooted in their culture. The way characters communicate, including their slang, jargon, or cultural expressions, offers insights into their personalities and backgrounds. Avoid using dialogue to provide heavy-handed exposition; instead, let their words hint at deeper aspects of their character, revealing personality, cultural heritage, or underlying fears and ambitions.

Complex characters often have relationships that reveal their values, biases, and internal struggles. Consider how your sci-fi character's interactions with others reflect the story's broader themes. A protagonist in a galaxy-spanning conflict might feel torn between loyalty to their crew and a duty to their species, or they may have unresolved tension with a family member who embraces or rejects a controversial technology. An AI and its human creator might share a relationship that is equal parts respect and rivalry, complicating the line between creator and creation. These dynamics give characters dimension, grounding their emotional lives even in settings that are fantastical or futuristic. Relationships show that, no matter how far the sci-fi world diverges from our own, characters experience universal human connections like loyalty, jealousy, admiration, and love.

In sci-fi, characters' arcs should reflect not just personal growth but also their changing roles in a world of rapid technological or societal evolution. Characters may start with one set of values and slowly adopt new perspectives as they encounter different cultures, face ethical dilemmas, or witness the impact of technology firsthand. A character who initially champions technological advancement may turn against it after seeing its darker consequences, or a soldier bred for war might struggle to find meaning in peacetime. These arcs reinforce the themes of a sci-fi story, showing how the world's speculative elements challenge and change the characters, just as they would real people facing change on a massive scale.

Finally, to create truly memorable sci-fi characters, give them a sense of agency and the power to affect change within their world. Even if they are part of a larger system—like a planetary colony, military, or AI network—they should have their own goals, ambitions, and beliefs that shape their actions and choices. A character in a sci-fi world should never feel like a passive observer of futuristic wonders; instead, they should be actively involved in shaping or challenging the world around them. This agency makes the character feel dynamic and prevents them from becoming just a bystander in a technologically advanced setting. Whether they're fighting for freedom, exploring the stars, or attempting to bridge cultural divides, characters with purpose and autonomy will resonate with readers, elevating the sci-fi world from an intriguing concept to an emotionally engaging experience.

Creating characters for a sci-fi world means embracing their complexities, imperfections, and connections to the world around them. By moving beyond stereotypes, grounding characters in specific motivations, and giving them layered relationships, you bring authenticity to the speculative setting. In the end, a well-crafted sci-fi character is someone readers can relate to, even if they live on distant planets, inhabit alien bodies, or interact with technology beyond our current understanding. It's through these relatable qualities that sci-fi characters make futuristic worlds feel human, reminding us that no matter how advanced the setting, it's the people—or beings—within it who make the story come alive.

The Hero's Evolution: Building a Sci-Fi Protagonist with Depth"

Building a sci-fi protagonist with depth requires more than equipping them with advanced gadgets or placing them in an exotic setting. A compelling hero in science fiction must embody a journey of evolution and self-discovery that mirrors the genre's themes of exploration, transformation, and boundary-pushing. The protagonist's depth comes from their internal struggles, moral complexities, and the dynamic ways they interact with the sci-fi world around them. Crafting a protagonist who grows and adapts not only enriches the story but also makes the futuristic or alien elements feel grounded and relatable.

The first step in creating a layered sci-fi protagonist is defining their motivations and core values. Why does this character exist in your world, and what drives them forward? Are they seeking knowledge, power, freedom, or redemption? Starting with strong motivations helps anchor the protagonist, giving them a personal investment in the plot beyond simply reacting to the world around them. A scientist on a space expedition may be motivated by the pursuit of knowledge, but beneath that could be a need to prove themselves or escape their past. Identifying these core motivations early on provides a foundation for their actions and decisions, shaping the journey they'll undertake as they evolve.

Complex sci-fi protagonists are often defined by the internal conflicts they carry. In a genre where technology, societal constructs, or alien species can reshape everything from identity to purpose, the hero's inner conflicts should reflect the challenges of adapting to a world that's constantly changing. A protagonist might struggle with their reliance on artificial enhancements, questioning whether they are losing their humanity, or grapple with the ethics of colonizing an alien world. These internal conflicts add depth and dimension, showing that the hero isn't just moving through a series of external obstacles but also confronting personal fears, doubts, and ethical dilemmas that force them to grow. This psychological journey is essential for building a hero with depth, inviting readers to explore the boundaries between humanity, technology, and morality through the protagonist's eyes.

To create a sense of growth, it's important to give your sci-fi hero a starting point that contrasts with where they'll end up. Consider how they perceive the world or themselves at the story's beginning versus the realizations they'll arrive at by the end. This journey could be a shift in belief, a newfound strength, or a release of past traumas. A character who starts off naïve or idealistic may become jaded as they encounter the harsh realities of their world, or an anti-hero who only cares about personal gain might learn the value of sacrifice. This arc allows readers to experience the evolution of the protagonist alongside them, making their triumphs, mistakes, and revelations feel meaningful and earned.

The sci-fi setting offers endless opportunities for building a protagonist who adapts and evolves in response to external challenges. A sci-fi hero might face threats that would be unthinkable in any other genre—such as navigating a collapsing wormhole, outsmarting a hyper-intelligent AI, or surviving in an alien ecosystem. These high-stakes situations test the protagonist's resilience, intelligence, and adaptability, forcing them to evolve in response to an ever-shifting environment. This adaptability doesn't just reflect their problem-solving skills; it reveals their values, courage, and willingness to push beyond their own limitations. Showing the protagonist finding new ways to overcome these challenges builds their depth, demonstrating that their evolution is a product of both internal and external forces.

Moral and ethical dilemmas are central to shaping a sci-fi protagonist with depth. Science fiction often grapples with profound questions about humanity, progress, and the nature of reality, and the protagonist's choices should reflect these themes. If the hero discovers that their mission involves exploiting a sentient alien species, they must confront questions of responsibility, ethics, and empathy. How they respond to these dilemmas—whether they challenge the mission, make compromises, or try to justify their actions—reveals layers of their character, making them multidimensional and relatable. These ethical struggles bring out the hero's humanity, allowing the audience to connect with them on a deeper level as they navigate choices that don't have easy answers.

Relationships are another powerful tool for building a sci-fi protagonist with depth. Consider how their relationships with other characters challenge, support, or change them. A mentor figure could influence the hero's understanding of their mission, while a rival might push them to confront their own weaknesses. Relationships with non-human characters, such as aliens or AI, introduce unique dynamics, prompting the protagonist to reassess their biases and broaden their perspectives. A deep bond with an AI companion could challenge the hero's views on artificial intelligence, perhaps leading them to see the AI as a friend rather than a tool. Through these relationships, the protagonist's understanding of themselves and their world is tested, showing the importance of connection and empathy even in a futuristic or alien setting.

Backstory and personal history play a significant role in shaping a sci-fi hero's depth. Instead of relying on surface-level traits, delve into formative experiences that have shaped their worldview and drive. Perhaps the hero has suffered a personal loss due to a failed technology experiment, making them wary of scientific progress. Or maybe they grew up in a rigid, controlled society and now seek freedom, which explains their willingness to take risks. By giving the hero a rich history, you make their actions feel motivated and organic, creating a character whose journey feels inevitable yet surprising. Their past experiences add layers to their decisions and responses, revealing who they are beneath the armor of their futuristic role.

To create a protagonist who feels realistic within a sci-fi world, consider how they relate to technology and the advancements around them. A character who views technology as a means of personal empowerment will approach situations differently from one who sees it as a potential threat to humanity. Perhaps they have cybernetic enhancements that give them physical advantages but alienate them from others. Or maybe they grew up in a low-tech environment and feel overwhelmed in a society where everything is automated. This relationship with technology influences the protagonist's view of their society and their place within it, adding layers to their character that feel unique to a sci-fi setting.

Vulnerability and failure are critical to a sci-fi hero's evolution, as they make the journey feel authentic and relatable. In a genre where characters often wield advanced tools or superhuman abilities, it's easy to fall into the trap of making the protagonist feel invincible. Instead, allow them to experience failure, fear, or self-doubt, showing that they are as susceptible to mistakes as anyone else. These moments of vulnerability create empathy, showing that even in a world of immense technological possibilities, the protagonist's struggles are deeply human. A hero who must learn from their failures or come to terms with their limitations feels layered and authentic, making their ultimate growth and achievements all the more satisfying.

Lastly, crafting a memorable sci-fi protagonist requires a degree of mystery and self-discovery. Often, the best protagonists are those who are also on a journey of self-understanding, discovering their own potential, flaws, or purpose as they go. This could mean uncovering hidden abilities, such as a latent telepathic skill, or confronting aspects of their identity they hadn't previously acknowledged, such as realizing they are partly cybernetic. By keeping aspects of the protagonist's nature or past hidden until the right moment, you create a sense of suspense and reveal, making their journey one of both external and internal discovery.

In a sci-fi setting, a well-crafted protagonist brings humanity to the futuristic or alien elements, anchoring the story's themes and conflicts within a relatable experience. By building a hero who is complex, evolving, and ethically challenged, you invite readers to invest not only in the world but in the individual's personal journey. The hero's evolution reflects the sci-fi genre's essence: the exploration of what lies beyond—both in the cosmos and within oneself. Through this journey, the protagonist's depth and growth transform the narrative from a story about high-tech adventures into a meaningful exploration of resilience, morality, and the human condition.

Alien Minds: Crafting Non-Human Characters with Relatable Traits

Crafting non-human characters with relatable traits is a powerful way to make your sci-fi world feel both vast and accessible. Alien characters can offer fresh perspectives and unique personalities that enrich the story, but they also need to resonate emotionally with readers. By imbuing alien characters with qualities that readers can connect to, you can bridge the gap between human and non-human experiences, creating characters that feel truly alien while still stirring empathy, curiosity, and understanding.

The first step in crafting a compelling alien character is establishing their distinct physical and psychological traits. Consider how their physiology might affect their experiences, perceptions, and interactions. For instance, an alien with heightened sensory abilities, like advanced sight or smell, may experience the world in a way that humans cannot. A character with multiple limbs could have different social customs or unique ways of interacting with their surroundings. These physiological traits make the alien feel otherworldly, but they also open up new narrative possibilities, such as the difficulties of communicating with humans who lack these sensory perceptions. However, keep in mind that while these traits set the character apart, their reactions, emotions, and struggles should include elements that readers recognize, creating a foundation for relatability.

One of the most effective ways to make alien characters relatable is to root their personalities in universal emotions or desires. Aliens might feel love, fear, ambition, or loyalty, even if these emotions are expressed differently than in humans. A character who values family and loyalty, for instance, may belong to a species that communicates through touch or scent, expressing affection in non-verbal ways. Alternatively, an alien character who fears solitude might develop complex social rituals to stay connected to their kin, reflecting the universal need for community. These emotions make the character relatable without sacrificing their alien nature, showing readers that, beneath the physical differences, they experience many of the same emotional highs and lows.

To make your alien character feel well-rounded, give them a backstory rooted in the culture and society they come from. Every society, no matter how alien, is shaped by its environment, history, and values. Perhaps your alien character comes from a war-torn planet where survival instincts are deeply ingrained, making them pragmatic and wary of risk. Or maybe they're part of a collectivist society where the needs of the group always come before the individual, leading to tensions when they interact with humans who prioritize independence. These cultural differences add depth, showing that the character's beliefs and behaviors are shaped by their background rather than being inherently "alien." By tying their worldview to cultural norms, you make them more understandable, giving readers insight into their values and conflicts.

Communication styles play a key role in defining alien characters and can reveal a lot about their personalities and thought processes. Consider how they might communicate based on their physiology, culture, or psychological makeup. A species that communicates through vibrations might struggle to understand spoken language, interpreting emotions or intent differently from humans. Perhaps they rely on symbols, telepathy, or pheromones, leading to misunderstandings and revelations as they interact with other species. If the character is uncomfortable with human expressions of emotion or gestures, it can lead to humorous or tense moments that highlight cultural gaps. By building unique communication styles, you not only enrich the character's identity but also create opportunities for growth as they learn to bridge these gaps with human characters.

Relatable traits often emerge through shared goals or struggles, even when motivations differ. Maybe your alien character is on a journey to understand their place in the universe, a theme that resonates universally despite their alien form. Or perhaps they're seeking revenge, justice, or knowledge, but the reasons are rooted in their cultural values. A scientist from an insectoid alien species, for instance, might value knowledge as the highest honor, not for personal gain but to advance their hive's collective understanding. Aligning these goals with human values shows that, while the alien's motives might be influenced by their biology or society, the emotions driving them are ones we can understand—curiosity, pride, honor, or love for their community.

Conflict and tension add layers to alien characters, making them feel three-dimensional. Consider the challenges they face within their own society or in their interactions with others. An alien who questions their society's values or rules might face ostracism, guilt, or doubt, creating internal conflict that feels relatable despite the character's otherworldly nature. Alternatively, an alien who disapproves of human behavior—such as humanity's tendency toward violence or environmental neglect—might struggle to reconcile these differences while working alongside humans. These conflicts bring out the character's strengths and vulnerabilities, showing that they, too, are susceptible to self-doubt, ethical dilemmas, and the desire for acceptance.

Relationships are another way to bridge the alien-human divide and make non-human characters relatable. Give your alien characters connections to others—whether they're family, friends, or rivals—that reveal their emotional range and deepen their story arc. An alien parent trying to protect their offspring might relate to a human's parental instincts, despite having different customs or expressions of love. Friendships between alien and human characters can show both the differences and similarities in how they express loyalty, trust, or conflict. Through these relationships, your alien character can experience growth, self-reflection, or even humor, showing that even in a sci-fi setting, bonds of kinship and friendship transcend species boundaries.

Another effective technique is to give your alien character a distinct moral code or philosophical outlook that challenges the protagonist—and, by extension, the reader. An alien who places the collective welfare above individual rights might struggle to understand a human's desire for personal freedom, sparking conversations and conflicts that force both characters to reconsider their values. Or, a non-violent alien might question humanity's reliance on war to solve disputes, sparking internal debate and new perspectives. By contrasting their ethical views with human norms, you create moments of introspection that highlight the character's depth, showing that while they may not share human beliefs, they grapple with universal questions of morality and purpose.

While alien characters should have relatable traits, don't shy away from their distinct "alien-ness." Let them retain behaviors, habits, or ways of thinking that set them apart and emphasize the mystery of their origins. For example, they might have rituals that seem strange or unsettling to humans but hold deep significance within their culture. An alien species that performs elaborate ceremonies for even the smallest achievements might seem peculiar, but once the meaning behind these rituals is revealed, they become endearing or inspiring. Embracing these quirks keeps the character feeling authentic to their non-human roots while also building curiosity and empathy.

Finally, it's essential to allow room for change and growth in your alien characters. While they may start with beliefs or habits that seem incompatible with human perspectives, they should experience arcs that allow them to learn, adapt, or find common ground. Perhaps an alien who is initially distrustful of humans begins to appreciate human resilience or creativity. Or a character who once looked down on human emotions learns to understand their value. This growth reinforces their relatability and shows that, even for alien beings, life experiences can shape, change, and deepen one's outlook on the world.

Crafting alien characters with relatable traits doesn't mean making them less alien—it means finding the balance between what is uniquely "other" and what is universally human. By grounding them in familiar emotions, shared struggles, and meaningful relationships, you create non-human characters who feel fully realized and compelling. Through their unique perspectives, you offer readers insights into the themes and questions at the heart of your story, creating a narrative where the alien and the familiar merge, reminding us of our shared experiences even in the most unfamiliar corners of the universe.

Technological Transformations: When Machines and Humans Collide

In science fiction, few themes are as powerful as the collision between humans and technology. Technological transformations—when machines and humans merge or clash—explore humanity's ever-evolving relationship with innovation, raising questions about identity, morality, and the limits of human control. These transformations can come in many forms, from cybernetic enhancements to AI partnerships, each presenting unique conflicts and potential for character growth. By exploring the interplay between machines and humans, sci-fi writers tap into both the promise and peril of a future where technology is an integral part of our existence, challenging us to reflect on what it means to be human.

The concept of technological transformation begins with the question of "how much" technology is too much. Start by deciding how integrated technology is within your world and how comfortable or dependent your characters are on it. For instance, in a society where cybernetic enhancements are common, people may see artificial body parts as normal or even desirable. Alternatively, in a world where technology has caused harm or failed in the past, characters might view it with suspicion. This foundational relationship with technology sets the stage for the central conflicts of your story, creating characters who either embrace, resist, or are transformed by the machines around them.

One of the most compelling aspects of technological transformations is the way they blur the line between human and machine. Characters with cybernetic enhancements, for instance, might struggle with their sense of identity as they grapple with the balance between natural and artificial parts. A character with an implanted memory chip that records their experiences might question whether their thoughts are their own or influenced by the device. Similarly, an AI that has developed human-like emotions or behaviors might wonder if it is still just a machine. These internal conflicts highlight the tension between self-perception and technological enhancement, challenging the characters—and readers—to consider the nature of consciousness and autonomy.

Technology-driven transformations also provide a platform for exploring physical and psychological vulnerabilities. While a character may gain strength, agility, or intelligence through machine integration, these enhancements often come with drawbacks or risks. A character with a neural interface for rapid data processing might experience sensory overload or dependency, losing touch with reality. A person with robotic limbs may face psychological barriers as they confront their altered appearance or the societal stigma attached to technological augmentation. By revealing the costs of these transformations, you add complexity to the story, showing that even in a world of advanced technology, there is no escape from human limitations and trade-offs.

The theme of control is central when machines and humans collide. Technology can be liberating, empowering individuals with abilities far beyond natural limits. However, it can also become a means of control, especially if powerful entities—like governments, corporations, or AI systems—monitor, restrict, or manipulate technology. A character who relies on cybernetic enhancements controlled by a central network might face issues of autonomy, wondering whether their actions are truly their own. In a world where personal data is constantly tracked, characters may struggle with privacy, rebellion, or even identity theft, as their digital selves are used in ways they can't control. These conflicts highlight the tension between empowerment and surveillance, raising questions about how much freedom individuals retain in a tech-driven society.

Ethical dilemmas abound in stories where machines and humans intersect, as characters confront the moral implications of technological transformation. For example, a society that encourages genetic modification or cybernetic enhancement might inadvertently marginalize those who choose to remain unmodified, creating class divides. If certain technological advancements give characters a significant edge over others, they must grapple with the ethical implications of wielding that power. Is it fair to possess superhuman abilities? Should technology be freely available, or should its use be regulated? By embedding ethical conflicts into your narrative, you show that technology isn't neutral—it shapes and is shaped by the values and decisions of those who wield it.

The collision between humans and machines also brings up the question of purpose and obsolescence. In a world where AI performs most jobs, characters might feel replaced, grappling with the fear of becoming obsolete or irrelevant. Imagine a human pilot in a future where space-faring AI has taken over most of the navigational duties, questioning their place in a society that no longer values human skills. Alternatively, an AI programmed for a specific task might begin to question its purpose once its job is automated, developing an existential crisis over its value. These crises of purpose and identity mirror real-world anxieties about automation and technological progress, grounding the story in a relatable, emotionally resonant theme.

In stories where technology becomes a part of the human body or mind, memory and perception are particularly fertile areas for exploration. Memory implants or perceptual enhancements might allow characters to record and relive experiences, but they could also raise questions about authenticity. A character who relies on a memory implant might wonder if the experiences they recall are accurate or if they've been tampered with. Similarly, a perceptual enhancement that filters reality to make it more "pleasant" could lead to a warped sense of truth. These transformations explore the fragility of human experience, suggesting that even our most intimate memories and perceptions can be influenced by the machines we use, blurring the lines between reality and constructed experience.

Creating emotional and psychological depth in stories of human-machine integration often means exploring dependency and addiction. Characters who rely on technological enhancements might develop a dependency on these tools, struggling when they're taken away. A character with a neural implant for pain suppression, for example, might become addicted to the relief it offers, fearing the vulnerability of life without it. This dependency can lead to powerful conflicts, showing how characters wrestle with the seductive allure of technology while yearning for self-control. These struggles humanize the characters, adding a layer of vulnerability that underscores the dangers of relying too heavily on machines for security, happiness, or identity.

Relationships between humans and machines also offer a unique angle for sci-fi stories. In a world where people interact with sentient AIs, robots, or digital avatars, emotional attachments can form, challenging characters to redefine concepts like love, loyalty, and friendship. A human character might develop a close bond with an AI companion, only to question the depth of the AI's feelings—is it capable of true friendship, or is it merely programmed to act as if it cares? Conversely, an AI that develops a deep connection to a human might question its own nature, wondering if its affection is genuine or merely a by-product of code. These relationships explore the emotional landscape of technology, showing that even machines can inspire loyalty, affection, or jealousy, blurring the lines between artificial and genuine emotions.

In many sci-fi stories, the collision of humans and machines raises the possibility of rebellion and self-discovery. Characters may begin with a passive relationship with technology, accepting its limitations and uses without question. But as they experience the drawbacks or manipulations of tech-driven life, they might start to question, challenge, or rebel against it. A character who once trusted their neural implant for daily functionality might disable it after realizing it's being used to track them, setting off a journey of independence and self-discovery. This rebellion can be a metaphor for the human spirit's resistance to control, symbolizing the search for identity and autonomy in a world increasingly defined by machines.

Finally, a powerful way to explore the impact of technological transformation is to show its effect on society as a whole. A world where humans and machines coexist harmoniously will have different social dynamics than one where there is tension or animosity. Consider how technology affects everything from class and culture to politics and religion. If certain technologies are accessible only to the wealthy, they may create divisions between those with enhancements and those without. A society that reveres AI might develop rituals or beliefs that integrate machines into their culture, while a society that fears it might impose strict regulations or even shun technology altogether. By depicting the social impact of technological transformation, you deepen the world-building, showing that this collision isn't just a personal struggle but a fundamental shift that reshapes the fabric of society.

When machines and humans collide, science fiction explores some of the most profound questions about humanity's future. By creating characters who confront ethical dilemmas, grapple with autonomy, and seek meaning in a tech-driven world, you turn technological transformations into a powerful narrative force. These stories reveal that technology is both a tool and a mirror, reflecting our deepest desires, fears, and ambitions. As humans and machines merge, clash, or evolve, sci-fi reminds us that in the end, our creations inevitably reshape us, challenging our understanding of freedom, identity, and the very essence of what it means to be alive.

Psychology of the Future: Understanding Character Motivations in Sci-Fi

Understanding character motivations in science fiction is about delving into the psychology of a world shaped by advanced technology, altered societies, and alien environments. In sci-fi, motivations often stem from a mix of familiar human drives and new factors influenced by futuristic settings. This unique combination gives sci-fi characters a sense of depth, making them relatable even in far-fetched situations. The psychology of the future requires us to think about how emerging technologies, societal shifts, and alien discoveries influence what characters want, fear, and believe, shaping their decisions and actions in compelling ways.

The first step in crafting believable motivations for sci-fi characters is considering the impact of their environment. Futuristic societies, whether utopian or dystopian, have norms, expectations, and pressures that influence how characters view the world and what they value. In a society where AI governs every aspect of life, a character may crave autonomy, leading them to resist technology or even seek ways to outsmart the system. Conversely, in a resource-scarce world, characters might prioritize survival and scarcity management, shaping a mindset that influences their every action. By grounding character motivations in the unique aspects of the setting, you create motivations that feel authentic and specific to the story's world.

Technology often plays a crucial role in shaping character motivations in sci-fi. A character's access to, dependence on, or skepticism of technology can heavily influence what they desire or fear. Imagine a protagonist who has undergone extensive cybernetic enhancements to improve their job performance. This character might be motivated by a need to prove their worth, yet at the same time harbor anxieties about their diminishing "human" qualities. Similarly, a character who grew up without access to technological advancements might be driven by a desire for equal footing, seeking out ways to secure their place in a tech-dominated society. Technology, then, becomes more than a tool; it's a symbol of power, identity, or control, providing fertile ground for complex motivations.

In sci-fi, the motivation to explore, discover, or understand the unknown is a common driver, often fueled by a sense of wonder or curiosity about the cosmos or unfamiliar species. Characters might seek to uncover the mysteries of the universe, discover alien civilizations, or unlock new dimensions, motivated by personal ambition, intellectual curiosity, or a quest for meaning. Yet this drive can be double-edged. A character's desire for knowledge might lead them to cross ethical boundaries, sacrifice personal relationships, or even endanger their life. This motivation to explore is often grounded in a fundamental human yearning to push limits and transcend known boundaries, making it universally relatable even in a far-off sci-fi setting.

Survival and security are powerful motivators in sci-fi, particularly in stories where characters face existential threats, like apocalyptic environments, hostile alien forces, or rogue technologies. In these scenarios, characters are driven not just by the instinct to stay alive but by the desire to protect their communities, families, or ideals. A scientist who discovers a way to stop a deadly virus might be motivated by a sense of responsibility, risking everything to find a cure. Alternatively, a character in a dystopian regime may focus on securing resources, finding safe havens, or fighting against oppressive powers to ensure their future. These motivations give characters a relatable edge, showing that even in futuristic worlds, the instinct for survival and protection remains deeply human.

In worlds where societal structures have evolved due to technological or environmental changes, motivations often revolve around power, status, or social mobility. Characters might be driven to climb the ranks within a powerful corporation, secure rare resources, or gain influence in a political system dominated by AI or alien governance. In a world where genetic modifications can enhance social standing, a character's motivation to "fit in" or "rise above" could drive them to embrace or reject such changes, sparking internal and external conflicts. These status-driven motivations reflect the universal desire for recognition and purpose, giving the characters a relatable sense of ambition, albeit in an unfamiliar context.

Psychological conflict also arises in sci-fi from the tension between tradition and progress, especially in societies where technology disrupts long-standing beliefs or cultural practices. A character raised in a traditionalist society may find themselves torn when faced with the chance to become cybernetically enhanced or to participate in a collective AI consciousness. These characters may be motivated by loyalty to their heritage, fear of losing their identity, or skepticism of technology's impact on humanity. Alternatively, characters who embrace technological advancements might feel disconnected from their roots, creating a conflict between who they are and who they wish to become. This internal struggle between tradition and innovation adds depth, showing that even in a world of advanced tech, the pull of one's origins and identity remains powerful.

One particularly unique motivator in sci-fi is the quest for self-understanding and identity, especially in worlds where characters might be genetically engineered, cloned, or raised by alien species. A character who discovers they're an AI, for instance, might embark on a journey to define what it means to be "alive." Another character, created in a laboratory, might seek out information about their origin, craving a sense of belonging or a connection to a family they've never known. These identity-driven motivations highlight the deeply personal journey of defining oneself in a world where biology, consciousness, and memory can be artificially altered. They touch on timeless questions of existence and purpose, elevating the narrative from a sci-fi adventure to a meditation on what it means to be human.

Relationships and emotional bonds can provide powerful motivation for sci-fi characters, especially in settings where the nature of relationships is challenged by technology. In a world where virtual relationships or AI companionships are common, a character might yearn for authentic, human connection, driving them to seek out genuine interactions. Alternatively, a character might fall in love with an AI or a genetically engineered being, grappling with society's judgment or questioning the authenticity of their feelings. These motivations for connection show that, despite technological advances, the need for emotional closeness and understanding remains. By focusing on the personal side of sci-fi characters' relationships, you add emotional depth to the story, making futuristic settings feel real and resonant.

Ethical and moral dilemmas play a significant role in shaping sci-fi characters' motivations, particularly when they face decisions about technology's impact on society or individual lives. A scientist who has the chance to clone extinct species may struggle with the environmental and ethical consequences of reintroducing them. Another character might be a corporate leader motivated by profit but haunted by the potential harm their technology could bring. These ethical conflicts add complexity, showing that in a world where technological progress can lead to unpredictable consequences, characters must weigh their ambitions against their values. This moral dimension humanizes characters, showing readers that in the future, just as in the present, choices come with a price.

Characters in sci-fi are often driven by existential questions, motivated by a desire to understand their place in a universe filled with mystery and wonder. In a world where interstellar travel is possible, a character might be motivated by a longing for connection beyond Earth, driven to explore the cosmos in search of kindred spirits or spiritual enlightenment. In a society where memory and consciousness can be uploaded or cloned, characters might grapple with what it means to be unique or whether an afterlife exists within the digital realm. These motivations tap into deep philosophical questions, inviting readers to ponder the meaning of life, identity, and the universe alongside the characters.

Ultimately, understanding character motivations in sci-fi means combining familiar human desires with the unique pressures and questions of a futuristic setting. By rooting motivations in the world you've built—whether through societal structures, technological advancements, or existential mysteries—you create characters whose goals feel both universal and distinctly sci-fi. This careful balance gives your story depth, as characters grapple with what it means to be human in a world shaped by forces that push beyond our current understanding. These motivations make sci-fi more than just an exploration of the unknown; they turn the genre into a reflection of our own hopes, fears, and desires, set against the backdrop of a future still waiting to be imagined.

Heroes and Anti-Heroes: Moral Complexity in a Sci-Fi Setting

In science fiction, moral complexity is a powerful tool for creating compelling heroes and anti-heroes, characters who navigate gray areas in worlds often driven by advanced technology, alien cultures, and shifting ethical landscapes. Sci-fi settings inherently lend themselves to exploring moral ambiguity, as characters grapple with choices that challenge conventional definitions of right and wrong. By crafting heroes and anti-heroes with moral complexity, you can create characters who feel authentic, whose journeys engage readers by forcing them to confront ethical questions and reflect on what it means to be human in a world where technology, power, and survival reshape morality itself.

To create a morally complex hero, start with their principles and values. Heroes in sci-fi settings often stand for ideals—justice, compassion, or the pursuit of knowledge—but in a world shaped by advanced technology or societal upheaval, these values are tested in ways that don't always have clear answers. For instance, a character committed to protecting life might struggle when they're forced to choose between saving one group at the expense of another. Or a scientist hero dedicated to discovery may confront the consequences of their work, realizing that knowledge can bring danger as well as enlightenment. These ethical dilemmas challenge the hero's ideals, forcing them to reconsider what their values mean when taken to extremes in a futuristic or alien world.

Anti-heroes, by contrast, often start with values that defy traditional heroic qualities—they may be self-interested, skeptical, or morally flexible. In sci-fi, these characters can thrive because the genre's speculative elements allow for unique character motivations and questionable choices. An anti-hero might be motivated by a personal vendetta, a need for survival, or a distrust of authority, pushing them to make choices that others see as ruthless or unethical. However, their willingness to act in morally gray areas often makes them more adaptable, better suited to navigating a world where conventional ethics don't always apply. As they confront the moral costs of their actions, anti-heroes reveal vulnerabilities and inner conflicts that humanize them, showing that even flawed characters grapple with questions of right and wrong.

One effective way to create moral complexity in sci-fi heroes and anti-heroes is through the influence of technology. Technology can blur moral boundaries, offering capabilities that push characters into ethically ambiguous territory. A hero with access to a powerful weapon or surveillance technology might question the ethical limits of its use—are they justified in violating privacy to stop a threat, or using force to protect others? An anti-hero, meanwhile, might initially use technology to serve their own goals but come to realize its potential consequences, facing the moral fallout of wielding power in a world of rapid technological change. These dilemmas highlight the genre's exploration of ethics in a tech-driven world, showing how access to advanced tools can lead characters to question their own morality and control.

Another powerful source of moral complexity in sci-fi settings is the presence of alien cultures or AI, whose values and logic differ from human norms. Heroes in these settings often face ethical challenges when interacting with these beings, particularly when their actions might be viewed as invasive, harmful, or incomprehensible to alien perspectives. A hero sent to terraform an alien planet might grapple with guilt as they realize the process threatens an ecosystem they don't fully understand. Anti-heroes might take a pragmatic stance, seeing aliens or AI as obstacles to their goals, only to face personal conflict when they realize the depth and complexity of these non-human beings. These interactions force characters to confront questions of empathy, coexistence, and respect, showing that morality is relative and shaped by perspectives far beyond the human experience.

Moral ambiguity also arises when heroes and anti-heroes operate within systems of power—such as governments, corporations, or military organizations—that enforce their own versions of right and wrong. Sci-fi settings often amplify the reach and control of these systems, turning them into forces that characters either resist or exploit. A hero working for a tech corporation might justify morally dubious practices because they believe they're ultimately serving a greater good. Meanwhile, an anti-hero might see these structures as inherently corrupt, motivated by power and control, leading them to justify rebellion or sabotage as a means of balancing the scales. These settings allow for rich exploration of institutional morality, showing how individuals within larger systems navigate conflicts between personal ethics and organizational demands.

In sci-fi, the theme of survival often drives characters to confront their own moral limits. Survival in a futuristic setting—whether it's on a distant planet, in a dystopian society, or against hostile AI forces—can force even the most principled hero or cynical anti-hero to make hard choices. A hero committed to saving lives might end up prioritizing their own survival when resources run low, questioning the limits of their empathy and altruism. An anti-hero might be driven by survival from the start, taking actions that others deem ruthless but which are necessary for their own protection. These characters often reflect the harsh reality that in extreme circumstances, traditional ethics are compromised, and the fight for survival demands sacrifices that reveal the true nature of heroism and self-interest.

One of the most effective ways to build moral complexity is to create conflicting loyalties for your characters. In a sci-fi setting, heroes and anti-heroes often find themselves torn between personal relationships, ideological commitments, and societal expectations. A hero who values loyalty to their crew might be forced to choose between helping a friend and protecting a mission, revealing the difficult compromises that come with moral conviction. Similarly, an anti-hero might face a moral shift when their loyalty to a cause or person is challenged by unexpected feelings or revelations, adding depth to their character. These conflicting loyalties emphasize the personal stakes in moral choices, showing that even heroes with the best intentions or anti-heroes with the toughest exteriors are influenced by emotional bonds and ethical dilemmas.

When writing morally complex characters in sci-fi, it's also useful to explore the consequences of their actions, especially when they make morally questionable choices. Sci-fi heroes and anti-heroes often act with high stakes, and the impact of their decisions can ripple across entire worlds or species. A hero who sacrifices a few for the greater good might find themselves haunted by guilt or the consequences of their actions on those left behind. An anti-hero who manipulates technology or breaks laws to achieve a goal might achieve temporary success but later face backlash from those affected by their choices. By showing the ripple effects of these decisions, you add layers of moral weight to the characters, forcing them to reckon with the impact of their actions and explore the complexities of accountability.

Sci-fi allows for an exploration of how time and experience shape characters' morality. Heroes and anti-heroes who initially take principled or self-interested stances may evolve over time as they experience the costs and rewards of their choices. A hero who starts with a strong moral compass might become disillusioned after witnessing repeated failures, becoming more flexible—or even cynical—about right and wrong. An anti-hero, on the other hand, might develop a stronger ethical foundation after realizing the impact of their actions on others. This evolution reflects the genre's capacity to explore long-term consequences and the gradual shifts in perspective that come with age, experience, and repeated moral tests, showing that in a sci-fi setting, morality is often a fluid, changing construct.

Finally, in sci-fi, characters' morality can be challenged by forces outside their control, such as memory alteration, mind control, or genetic programming. These elements raise intriguing questions about free will, agency, and responsibility, as heroes and anti-heroes alike grapple with the influence of external forces on their choices. A hero who learns that their memories have been altered might question the validity of their past actions, while an anti-hero genetically engineered to follow orders might struggle to break free from their programming. These scenarios challenge characters to reclaim their sense of self, exploring whether morality can exist independently of outside influence, and how much of one's actions are genuinely their own.

In the end, crafting morally complex heroes and anti-heroes in sci-fi settings invites readers to examine the fluidity of right and wrong in worlds where technology, survival, and power dynamics challenge traditional ethics. These characters aren't simply good or bad; they are nuanced individuals whose decisions are shaped by their environment, experiences, and personal dilemmas. Through their struggles, sci-fi reveals that morality is often a matter of perspective, constantly tested by forces beyond human control. By presenting heroes and anti-heroes who navigate these gray areas, you create a narrative that resonates on a deep level, inviting readers to explore the boundaries of human integrity, resilience, and the timeless question of what it truly means to be good.

Relationships in Space: Exploring Connections across Dimensions

Exploring relationships in a sci-fi setting—particularly across the vast expanses of space and even across dimensions—adds a unique depth and richness to the narrative. In these stories, characters face challenges to connection that test the limits of loyalty, empathy, and understanding. Relationships in space settings transcend conventional boundaries, forcing characters to adapt to new forms of communication, cope with distance, and confront the complexities of interacting with beings from different worlds or realities. By examining these connections in a sci-fi context, you delve into timeless themes of love, friendship, and trust in a way that is distinctly futuristic and imaginative, yet universally relatable.

The vast distances of space create both physical and emotional separation, which often pushes characters to form creative, unconventional ways of connecting. Long-distance relationships in space can't rely on regular, instant communication, so characters might record messages, send visual memories, or invent technology that bridges these distances in unique ways. A crew member separated from their loved ones on Earth might only receive delayed transmissions, relying on these fragmented conversations to sustain their bond. This delay adds a sense of melancholy and longing, showing how relationships adapt and endure even when separated by light-years. The tension between closeness and isolation becomes a central theme, as characters navigate the challenge of staying emotionally connected despite physical separation.

In a sci-fi setting, communication technology is often more advanced, enabling characters to connect in ways unimaginable today. Telepathic links, holographic projections, and immersive simulations allow characters to experience intimacy across distances or even dimensions. Imagine a protagonist who maintains a telepathic bond with a partner, experiencing their emotions and thoughts in real-time even when they're galaxies apart. Or consider a crew member who spends time in a virtual reality simulation with a loved one, allowing them to "be together" across vast distances. These technologies bring characters closer, but they can also complicate relationships. The immediacy of telepathic or virtual connections might lead to misunderstandings, misinterpretations, or even conflicts over privacy and emotional boundaries, highlighting the complexity of closeness in a hyper-connected sci-fi world.

One of the most fascinating aspects of relationships in a space setting is the influence of cultural and biological differences, particularly when characters form connections with aliens or AI. Interspecies relationships require characters to bridge vast gaps in language, values, and even physiology. A human character in a relationship with an alien might struggle to understand customs that feel deeply foreign to them, like an alien partner's approach to time, emotion, or physical affection. A human might find themselves in love with an AI, grappling with the fact that their partner perceives emotions differently or may not experience "love" in a human sense. These relationships challenge characters to confront their own biases and assumptions, pushing them to adapt and expand their understanding of connection. Through these bonds, sci-fi explores the universality of love and friendship, showing that even across species and dimensions, empathy and respect create bridges.

Relationships in space often involve shared missions or survival situations that intensify bonds quickly, making connections feel profound and immediate. Characters who rely on each other to survive hostile environments, navigate alien worlds, or operate spacecraft develop a type of camaraderie that transcends ordinary friendships. These relationships are marked by mutual dependence, loyalty, and trust, as the characters know that their lives are intertwined. A crew member who trusts their partner implicitly in the middle of a space battle or an explorer who depends on their companion to navigate an alien terrain feels a profound bond that is often deeper than friendship.

The intensity of these shared experiences forges connections that can endure extreme circumstances, revealing how the human need for companionship remains vital even in the most hostile or foreign environments.

Another element of sci-fi relationships is the theme of time, particularly in stories involving space travel at near-light speeds, cryogenic sleep, or alternate dimensions. Characters might experience time differently, with one partner aging while the other remains the same due to time dilation, or one character waiting for decades while another experiences only a few days. This disparity creates emotional tension, as characters grapple with how they've changed in the other's absence or how memories fade while one partner has remained unchanged. Such scenarios explore the resilience of relationships over time, asking whether love or loyalty can survive the transformative effects of prolonged separation or differing timelines. These unique sci-fi scenarios reveal that while time may distort memories or distance, genuine bonds can endure across lifetimes, highlighting the timeless quality of true connection.

Relationships that cross dimensions or involve parallel worlds add yet another layer of complexity. Characters who form bonds with versions of themselves from other realities, or who encounter alternate versions of loved ones, experience a unique form of emotional conflict. A character might meet an alternate version of their partner who made different life choices, stirring feelings of jealousy, curiosity, or regret. Alternatively, a character might find themselves in a relationship with a person who only exists in another dimension, leading to an impossible longing and a sense of being torn between worlds. These connections force characters to confront questions of identity, fate, and the nature of their relationships, showing that love and connection are not confined by single realities. The exploration of multiple dimensions invites readers to consider how each version of ourselves is shaped by different choices, and how connections in one reality can resonate across others.

Exploring the impact of memory on relationships is particularly poignant in a sci-fi setting, where technology often allows for memory manipulation, cloning, or artificial consciousness. Imagine a character who's lost their partner but has access to a digital replica of them—a simulation that looks, speaks, and remembers their life together. This raises profound questions: is the connection genuine, or a shadow of what once was? Alternatively, a character might fall in love with a clone, struggling with the realization that while their memories are shared, the individual in front of them is different. These stories reveal the fragility and resilience of relationships, as characters grapple with the nature of memory and the question of whether love can survive beyond the original moment. In these emotionally charged scenarios, sci-fi shows that relationships are defined by more than just shared history—they are a continuous act of recognition, acceptance, and renewal.

Power dynamics also play an essential role in relationships within sci-fi settings, particularly in stories involving AI, advanced species, or hierarchical societies. A relationship between a human and an advanced AI might blur lines of control, as the AI possesses greater knowledge or abilities that give it an advantage. In another scenario, a human who falls in love with a member of a highly evolved alien race might feel both awe and insecurity, fearing that their partner views them as primitive or fragile. These power imbalances can lead to tension, jealousy, or even manipulation, as characters navigate complex emotional landscapes shaped by differences in status or capability. Exploring these dynamics adds depth to relationships, showing that power—whether technological or biological—can both unite and divide, pushing characters to confront their insecurities and ultimately find a balance.

Finally, one of the most profound elements of relationships in a sci-fi setting is the theme of sacrifice. In space, characters are often faced with life-or-death situations, forcing them to make difficult choices about their bonds with others. A character might sacrifice their chance to return home to ensure the safety of their crew, or a protagonist might part from a loved one to fulfill a mission that benefits countless others. These sacrifices add emotional weight, underscoring the depth of characters' connections even when it leads to separation or loss. In the vastness of space, where life is fragile and missions are perilous, acts of sacrifice become acts of love, loyalty, and honor, giving relationships a sense of gravitas that resonates with readers.

In exploring relationships across space and dimensions, sci-fi offers a unique lens on the enduring power of connection. The genre's speculative elements allow us to examine timeless emotions in extraordinary circumstances, showing that while the settings may change, the essence of love, friendship, and loyalty remains universal. Through telepathic bonds, long-distance transmissions, and alliances across species, sci-fi reveals that relationships are adaptable and resilient, capable of enduring and evolving even in the face of impossible challenges. These stories remind us that, in the end, it's our connections with others that anchor us—whether across galaxies, lifetimes, or dimensions—making us feel a little more at home in the vastness of the universe.

Arcs in Alien Worlds: Character Growth amidst Futuristic Challenges

Building character arcs in alien worlds allows sci-fi writers to explore growth, change, and self-discovery against a backdrop of futuristic challenges that push characters beyond their limits. The combination of uncharted planets, advanced technologies, and encounters with alien societies creates an environment ripe for personal evolution. As characters navigate these unique settings, they face obstacles that test their values, challenge their beliefs, and force them to adapt in ways they never imagined. Character growth in alien worlds is about more than adapting to new surroundings; it's about confronting the unknown within themselves, spurred by the unfamiliar and often unpredictable forces of the world around them.

To craft compelling arcs in alien worlds, it's essential to start with the character's baseline beliefs and values—their worldview as it exists before they encounter the alien world. This gives readers a foundation for understanding who the character is and sets up a contrast with who they will become. For instance, a character who begins with an unwavering belief in human superiority might find that encountering an advanced alien civilization humbles them, forcing them to reevaluate their assumptions. Or a by-the-book scientist may find themselves questioning the value of empirical data when faced with an alien species whose reality defies human logic. Starting with clear beliefs and values provides a framework for character growth, giving the arc direction and purpose as the character encounters challenges that force them to evolve.

Futuristic challenges in alien worlds often involve physical and environmental obstacles that test a character's resilience and adaptability. Imagine a character stranded on a planet with extreme weather, limited resources, or an ecosystem that seems hostile to human life. To survive, they must push past their fears, learn new skills, and rely on instincts they may have never trusted before. These physical challenges create immediate stakes, forcing the character to confront their limitations and push past them. As they overcome each obstacle, they gain confidence, resourcefulness, and self-assurance, showing readers that their growth is not just intellectual but also physical and practical, driven by their evolving relationship with the environment around them.

Encounters with alien societies provide a unique opportunity for characters to question their cultural biases and expand their perspectives. In alien worlds, characters often come face-to-face with beings who think, feel, and live in ways completely foreign to their own experiences. This encounter challenges their assumptions, forcing them to either double down on their beliefs or open themselves to new ideas. A character who starts out as ethnocentric might learn the value of diversity, while another who prides themselves on their empathy might realize that they need to work harder to understand cultures that don't share human emotions or customs. These moments of cultural exchange are often transformative, leading characters to reexamine their own values and adopt a broader, more inclusive view of the universe.

Technology and alien innovations often serve as catalysts for character growth, pushing characters to adapt in unexpected ways. A character who initially mistrusts technology, for instance, might find themselves relying on alien tech for survival, gradually coming to appreciate its utility and ingenuity. Alternatively, a character who begins the story as overly dependent on technology may have to rely on their natural instincts and ingenuity when their equipment fails. These experiences shape the character's relationship with technology, revealing its limitations or its potential for good. Through this relationship with futuristic tech, characters discover that growth often means moving beyond the tools that once defined them, finding strength and resourcefulness within themselves.

Exploring the theme of isolation is particularly powerful in alien settings, where characters may find themselves cut off from everything they know. Isolation in an alien world can amplify feelings of loneliness, fear, and vulnerability, creating an emotional crucible that pushes the character to confront their inner demons. A character who relies heavily on social connections may struggle in isolation, ultimately learning self-reliance and resilience. Alternatively, a loner who thrives in solitude might discover the importance of companionship when forced to form bonds with alien allies for survival. These arcs show how the alien world acts as a mirror, reflecting and magnifying the character's insecurities and strengths, catalyzing growth through both hardship and discovery.

Alien worlds often introduce characters to ethical and moral dilemmas they would never face in familiar settings, forcing them to make difficult choices that define who they are. Imagine a character who arrives on a planet rich in resources, only to learn that exploiting these resources will harm the native species. This forces them to confront questions about colonialism, exploitation, and responsibility. Or a character might have to choose between following human protocols and respecting alien customs, putting them in conflict with their own people. These moral challenges create turning points in the character's arc, pushing them to define their values and principles in the face of impossible choices. Through these ethical dilemmas, characters emerge with a stronger sense of self and a deeper understanding of what they stand for.

Exploring personal fears and vulnerabilities is another powerful aspect of character growth in alien worlds. Encounters with the unknown often force characters to confront fears they may have ignored or denied. A character who fears death, for instance, might learn to accept it as they experience a culture that celebrates life and death as two parts of a natural cycle. Or a character who fears failure might have no choice but to take risks, facing setbacks that ultimately build resilience. Alien worlds serve as a backdrop that amplifies these fears, giving characters no choice but to confront and work through them. This process of facing fear head-on is central to meaningful character growth, showing that true courage comes not from the absence of fear, but from overcoming it.

Forging relationships with alien beings also plays a critical role in character growth, often forcing characters to overcome prejudice, fear, or cultural barriers. A human character might form a deep bond with an alien who teaches them a new way of seeing the world, challenging their beliefs and encouraging empathy. Alternatively, a competitive relationship with an alien rival might push both characters to grow as they learn to respect one another's strengths and values. These relationships broaden the character's worldview, showing that connection and understanding are possible even across vast cultural divides. By the end of their journey, these relationships often leave lasting impacts, reshaping the character's sense of belonging and teaching them lessons about tolerance, cooperation, and the strength of diversity.

In alien worlds, survival often depends on collaboration and trust, and characters grow by learning to work with others, even if those others are vastly different from themselves. Characters who start as fiercely independent may find themselves forced to rely on an alien ally or group, realizing that trust and teamwork are essential for survival. Conversely, a character who begins as dependent on others might discover a hidden strength as they learn to act independently. These alliances and friendships drive character arcs, revealing that growth often comes from acknowledging one's limitations and learning to lean on others for support. Through these bonds, characters develop humility, loyalty, and mutual respect, transforming the alien world from a place of hostility to one of shared experience.

Finally, character growth in alien worlds often culminates in a sense of purpose or self-discovery, as characters gain insights about who they are and what they value. A scientist who set out purely for knowledge might return with a deeper respect for life and the mysteries that remain unsolved. A soldier sent on a mission of conquest might come back as a defender of peace, shaped by their experiences among alien species who showed them new perspectives on coexistence. These revelations represent the pinnacle of the character's arc, showing that growth is often about finding purpose in the unfamiliar and embracing change.

In the end, crafting character arcs in alien worlds is about allowing the setting itself to influence the characters, revealing who they are as they confront futuristic challenges. As they navigate these worlds, the characters evolve, becoming more resilient, open-minded, and self-aware. Through encounters with new cultures, ethical dilemmas, survival struggles, and the challenges of forming cross-species bonds, characters grow in ways that feel both surprising and inevitable. Their journeys remind readers that growth is a universal experience—whether on Earth or in the furthest reaches of the galaxy, the path to self-discovery often begins with stepping into the unknown and embracing the transformative power of change.

Speaking the Future: Crafting Dialogue for a Sci-Fi Setting

Crafting dialogue for a sci-fi setting involves a careful balance of realism, futurism, and accessibility. Dialogue in science fiction not only serves to reveal character and advance the plot but also helps build an immersive world by reflecting the setting's unique social norms, technologies, and cultural influences. In a genre that often explores advanced technology, alien languages, or unfamiliar social structures, dialogue must feel authentic yet understandable, grounded yet imaginative. When done right, dialogue in a sci-fi setting becomes a powerful tool for building believability, pulling readers into a world that feels distinct and alive, yet emotionally resonant.

The first step in creating authentic sci-fi dialogue is to consider how technology shapes communication in the story's world. In a setting where neural interfaces, telepathy, or translation devices are common, characters may use these tools in ways that influence the rhythm, tone, or speed of their dialogue. For example, a society accustomed to instant mental communication might find spoken language cumbersome or might use shorthand expressions for efficiency. Alternatively, a character with a built-in AI assistant might frequently "consult" it mid-conversation, pausing for input or guidance, giving their dialogue a layered, fragmented feel. These small details help establish the technological background subtly, showing how advancements in communication shape the way characters talk and interact.

To keep sci-fi dialogue accessible, avoid overloading it with jargon or invented terms, especially in the early parts of the story. While futuristic or alien terms can add flavor, too much can alienate readers, pulling them out of the story. Start by introducing only a few specific terms, then gradually build on them as the context becomes clear. If characters frequently mention a "stasis shield" or "quantum core," make sure these terms are understandable through their reactions and the dialogue's context, rather than through heavy exposition. This approach keeps the dialogue natural and immersive, allowing readers to pick up on the terminology over time without feeling overwhelmed.

Building distinct voices for characters is crucial in a sci-fi setting, where characters may come from different species, planets, or even dimensions. Each character's background should influence how they speak, including their vocabulary, tone, and even cadence. An alien ambassador, for instance, might speak in a formal, precise manner, using metaphors tied to their homeworld's unique environment. Meanwhile, a human engineer raised in a tech-dominated colony might use slang or shorthand, favoring practical, straightforward speech. These differences in voice provide insight into each character's background and perspective, enriching the world by showing how culture and origin shape language. It's important to maintain these distinct voices consistently, ensuring that each character's speech patterns feel as integral to them as their physical traits or personality.

Incorporating invented language or slang adds depth to the world, highlighting its distinct social and cultural influences. Sci-fi settings often introduce phrases or idioms that reflect the characters' experiences or environments. A miner on a barren moon might have sayings inspired by the desolate landscape, like "dry as dust" to mean something lifeless or "rockslide" to signify sudden danger. Similarly, characters might use specialized slang related to their technology or lifestyle, like calling a risky venture "a black hole dive" or describing unreliable machinery as "sparkbound." These linguistic quirks give the world a lived-in feel, making it clear that this setting has its own history, norms, and culture.

When crafting dialogue for alien characters or advanced AIs, consider how their language might differ fundamentally from human norms. Alien characters might lack certain emotional expressions or place emphasis on values unfamiliar to humans, influencing their speech. An alien that communicates through color or sound might struggle to convey nuanced emotion in spoken language, leading to interactions that feel formal or detached. An advanced AI, by contrast, might be extremely literal, avoiding metaphors or humor, or might adopt an overly precise, clinical tone. These differences not only set non-human characters apart but also reveal the limitations and adaptations involved in cross-species or human-machine communication. By designing alien or AI dialogue with unique structures or tones, you deepen the sense of otherness while allowing for moments of humor, misunderstanding, or revelation.

Using dialogue to reveal the sci-fi setting's political or social landscape is another powerful way to build world depth. In a story where certain factions hold opposing views, characters' dialogue can reveal allegiance or distrust. For instance, a character might refer to rebels with disdain as "dissenters" while those in support call them "freedom fighters," hinting at the underlying tension. In a society where AI is controversial, someone might pointedly call an AI "it" instead of "they," exposing biases or conflicts within the society. These small language choices give clues about the story's social hierarchies, tensions, or alliances, allowing the dialogue to convey background information organically without explicit exposition.

Dialogue is also an excellent way to build suspense and mystery in a sci-fi setting by hinting at unknowns or suggesting hidden dangers. Characters might use cryptic terms or discuss rumors that pique curiosity, like mentioning a place called "the Dead Zone" without further explanation. Characters could share hushed whispers about a mysterious alien artifact, leaving some phrases unexplained or half-finished, allowing the unknown to linger in readers' minds. This approach adds tension, drawing readers in as they pick up on the ominous or mysterious aspects of the setting, creating a sense of intrigue without slowing down the pace with exposition.

When writing dialogue for sci-fi characters, remember that emotional truth remains crucial, no matter how advanced or alien the setting. Even in a futuristic or high-tech world, characters experience universal emotions like fear, love, frustration, and hope. Conveying these emotions in their dialogue makes them relatable and grounds the sci-fi setting in familiar experiences. A character may express grief over a lost comrade even if their expression includes references to a "memory implant" or "neural backup." When the emotional stakes are real, readers connect to the dialogue, regardless of how alien or futuristic the vocabulary may be. Emotionally grounded dialogue ensures that the story resonates with readers on a human level, making the characters' journeys meaningful and impactful.

Finally, dialogue in sci-fi settings should be concise and purposeful, as the genre often involves fast-paced action and complex ideas. Each line should serve a purpose—whether it's advancing the plot, revealing character, or building the world. This doesn't mean dialogue should be devoid of nuance or detail; rather, it should flow naturally and avoid unnecessary filler. By keeping dialogue focused, you maintain the momentum essential to sci-fi storytelling, giving readers just enough context to stay immersed without slowing down the pace. Efficient, well-crafted dialogue ensures that readers stay engaged, picking up on world details and character motivations through quick exchanges that keep the story moving forward.

In a sci-fi setting, dialogue is a dynamic blend of futuristic and familiar, a vehicle for building worlds, conveying technology, and exploring relationships across alien or technological boundaries. By grounding futuristic language in accessible emotions, tailoring voices to character backgrounds, and carefully balancing jargon with clarity, you create a dialogue that feels authentic to the sci-fi world while remaining relatable and immersive. Through skillful dialogue, you can invite readers into a world that feels as rich in its spoken nuances as it does in its visual wonders, making the story's universe both expansive and intimately connected through the words spoken within it.

Beyond Technobabble: Balancing Jargon and Clarity

In sci-fi, technology is often at the heart of the story, shaping the world, defining the stakes, and propelling the plot. However, using technical jargon effectively is a balancing act; too much "technobabble" can overwhelm or confuse readers, while too little can make the setting feel underdeveloped or implausible. The goal is to create a sense of realism by incorporating specific language and concepts that feel advanced and futuristic, without sacrificing clarity or accessibility. Balancing jargon and clarity allows readers to immerse themselves in the world's technology and innovations without feeling alienated, keeping them engaged in both the story and the science behind it.

The first step to achieving this balance is understanding what each piece of technology contributes to the story and focusing on its narrative purpose rather than the minutiae of its mechanics. Before diving into technical explanations, consider what role the technology plays. If a "quantum processor" is essential for a character's plan to succeed, readers don't need a detailed breakdown of how quantum computing works; they need to understand its relevance. Describing it as "a device that can process probabilities, giving the user real-time predictive insights" grounds the technology's function without diving into complex theory. This approach helps readers grasp the technology's significance, allowing the story to flow without technical interruptions.

When introducing new technology, use context to provide clues about its nature and purpose. Characters' actions, dialogue, or reactions can communicate an unfamiliar concept in a natural way. Instead of explaining the entire functionality of a "biochemical resonator," show a character using it to heal wounds or neutralize toxins. Another character might be wary of it, hinting at potential side effects or limitations. This technique allows readers to infer the basics through observation, making the technology feel like an organic part of the world. By focusing on practical applications and observable effects, you avoid info-dumping and keep the narrative moving.

Selective jargon is often more effective than extensive technical language. Introducing a few specific terms can add flavor to the story, giving it a sense of futurism without overwhelming readers. Choose words that feel natural to the setting and that the characters would realistically use. A character in a tech-driven society might refer to a "data wipe" instead of a reset, or mention "translight drives" for faster-than-light travel. These terms signal technological advancement while remaining intuitive, encouraging readers to infer their meaning without needing exhaustive definitions. Keeping jargon minimal and impactful allows readers to acclimate to the language of the story without feeling bombarded.

Consider how you can weave technical explanations into dialogue or action scenes to maintain momentum and make the information feel relevant. For instance, a character might explain a crucial piece of tech under pressure, giving just enough information to help others (and readers) understand its function in that specific moment. If two engineers are discussing a "neural link," one might say, "It syncs the mind directly with the ship's AI, but don't stay connected too long or you'll start losing yourself." This approach allows the explanation to be brief, relevant, and embedded within the story's action, ensuring that the focus stays on the characters and plot.

Using metaphors and analogies is a valuable technique for simplifying complex ideas without "dumbing them down." Comparisons to familiar concepts make futuristic technology more accessible, helping readers visualize or grasp its function quickly. For example, describing a spaceship's propulsion system as "like a slingshot that pulls energy from nearby stars" creates a mental image without an in-depth scientific breakdown. Or, a quantum communicator could be explained as "like having a phone that rings before you dial." Metaphors like these keep the story moving and allow readers to engage with the tech more intuitively, making advanced concepts feel grounded and relatable.

When the story does require more detailed explanations, consider the pacing and timing. Give technical details only when they enhance the narrative, such as when the science becomes a crucial obstacle or solution. If a character must repair a piece of machinery to survive, describing the components they're using makes sense and can add tension to the scene. Conversely, if the science is just part of the background, keep explanations brief and focus on how it affects the characters. By embedding technical details at key moments, you enhance the storytelling rather than interrupting it, maintaining the reader's immersion.

The characters' familiarity with technology can also provide clues to readers, shaping the tone and depth of technical explanations. A seasoned scientist might use complex terms without explanation, reflecting their expertise and comfort with the tech. Meanwhile, a non-expert character might use simpler language or even express confusion, which can guide readers in interpreting the technology's impact on the story without needing a full explanation. Allowing characters to respond naturally to technology—whether with mastery, apprehension, or curiosity—gives the tech context within the world, making it feel both real and relatable.

Including limitations or consequences associated with technology helps ground the story and make the science more believable. If a "fusion disruptor" can halt an enemy's weapon, it should have drawbacks—perhaps it's bulky, drains a lot of energy, or only works at close range. These constraints give readers a sense of the technology's scope without detailed mechanics, making it feel realistic. When characters face trade-offs with the tools they rely on, the technology feels balanced and well-integrated, enhancing the world's depth and making it more interesting than a setting where every piece of tech works perfectly and without consequence.

Consider adopting a "show, don't tell" approach when possible, allowing the effects of technology to illustrate its purpose. Rather than explaining that a "refractor shield" can deflect energy blasts, show it in action, perhaps as it deflects an enemy shot but starts to flicker from overuse. This approach invites readers to learn through observation, creating a natural, immersive experience. Readers don't need to know the exact science behind the refractor shield; they simply need to see that it's powerful but not invincible. Through showing rather than telling, you avoid bogging down the story with unnecessary details and instead let readers experience the technology as part of the action.

When writing in a sci-fi setting, remember that not every reader will have a background in science or technology. Balancing clarity with jargon means crafting an experience that appeals to both seasoned sci-fi fans and newcomers. Aim to use accessible language, and reserve in-depth technical descriptions for moments where they serve a clear narrative purpose. This approach broadens the story's appeal, allowing readers of various backgrounds to enjoy the immersive aspects of the world without needing a degree in astrophysics.

Ultimately, the key to balancing jargon and clarity is remembering that technology in sci-fi serves the story rather than being the story itself. By focusing on the narrative function of each piece of tech, using selective terminology, relying on context and character reactions, and simplifying complex concepts, you create a setting that feels futuristic and grounded at once. Well-crafted technobabble becomes a tool for immersion, drawing readers deeper into the world rather than creating barriers. By using jargon thoughtfully, you enhance the realism of the sci-fi universe while keeping the story accessible, allowing readers to explore the future without losing sight of the characters and conflicts at its core.

Voices from Other Worlds: Creating Distinctive Alien and AI Dialogue

Creating distinctive dialogue for alien and AI characters is a hallmark of immersive sci-fi storytelling, giving these non-human voices a presence and personality that makes the world feel diverse, complex, and truly "other." Alien and AI dialogue can offer fresh perspectives on familiar themes while challenging readers to connect with characters whose thought processes, experiences, and expressions are vastly different from human norms. Crafting unique dialogue for these beings involves considering their cultural backgrounds, biological constraints, and artificial constructs, while making sure their voices are relatable and understandable.

To create authentic alien dialogue, begin by considering the character's culture and worldview. Language is heavily influenced by a society's values, traditions, and environment, so an alien species raised in an oceanic world, for instance, might use water-related metaphors or expressions that emphasize fluidity, depth, or flow. Similarly, an alien civilization that prioritizes collective harmony over individuality might use "we" instead of "I" when speaking, or frame questions as statements to avoid confrontation. By letting each alien's speech reflect their societal values and physical surroundings, you give their dialogue a layered, lived-in feel, showing that their language is a natural extension of their world rather than a human template.

Alien dialogue can also be shaped by physiology and sensory abilities, which often differ significantly from human norms. An alien with multiple vocal cords or tonal variations might speak in harmonics or layered sounds, conveying emphasis or emotion through pitch rather than vocabulary. A species with heightened senses might have terms that reflect complex sensations that humans lack words for, like color tones only visible to them or scents that convey specific emotions. Describing these unique sounds or sensory-based expressions gives readers insight into the character's physiology without directly explaining it. This approach allows readers to feel the otherness of alien voices while imagining the fascinating ways in which these beings perceive and communicate.

Alien dialogue benefits from inventive vocabulary that hints at the species' unique experiences and concepts. Consider developing specific terms or idioms that only make sense within their cultural or environmental context. An alien with a long lifespan might say "in a heartbeat" to mean decades, emphasizing their concept of time. Another might use phrases that reflect their life cycle, like "rebirth" to signify a major personal transformation. When carefully chosen, these unique expressions enrich the character's dialogue without overwhelming the reader. Aim to introduce these terms gradually, using context to help readers understand their meanings naturally.

To create distinctive AI dialogue, start by considering the AI's origin, purpose, and programming. An AI's language often reflects its intended function and constraints. An AI designed for medical purposes, for instance, might use clinical, precise language, referring to humans as "patients" and avoiding emotionally charged terms. A security-focused AI might use military jargon or data-driven language, emphasizing risk and probability. These details anchor the AI's dialogue in its role, helping readers understand its objectives and limitations without needing technical exposition. By letting an AI's purpose inform its speech, you create a dialogue style that feels uniquely tailored, reflecting the "personality" of its programming.

AI dialogue is often marked by formality or directness, avoiding idioms, metaphors, or humor unless it's been programmed to mimic human speech patterns. For instance, an AI that states facts without embellishment might say, "Error: system failure at 98% probability," rather than "It looks like something went wrong." This precision gives AI dialogue a stark quality, reinforcing its machine nature and differentiating it from human speech. If the AI has an evolving algorithm or adaptive learning capabilities, you could introduce subtle changes in its language over time, showing a shift from pure logic toward more nuanced, human-like expressions as it learns or interacts more with humans.

For both alien and AI characters, experimenting with sentence structure is an effective way to make their dialogue stand out. Alien species might communicate in a pattern different from human norms, such as starting with verbs, omitting articles, or structuring sentences in a way that reflects their thought processes. An alien whose language values essence over specifics might say "Move, time for rest is" instead of "It's time to rest." Similarly, an AI might avoid pronouns to emphasize objectivity, saying "Observation indicates error" rather than "I think there's an error." These changes in syntax signal an unfamiliar perspective, hinting at the character's unique way of interpreting the world while still being understandable to readers.

Creating emotional depth in alien and AI dialogue is crucial for making these characters relatable. For aliens, emotions might be expressed differently than in human dialogue. An alien might describe sadness through physical changes ("My colors have dimmed"), or an AI might acknowledge emotional data analytically ("Increased heart rate detected; distress likely"). When non-human characters express emotions within the framework of their unique physiology or programming, it helps readers connect with them on an emotional level while maintaining their distinctiveness. Readers feel the alienness of their emotions without losing the core human experience of empathy, making them simultaneously foreign and relatable.

Silence, pauses, or unconventional pacing in dialogue can convey alien or AI "thought" processes that are unfamiliar to humans. An AI character might pause mid-sentence as it calculates a response, or an alien might take longer to process human language, leading to brief gaps in conversation. These pauses suggest a different rhythm or method of processing information, adding to the sense that these beings operate on a different mental plane. Alternatively, an alien who communicates telepathically or non-verbally could use subtle physical cues or visual language, with descriptions of how they "speak" through movement, color shifts, or changes in scent. These non-verbal cues enrich the world-building, showing that communication in alien societies may not be bound to words alone.

When writing alien and AI dialogue, remember that characters from other worlds or created as machines may lack human cultural context, resulting in misunderstandings or literal interpretations. An alien might be puzzled by human phrases like "break a leg" or "sleep on it," taking them literally and providing humorous or thought-provoking reactions. An AI, limited by programming, might miss subtle human nuances like sarcasm, responding to it as if it were a sincere statement. These misunderstandings not only add authenticity to the non-human dialogue but also allow for moments of humor, learning, or conflict that deepen the relationship between human and non-human characters.

Finally, using dialogue to reveal character development is essential for both alien and AI voices. Just as human characters grow, alien and AI characters can change their perspectives or adapt their language over time, showing a journey of learning or self-awareness. An AI might begin by using rigidly formal language but gradually adopt more natural phrases as it learns from humans. An alien who initially speaks in formal, measured tones might adopt slang or human expressions as they grow closer to the crew, symbolizing the bond they've developed. These changes in dialogue reflect the evolution of the character, showing that even non-humans can experience growth, connection, and understanding.

Crafting distinctive dialogue for alien and AI characters involves more than just adding quirks or invented words; it's about building voices that reflect their origins, purpose, and perspectives. By considering cultural influences, physiological differences, programming constraints, and unique thought processes, you create dialogue that feels truly otherworldly while still resonating with readers on an emotional level. These voices deepen the sense of immersion, making alien and AI characters feel as real and nuanced as their human counterparts, while exploring the boundaries of language, empathy, and understanding in a vast and complex universe.

Emotion in the Unknown: Conveying Humanity through Sci-Fi Dialogue

In sci-fi, where settings often venture into the unknown—distant planets, alternate realities, or futuristic societies—dialogue becomes a vital bridge for conveying human emotion in unfamiliar surroundings. Characters' words and interactions reveal vulnerability, resilience, and connection, grounding the story's fantastical elements in relatable emotions. Through skillful dialogue, sci-fi writers can portray the raw humanity of their characters, showing that even amid alien landscapes and advanced technology, the fundamental aspects of love, fear, joy, and grief remain powerfully present.

The first step in conveying emotion through dialogue in a sci-fi setting is to anchor characters' responses to the unfamiliar. When faced with an alien world or advanced technology, characters often react with awe, curiosity, trepidation, or even cynicism. Their initial responses reveal their underlying emotions and hint at past experiences or values. For instance, a character might express wonder at a vibrant alien ecosystem with a simple, "It's...beyond anything I imagined," or, conversely, express skepticism with, "Nothing this beautiful is ever safe." These reactions show readers the character's perspective, grounding the unknown in emotional authenticity while adding depth to the setting.

Creating contrasts between familiar human emotions and extraordinary sci-fi environments is a powerful way to amplify emotional impact. When characters express love, fear, or loss in the context of an alien world or futuristic society, their emotions stand out vividly against the strange backdrop. Imagine a character gazing at the stars with a friend and saying, "I never thought I'd feel this far from home...with you." The mix of isolation and intimacy in that simple line captures the strangeness and the warmth of their connection, highlighting the depth of their bond against the vastness of space. This contrast makes the dialogue resonate, showing that emotions are universal, even when the surroundings are unfamiliar.

In a sci-fi setting, characters' emotional vulnerability often shines through during moments of crisis or uncertainty, and the language they use reveals their deeper fears and desires. When a character faces life-threatening situations—like malfunctioning equipment on a spacecraft or a hostile alien species—their words often strip down to essentials. A character might admit, "I'm not ready to die out here," or desperately reach out with, "Stay with me. Just stay with me." These brief but loaded phrases carry the weight of their fears and attachments, letting readers feel the urgency of the moment and the human bonds that transcend the situation's danger. These moments show that, even in futuristic settings, life's fragility and the need for connection remain at the forefront.

Sci-fi settings often push characters to face existential questions or conflicts, and dialogue is a natural way to explore these deeper themes. When characters grapple with concepts like mortality, identity, or belonging, their dialogue can reveal the emotional undercurrents of these philosophical dilemmas. A character discovering they are an AI might ask, "If my memories aren't real, then who am I?" Or someone facing an interplanetary war might ponder, "Is survival worth it if we lose who we are?" These lines are not just intellectual; they're deeply personal, showing that beneath the futuristic trappings, characters are wrestling with the same core questions that have shaped humanity for centuries. These moments of introspection connect readers to the character's journey, offering glimpses of their inner life that resonate despite the otherworldly setting.

Dialogue also provides an opportunity for characters to express resilience and hope in the face of the unknown. In a genre often marked by high stakes and challenging environments, characters' words of encouragement or resolve reveal the inner strength that drives them forward. A character facing a difficult mission might declare, "We've come too far to turn back now," or reassure a frightened friend with, "We'll find a way—together." These expressions of solidarity and determination show that even in the bleakest circumstances, the human spirit persists. Through these words, sci-fi dialogue reminds readers that hope and resilience are timeless qualities, and that characters, despite the futuristic setting, find strength in each other and their shared purpose.

Relationships in sci-fi often develop under unusual or high-stress conditions, and dialogue becomes essential for conveying the deep emotional bonds that form. When characters work together to survive in hostile environments, the language they use becomes an anchor, fostering connection even when they feel far from home or familiarity. A character who says, "I couldn't do this without you," in the middle of an intense operation or exploration is acknowledging both vulnerability and trust, emphasizing the role of companionship in overcoming adversity. These expressions of reliance and gratitude remind readers that even in the vast, indifferent landscape of space or alien worlds, characters are drawn to each other, finding comfort and belonging in their shared experience.

In sci-fi, technology itself can sometimes serve as a conduit for emotional dialogue, especially when characters communicate across vast distances. Messages sent through holograms, long-distance transmissions, or even time-delayed audio logs can capture the longing, urgency, or love that exists despite physical separation. A message from a distant loved one saying, "I miss you every day," takes on added weight when the delay means the words won't reach the other person for months or even years. Similarly, an AI programmed to relay messages between separated family members might say, "She wanted me to remind you that she loves you, today and every day." These mediated communications evoke a sense of distance and yearning, showing that technology, while helpful, cannot replace the warmth of human connection, thus heightening the emotional stakes.

To enhance emotional resonance in a sci-fi setting, consider using metaphor or poetic language that connects the futuristic environment with universal feelings. Characters might speak in metaphors tied to their surroundings, like describing love as "the only constant in a galaxy of change" or fear as "a shadow that even light-years can't outrun." This use of figurative language bridges the gap between the extraordinary and the relatable, allowing characters to express complex emotions in ways that feel rooted in their specific world yet universally understandable. It also enriches the dialogue, providing readers with a poetic lens that deepens the emotional impact of the characters' words.

For AI or alien characters, showing emotional evolution through dialogue adds an extra layer of complexity and connection. An AI initially programmed for efficiency might start developing a sense of care, subtly reflected in its language as it shifts from saying, "Objective completed" to "I'm here for you." Similarly, an alien who initially speaks in formal, detached tones might begin using more human expressions, showing a budding empathy or understanding. These shifts in dialogue reveal the growth of non-human characters, showing that emotions and connections can transcend programming or biological boundaries, reinforcing the theme of shared humanity.

Lastly, silence or fragmented dialogue can be just as powerful as spoken words in conveying emotion in a sci-fi setting. When characters face loss, grief, or fear, their struggle to find words or their choice to remain silent can speak volumes. A character who can't bring themselves to say goodbye before a risky mission might simply nod, letting the gravity of the moment fill the space. Or a character who has survived a harrowing experience might speak in short, fragmented sentences, showing the lingering trauma without needing elaborate description. These pauses and gaps in speech reflect the weight of unspoken emotions, making the dialogue feel raw and authentic.

Conveying humanity through dialogue in sci-fi is about distilling the characters' emotions and connections within an extraordinary context. By anchoring dialogue in familiar feelings of awe, fear, love, and resilience, sci-fi writers can reveal characters' deepest emotions, allowing readers to connect with them on a fundamental level. The unknown becomes a backdrop that magnifies the intensity of human experience, proving that even across light-years or in the presence of advanced technology, the essence of what it means to be human remains constant. This connection between emotion and dialogue brings a layer of intimacy to sci-fi storytelling, showing that in the vastness of the universe, it is still our humanity that makes each journey meaningful.

Dialect and Diction: Developing a Unique Linguistic Style

Creating a unique linguistic style for characters in a sci-fi setting enriches the world and adds depth to the story, helping each society, species, or even social class feel distinctive. Dialect and diction in sci-fi go beyond simply inventing new words or slang; it involves constructing a voice and cadence that reflects each character's cultural background, environment, and individual personality. By thoughtfully developing dialect and diction, you can create a language that feels as integral to the world as its landscapes and technologies, drawing readers deeper into a universe that feels both familiar and foreign.

The first step in crafting a unique linguistic style is considering the character's cultural and social background. Language often reflects the society it comes from, including its values, norms, and worldview. For instance, in a hierarchical society, characters might use formal language to show respect or reinforce social structure, while in a more egalitarian setting, speech might be relaxed and straightforward. A character from a technologically advanced world might use highly technical language in daily conversation, while someone from a resource-scarce colony might speak in terse, economical sentences, shaped by the need for brevity and practicality. By letting each character's speech pattern reflect their society, you create an authentic voice that feels rooted in the story's world.

Dialect is an effective tool for distinguishing characters from different regions, planets, or social groups. Subtle shifts in pronunciation, rhythm, and vocabulary can imply a character's origins, making the world feel expansive and diverse. A character from a densely populated planet might speak in rapid, clipped tones, while someone from a rural, open landscape might draw out their words, reflecting a slower pace of life. If a character hails from a coastal region on an alien planet, they might use idioms related to tides or ocean life, infusing their speech with regional flavor. By weaving these differences into the dialogue, you give each place a unique linguistic identity, showing readers that the world is varied and filled with its own pockets of culture.

Inventing slang and idioms is another powerful way to build a unique linguistic style that feels integral to the setting. Sci-fi worlds are shaped by their own histories, technologies, and social issues, and these elements naturally give rise to colloquial expressions. Characters in a world where technology is deeply integrated might say "crash out" to mean they're exhausted or "go binary" to indicate clear-cut choices. Slang terms for advanced technology, like "boosters" for energy sources or "gleamers" for personal data analyzers, add realism, showing that this world has lived with these technologies long enough for shorthand to develop. These idioms and slang words deepen immersion, providing a sense of history and everyday life that makes the setting feel fully realized.

Diction, or word choice, plays an essential role in crafting a distinct linguistic style, as it reflects not only background but also personality and perspective. Formal diction may signal authority, wisdom, or aloofness, while casual diction can suggest openness, friendliness, or defiance. For instance, an alien diplomat might use precise, ceremonial language to convey respect and neutrality, whereas a rebellious youth might use short, blunt sentences, reflecting impatience or resistance. The words each character chooses reveal aspects of their personality and emotional state, allowing readers to infer details about their character without needing explicit descriptions. By matching diction to character traits, you create voices that feel true to each individual's nature, making them instantly recognizable.

For non-human or AI characters, diction is particularly important for conveying their otherness. Alien characters might use vocabulary rooted in their environment, biology, or societal structure, showing readers how they perceive the world. For instance, an alien species that perceives time differently might use terms that lack tense, speaking in "all time" rather than past or future. Meanwhile, an AI character might have diction that reflects logical, unambiguous thinking, often avoiding slang, idioms, or ambiguous phrasing. This choice of language not only distinguishes non-human characters but also reveals their unique mindset, enhancing the reader's understanding of their worldview and limitations.

Experimenting with syntax, or sentence structure, can further differentiate characters' speech. Different cultures or species may naturally favor different sentence constructions, reflecting their thought processes. An alien species that prioritizes actions over identities might place verbs at the start of sentences ("Run we must" instead of "We must run"), subtly hinting at their values and perspectives. Similarly, a character with a scientific background might use compound sentences to layer observations or qualify statements, reflecting a precise and analytical mindset. Altering syntax adds depth to the language, giving each character or group a signature cadence that hints at their mental processes and cultural norms.

Language in sci-fi settings is also influenced by technological advancements, and this should be reflected in diction and dialect. In a world where AI, cybernetic enhancements, or space travel are common, characters may use terms and references specific to their tech environment. A character accustomed to virtual interfaces might speak in digital terms, like saying "offline" instead of "unconscious" or using "scan" to mean "take a look." By embedding technology-related language naturally into dialogue, you create a sense of familiarity between the characters and their environment, showing readers that this technology is deeply integrated into daily life and has reshaped their vocabulary accordingly.

To make the linguistic style cohesive and immersive, consider creating linguistic consistency across different groups, classes, or species. Just as different regions on Earth have accents and dialects, each faction or species in your sci-fi world can have unique linguistic traits that signify shared history or common values. Military characters might use clipped, direct speech filled with jargon and codes, while aristocrats might have a slower, more elaborate style, full of ceremonial phrases. These consistent linguistic differences give the world a structured, believable feel, making it clear that each group has developed its own language norms, shaped by experience and shared culture.

When using invented language or slang, it's important to introduce new terms gradually and with context, so readers aren't overwhelmed. Start by defining a few essential terms through dialogue or action, allowing readers to pick up on meanings naturally. For example, if characters frequently mention a "time slip" when discussing risky travel, readers will infer that it's a dangerous phenomenon tied to space or time travel. By repeating terms in various contexts, you reinforce their meaning, allowing the language to become part of the reader's vocabulary as they progress through the story. This gradual introduction of new terms keeps the world accessible while deepening immersion.

Emotions are also expressed differently across linguistic styles, and considering how characters convey feelings through language can add another layer of depth. In a restrained or formal society, characters might use indirect expressions of emotion, saying, "Your presence brings honor" instead of "I missed you." Alternatively, in a society that values directness, characters might favor blunt, literal expressions of feeling, like "I want you to stay." These choices in expressing emotion through dialogue reveal cultural attitudes toward vulnerability and intimacy, showing readers how societal norms influence the way characters communicate their feelings.

Finally, remember that dialect and diction should evolve along with the character's journey. As characters experience new worlds or form bonds with different groups, their language may change, adopting phrases or expressions that reflect their growth. A character who starts as formal and reserved might begin to pick up slang from a more relaxed crew, revealing their increasing comfort and connection with them. Conversely, a rebellious character might adopt more formal speech if they come to respect a structured society. This evolution in language shows that characters are shaped by their experiences and relationships, adding authenticity to their arcs.

Developing a unique linguistic style for a sci-fi setting goes beyond inventing new words; it involves carefully constructing how characters speak, what influences their language, and how these choices reflect their culture, personality, and experiences. By thoughtfully building dialect, diction, and syntax, you create voices that resonate with readers, making the world feel diverse and alive. This linguistic depth brings authenticity to the story, showing that language is a living reflection of a society's history, values, and worldview, and that even in the vast unknown of space, the way characters speak reveals the essence of who they are.

Exposition through Dialogue: Revealing the Sci-Fi World Naturally

Exposition through dialogue is a powerful tool in sci-fi storytelling, allowing you to reveal the intricacies of your world naturally, without resorting to dense narrative blocks. Sci-fi settings are often complex, with new technologies, societal structures, and alien cultures that need to be conveyed effectively to immerse the reader. By using dialogue for exposition, you can introduce these details in a way that feels organic, keeping the pace lively and engaging while gradually unfolding the world. Skillfully handled, dialogue-driven exposition enriches the narrative, inviting readers to discover the world piece by piece as characters interact and discuss their environment.

One of the most effective ways to integrate exposition into dialogue is to make use of characters' differing levels of knowledge or experience within the world. A newcomer, like a visitor to an alien planet or a recruit in a futuristic space force, is naturally unfamiliar with their surroundings. By having a more knowledgeable character explain essential concepts, you can reveal key information without it feeling forced. For instance, if a new crew member is getting a tour of a spaceship, the guide might explain, "This is the med bay—our AI medic can treat anything from radiation burns to a broken limb in seconds." This approach allows readers to learn alongside the character, maintaining a natural flow of information while avoiding an artificial lecture.

Another technique for delivering exposition is to use dialogue during moments of conflict or urgency, where explanations become essential to the plot. In a tense situation, characters might have to clarify what a piece of tech does or why a specific protocol must be followed, especially if others are unfamiliar with it. For instance, a scientist might shout, "Don't touch that! The containment field's destabilizing—we'll all be vaporized!" Here, the urgency drives the exposition, giving the information a clear purpose while heightening the story's tension. By embedding explanations in high-stakes dialogue, you can maintain the story's momentum while revealing critical aspects of the sci-fi setting.

Using context-specific dialogue to convey details about the world is another way to introduce exposition naturally. Characters often discuss day-to-day matters, tasks, or routines that can reveal aspects of their world without requiring a full explanation. A simple line like, "The gravity on this planet makes everything twice as heavy—your muscles will be sore for days," hints at both the planet's environment and the physical challenges characters face there. Such remarks add depth to the world without breaking from the conversation's flow, allowing readers to absorb details organically. This technique is particularly effective when the characters are handling a new task or navigating a different environment, as it allows the world's unique qualities to emerge naturally from their interactions.

Characters' memories or shared histories can also serve as a way to introduce world-building details without sounding artificial. When two characters reminisce or reference a past event, they reveal background information while also building emotional depth. For example, a pilot might say to a fellow soldier, "This mission is starting to feel like Jupiter all over again," hinting at a significant event in their shared history. Such references create a sense of continuity within the world, as characters speak to each other in ways that acknowledge their shared experiences. This technique also gives readers hints about the larger world, encouraging them to piece together context clues and gain a sense of the setting's history.

Using misunderstandings or questions within dialogue allows characters to reveal or correct information, especially when dealing with complex technology, alien customs, or cultural differences. When one character misunderstands a concept, another can clarify or explain it naturally. For example, a character might ask, "Why does everyone here wear a locator chip?" leading to a response like, "It's mandatory. Last year, we lost three miners in the lower caverns before they implemented it." This approach not only provides essential information but also feels realistic, as people often ask questions when they don't understand something. It also adds a layer of character interaction, as one character's curiosity or confusion prompts another's knowledge.

Exposition can also be incorporated through dialogue that references political, social, or ethical issues relevant to the story's world. When characters debate or express opinions, they reveal details about the societal structures and values around them. For instance, a character might comment, "The AI council is all about efficiency, but they don't care about the people left behind," hinting at potential social divides or ethical dilemmas within the society. By embedding exposition in opinionated or emotional dialogue, you add depth to the world and show how the setting impacts the characters' lives and beliefs. This method makes the exposition feel purposeful, as it directly influences the characters' motivations and conflicts.

To keep exposition subtle, consider using dialogue that hints at information without fully explaining it, leaving space for readers to infer details. A character might say, "That's a Class IV storm warning—nothing like the ones back home," allowing readers to understand the severity without a full weather report. Or a mechanic could mutter, "If this stabilizer blows again, we're grounded for days," implying that it's happened before and that it's a major inconvenience. These hints keep the dialogue realistic and avoid over-explaining, trusting the reader to pick up on the significance from context. This approach also builds intrigue, encouraging readers to engage more deeply as they piece together the details.

When characters talk about the world in passing, using casual references or "throwaway" lines, it reinforces the setting's authenticity without drawing too much attention to the exposition. A character might casually mention, "I've only got two recharges left on my suit," revealing details about the technology and limitations they live with. Or someone could complain, "I thought the terraforming was supposed to make this place habitable by now," hinting at long-standing environmental issues. These casual comments create a sense of realism, as characters are so familiar with their world that they mention these aspects in an offhand way. This method allows the world-building to feel natural and lived-in, giving readers a glimpse into the everyday concerns of the characters.

When crafting exposition-heavy dialogue, keep the character's voice and personality in mind to maintain authenticity. A technical-minded character might use more jargon or complex terms, while a more straightforward character would summarize or simplify. By adapting the style of exposition to each character's way of speaking, you prevent the dialogue from feeling generic or overly staged. For example, an engineer might say, "The drive's energy output is barely at sixty percent," while a soldier might simply remark, "This ship's running on fumes." Each line reveals the same information but feels unique to the speaker, allowing the exposition to be consistent with character development.

Finally, remember that dialogue-driven exposition works best when spread out and interwoven with action or character development. Instead of explaining everything at once, reveal the world's details in layers, letting readers absorb the information over time. As characters encounter new places, confront different technologies, or meet other factions, let each interaction provide fresh insights into the world. This gradual approach makes the world-building feel organic, as readers experience the world alongside the characters. It also keeps the narrative dynamic, ensuring that each piece of exposition serves the story's flow and progression.

Exposition through dialogue in a sci-fi setting is about balancing information with interaction, allowing the world to unfold naturally as characters explore, question, and respond to their environment. By focusing on character-driven moments and using hints, context, and conflict, you can reveal the complexities of the sci-fi world in a way that feels immersive and engaging. When done well, dialogue-driven exposition not only enriches the world but also deepens the connections between characters and readers, making the story's universe both fascinating and accessible.

Tension and Timing: Dialogue for Action-Packed Sci-Fi Scenes

Crafting dialogue for action-packed sci-fi scenes requires a keen sense of timing, brevity, and intensity. In these moments, the stakes are high, and every word must serve to heighten tension, reveal character, or advance the plot. Action scenes in sci-fi settings often add an extra layer of complexity with futuristic technologies, high-speed chases, or alien threats. Effective dialogue in these situations keeps readers on the edge of their seats while immersing them in the urgency and chaos of the moment. The goal is to balance clarity with pacing, ensuring the dialogue propels the action forward without slowing down the scene.

One of the key principles in writing dialogue for action scenes is brevity. Short, direct lines of dialogue convey urgency, allowing characters to communicate without breaking the flow of the action. In high-stakes moments, characters are focused on survival or achieving their immediate goals, so long-winded explanations are unrealistic and disrupt pacing. For instance, instead of saying, "I think we should probably run because that door's not going to hold for long," a character might shout, "Move! Door's about to go!" Each word counts, maximizing impact while keeping the momentum fast-paced. This terse style mirrors the characters' heightened adrenaline, placing readers right in the middle of the intensity.

Timing is crucial for effective dialogue in action scenes, as well-timed exchanges can amplify suspense and tension. Dialogue can be strategically placed between bursts of action to give readers a moment to breathe and absorb the stakes before diving back into the chaos. For example, after a high-energy chase scene, a character could gasp, "Please tell me we lost them." This brief pause in the action allows tension to build as readers wait for the response, only for another character to say, "Not yet," before the chase resumes. These small beats add rhythm to the scene, creating a dynamic flow that allows for quick exchanges without sacrificing momentum.

In sci-fi action scenes, dialogue can be a powerful tool for revealing immediate obstacles or threats, keeping readers informed of the dangers as they unfold. Characters might call out warnings, describe oncoming threats, or issue commands to convey critical information without lengthy exposition. For instance, a pilot might yell, "Brace for impact—shields are down!" or "Target lock in three seconds!" These lines provide readers with essential context about the threats facing the characters, allowing the action to progress clearly and coherently. By using concise, direct statements, you ensure readers understand the stakes without slowing down the scene for detailed explanations.

When writing sci-fi action dialogue, it's essential to use tension-filled exchanges to capture the characters' emotional states under pressure. Moments of fear, anger, or determination can be communicated in just a few words, adding emotional weight to the scene without detracting from the action. A character under fire might mutter, "Not like this," revealing vulnerability, or grit their teeth and say, "Let's finish this," conveying resolve. These short, emotionally charged lines add depth to the characters, showing how they cope with the intensity of the moment and giving readers an emotional anchor amid the high-stakes action.

Another effective technique is to use overlapping or interruptive dialogue, especially when characters are communicating in a fast-paced, chaotic setting. In the heat of an alien attack or during a ship malfunction, characters might cut each other off, speak over one another, or fail to finish sentences as they struggle to communicate. For example:

"Get the door—" "It's jammed!" "Use the override!" "No time!"

These quick, fragmented exchanges mimic the frantic nature of the scene, creating a sense of urgency and disarray. The overlapping dialogue shows that the characters are operating under pressure, struggling to stay focused as they manage the crisis. By capturing this disjointed communication style, you convey the chaos and tension of the action, immersing readers in the immediacy of the experience.

Sci-fi action scenes often involve complex technology, which can make dialogue challenging. To keep the pacing smooth, avoid overexplaining how technology works during action scenes. Instead, focus on its immediate function and limitations. Characters might refer to tech using shorthand or specialized terms, relying on their knowledge to communicate efficiently. For instance, a character could yell, "Engage thrusters, max power!" instead of describing how thrusters operate. If a particular piece of technology malfunctions, keep the explanation brief and relevant to the action. "Main engine's fried—we're dead in the water!" tells readers all they need to know. This approach keeps the dialogue grounded in the characters' immediate needs, allowing the tech to enhance the action rather than bogging it down.

In an action-packed sci-fi setting, characters' dialogue can be a powerful way to show their relationships and teamwork under pressure. Quick, coordinated exchanges reveal how well (or poorly) characters function together in high-stakes scenarios. A seasoned pilot and co-pilot, for instance, might anticipate each other's moves with little verbal exchange, saying only, "You see it?" followed by, "On it," as they maneuver through a debris field. Alternatively, characters with conflicting approaches might clash mid-crisis, with one shouting, "We need to regroup!" and the other retorting, "No time—just go!" These interactions reveal the characters' dynamics and level of trust, adding an interpersonal layer to the tension. By showing how characters communicate under pressure, you add emotional resonance to the scene, highlighting their strengths, vulnerabilities, and relationships.

Using humor or sarcasm in dialogue can provide moments of relief in action-packed sci-fi scenes, offering brief, natural pauses that enhance the pacing and give readers a chance to breathe. A character facing overwhelming odds might quip, "Well, this day just keeps getting better," or joke, "If I make it out of this, drinks are on me." These quick, wry comments convey resilience and defiance, showing that even in the face of danger, characters find ways to cope. The humor should be brief and well-timed, breaking up the intensity without diminishing the stakes. This touch of levity adds dimension to the characters, showing how they use humor as a defense mechanism amid the chaos.

In addition to verbal dialogue, consider using non-verbal cues—such as gestures, facial expressions, or body language—to convey communication in action scenes. Characters might exchange a tense nod before charging into danger, or make eye contact as they prepare to split up, saying everything they need to with a glance. These non-verbal cues allow for moments of silent understanding, adding subtlety to the interaction without slowing down the action. In high-stakes scenes where there isn't time for lengthy goodbyes or explanations, these quick, wordless exchanges convey the depth of characters' bonds, creating moments that resonate even in the midst of chaos.

Lastly, action-packed sci-fi scenes benefit from well-paced dialogue that punctuates, rather than dominates, the narrative. Allow the dialogue to act as beats within the action, guiding the reader's attention without overshadowing the physical stakes. Short, impactful lines that focus on immediate needs—"Left flank—now!" or "We're outnumbered!"—give rhythm to the action, emphasizing key moments. These sharp bursts of dialogue keep the reader grounded in the scene's progression, creating a cohesive blend of dialogue and action that feels immersive and cinematic.

Crafting dialogue for action-packed sci-fi scenes is about balancing urgency with clarity, intensity with brevity, and technology with humanity. By using concise language, well-timed exchanges, and emotionally charged lines, you create dialogue that drives the action forward while grounding it in character and tension. These techniques ensure that readers feel the high stakes and fast pace of the scene, while remaining engaged with the characters' struggles and triumphs, creating an experience that's as exhilarating as it is immersive.

Monologues from the Stars: Using Soliloquies to Reflect Themes

In sci-fi, monologues and soliloquies are powerful tools for exploring deeper themes, allowing characters to reflect on their place in the vastness of the universe, wrestle with existential questions, and reveal inner conflicts that resonate with readers. These moments of introspection—when a character voices their thoughts in solitude, sometimes to the stars, an AI, or even an empty space—provide a window into their soul, elevating the narrative beyond action and adventure. Sci-fi soliloquies invite readers to pause and ponder big questions alongside the characters, making the story feel intimate and profound, even amid galaxies, alien civilizations, and advanced technology.

One of the most effective uses of a soliloquy in sci-fi is to reflect on themes of isolation and the human desire for connection. Characters in sci-fi settings often find themselves alone, separated from loved ones by vast distances, or even isolated by technology or cultural differences. In such moments, a character's soliloquy can capture the ache of isolation and the longing for connection. A character might gaze out of a spaceship window and speak to the stars, saying, "Out here, surrounded by light-years of empty space, I've never felt more alone. Yet somehow, I feel closer to everything than ever before." This reflection taps into universal emotions, showing that no matter how far humanity ventures, the need for connection remains a defining feature of the human experience.

Soliloquies in sci-fi are also a powerful way to explore themes of discovery and wonder. When characters are faced with alien landscapes, new dimensions, or the discovery of unknown life forms, a soliloquy can capture their awe and sense of wonder, allowing readers to share in the experience. Imagine a scientist standing before an ancient alien relic, whispering, "What mind could have created this? What knowledge did they possess that we're only beginning to imagine?" This quiet reflection allows the character to voice their curiosity and reverence, drawing readers into the beauty and mystery of the sci-fi world while emphasizing the wonder of exploration and the thrill of uncovering the unknown.

Sci-fi often grapples with themes of existence and identity, and soliloquies are an ideal device for characters to explore these questions on a deeply personal level. A character who discovers they're an AI or a clone, for example, might wrestle with the nature of their identity in a soliloquy, questioning what makes them truly "alive." They might say, "If my memories are manufactured, my thoughts coded—does that make my feelings any less real?" This inner conflict not only brings depth to the character but also invites readers to consider their own beliefs about consciousness and what it means to be human. Through soliloquies, sci-fi can address these existential questions with emotional resonance, making abstract themes feel immediate and personal.

Monologues can also serve as a means of processing loss and grief, particularly in sci-fi, where characters may face the death of loved ones in far-flung locations or endure long separations due to space travel. A character might speak to the memory of someone they've lost, saying, "You would have loved this place. I wish you could see it. Somehow, I feel like you're here, in every star I pass." Such a soliloquy not only gives the character space to process their feelings but also illustrates the ways in which love and loss transcend time and space. These moments of vulnerability allow readers to connect with the character's grief, bringing emotional depth to the narrative even within the futuristic setting.

In sci-fi, soliloquies are often used to reflect on the theme of humanity's impact on the universe, exploring questions of responsibility, ethics, and legacy. When characters find themselves in a position of power—such as the discovery of a new resource, or the ability to shape entire ecosystems—soliloquies allow them to grapple with the moral implications of their actions. A character might stand alone on a terraformed planet and ask, "Who am I to shape this world? To decide what lives or dies?" This internal debate invites readers to consider the ethical boundaries of human progress, creating a philosophical layer that adds complexity to the character's choices and to the story's larger themes.

Sci-fi soliloquies also lend themselves well to themes of destiny and free will, especially when characters face futures that seem predetermined by advanced technology, genetics, or societal structures. A character who feels trapped by their circumstances might speak aloud to challenge fate, saying, "Am I just a product of my programming, or can I choose my own path?" These moments reveal the character's internal struggle, giving voice to the timeless human quest for autonomy and purpose. Soliloquies on destiny and free will highlight the sci-fi genre's exploration of choice and agency, showing that even in a world shaped by technology, characters yearn to forge their own identities.

Another powerful use of soliloquies in sci-fi is to allow characters to confront fear and mortality, especially in settings where they face life-threatening situations or the vast, indifferent emptiness of space. Alone in the cockpit of a damaged ship or marooned on an alien planet, a character might voice their fears, saying, "I thought I was brave, but out here, facing the abyss, I'm nothing but terrified." This raw admission of vulnerability deepens the reader's connection to the character, showing that even in a genre marked by courage and adventure, the fear of death is an experience that unites all sentient beings. By allowing characters to reflect on mortality, soliloquies bring a sense of humility and humanity to the sci-fi narrative, grounding it in a universal truth.

Monologues can also be used to voice philosophical reflections, particularly on the nature of knowledge, understanding, and progress. A scientist character might, after a breakthrough, stand in quiet contemplation and muse, "For every answer we find, a thousand new questions arise. Perhaps the universe is an endless puzzle—designed to keep us reaching." Such reflections offer readers insight into the character's mindset while exploring the broader theme of curiosity as a driving force in human nature. Soliloquies about knowledge and progress remind readers that sci-fi is as much about exploration of ideas as it is about physical space, inviting them to ponder the mysteries of existence alongside the characters.

In a futuristic or alien setting, soliloquies can help bridge the gap between the familiar and the strange, allowing characters to voice reflections that make the world feel grounded and relatable. A character might gaze at an alien sky and say, "In the end, it's not so different, is it? We look up and see stars. They looked up and saw the same." This reflection emphasizes the shared experience of wonder and curiosity, connecting readers to the alien world by highlighting universal themes. By grounding sci-fi themes in relatable observations, soliloquies make even the most fantastical elements feel accessible, allowing readers to see themselves within the story.

When crafting a sci-fi soliloquy, keep the language and tone reflective of the character's background, mindset, and unique situation. A scientist's monologue might be laced with curiosity and technical language, while a soldier's might focus on duty, honor, or survival. Tailoring each soliloquy to the character's voice ensures that it feels authentic and natural, drawing readers deeper into the narrative. These individual touches give each soliloquy a distinct emotional weight, making it a personal reflection as well as a thematic exploration.

Ultimately, using soliloquies in sci-fi allows characters to reflect on the themes that make the genre so compelling—identity, knowledge, wonder, destiny, and the human condition. By giving voice to their innermost thoughts, you create moments of introspection that resonate on a deeply personal level, turning abstract themes into lived experiences. Monologues from the stars remind readers that, no matter how advanced or alien the setting, the questions that drive us remain fundamentally human, bridging the vastness of space and time with the timeless reflections that define our species. Through these moments of solitude and reflection, sci-fi soliloquies invite readers to journey not only across galaxies but also into the depths of the human spirit.

Laying the Foundation: Building Worlds from Concept to Reality

Building a sci-fi world from concept to reality is a transformative journey, requiring careful attention to detail, creativity, and consistency. A strong foundation in world-building not only immerses readers but also gives the story depth and coherence. In sci-fi, where settings often include futuristic technologies, alien cultures, and complex societal structures, effective world-building is essential to making these elements feel authentic and engaging. This process starts with a clear concept and gradually adds layers, transforming an idea into a vivid, dynamic reality that supports both plot and character development.

The first step in world-building is defining the core concept or "big idea" that will shape the setting. This could be an overarching theme, a unique technological advancement, or a distinct environment that sets the tone for the world. For instance, consider a concept based on a society that has achieved interstellar travel but at a steep environmental or ethical cost. This central concept serves as the foundation for the world, influencing its values, conflicts, and technologies. A strong concept not only sets the direction for world-building but also gives readers a lens through which they can understand the world's unique challenges and norms.

Once the concept is established, it's important to consider the setting's physical characteristics, including geography, climate, and ecosystems. These factors influence how societies develop, shaping everything from architecture to transportation. A world with low gravity, for example, might feature sprawling cities with suspended walkways or floating structures, while a planet with frequent solar storms could necessitate underground shelters or shielded habitats. Thinking through these physical details helps the world feel tangible, as each environmental factor affects daily life and the way people adapt. A consistent and well-defined physical setting grounds the story, making even the most fantastical elements feel plausible.

Technology plays a central role in sci-fi world-building, as it often defines the boundaries of what characters can achieve. When creating futuristic technology, it's crucial to decide how advanced it is, how accessible it is to the population, and how it impacts daily life. Consider the role of AI, medical advancements, space travel, and energy sources in your world. For instance, if AI is ubiquitous, it might change how people communicate, work, and even interact emotionally. The impact of these technologies should be woven into the fabric of society, shaping everything from social hierarchies to personal relationships. By considering both the possibilities and limitations of technology, you create a setting where innovation feels like a natural extension of the world.

Societal structure is another vital layer in world-building, as it defines how people interact within the setting. A society's values, political systems, and social norms create a framework for the characters' motivations and conflicts. For example, a rigid caste system with access to advanced genetic engineering might dictate not only one's profession but also social worth, influencing how people relate to each other. Alternatively, a utopian society where resources are abundant might have minimal conflict but grapple with other issues, like purpose or existential ennui. By defining societal structures, you give readers a sense of the challenges and opportunities unique to this world, deepening their understanding of character dynamics and motivations.

In a sci-fi world, alien species or genetically altered humans can add richness and diversity, providing opportunities to explore themes of difference, acceptance, and conflict. When creating alien cultures or modified human societies, consider how they view concepts like time, identity, and community, as these might differ significantly from human norms. Perhaps an alien race values collective memory over individual achievement, or a group of genetically enhanced humans sees themselves as superior. These cultural or biological differences add depth to the world, making interactions between species or groups layered with complexity. Thoughtfully developed alien or hybrid societies challenge characters to confront their own values, driving tension and understanding within the narrative.

Magic or "soft science" elements—like telepathy, advanced psychic abilities, or otherworldly powers—are often included in sci-fi settings, though they require careful integration to avoid inconsistencies. Establish clear rules for how these abilities work, who can use them, and what limitations exist. For instance, a society where psychic abilities are common might have strict laws governing their use, while a rare power might be revered or feared. Creating logical constraints around these elements prevents them from becoming convenient plot devices, giving them a sense of realism. Consistent rules also add stakes and consequences, as characters face both the benefits and costs of wielding such abilities within the constraints of their world.

Economic and resource systems are essential for grounding sci-fi worlds, as they influence social dynamics, trade, and conflict. Decide on the primary resources—like energy sources, precious metals, or even water—that sustain the world's economy. A society reliant on a rare mineral might have strict policies around mining and distribution, while a world abundant in clean energy might lack traditional wealth disparities but face other forms of division. These economic systems give the world depth, providing motivation for conflicts or alliances between different factions, planets, or species. By developing a coherent economy, you create a world that feels self-sustaining and layered with realistic stakes.

Language and dialect are powerful tools for adding authenticity to a sci-fi setting. Consider whether there are regional dialects, specialized terminology, or even entirely different languages in the world. A galactic society might have a "common tongue" that everyone uses, alongside individual languages that signify cultural heritage. Characters could use specific slang or idioms related to their trade or background, like "binary talk" for AI programmers or "stardust" as slang for space travel. This linguistic diversity enriches the world by reflecting its various influences, histories, and technological advancements, giving each character or faction a distinctive voice.

Adding historical context and mythology to your sci-fi world can deepen its complexity and sense of authenticity. Societies are shaped by their histories, and a rich backstory filled with key events, wars, or discoveries can influence the beliefs and behaviors of your characters. Perhaps the world endured a catastrophic war over technology, resulting in widespread distrust of certain innovations, or maybe an ancient alliance between species led to longstanding peace treaties and trade agreements. Historical context provides readers with a sense of continuity, showing that the world extends beyond the current story, while myths or legends offer insight into cultural beliefs and fears, adding another layer of realism to the world.

When building a sci-fi world, it's important to establish the boundaries of exploration, from known territories to uncharted space. Defining the limits of the known universe and the presence of dangerous or mysterious regions creates intrigue and provides natural plot points for adventure. Known sectors might be mapped and regulated, while uncharted zones could hold the potential for discovery, danger, or hidden knowledge. These boundaries provide tension and opportunities for exploration, as characters venture into unknown realms or uncover secrets about their world. By setting clear boundaries, you invite readers to wonder about what lies beyond, enhancing the sense of scale and possibility within the story.

Finally, when building a sci-fi world, remember to maintain consistency and avoid overloading the story with excessive details. Not every aspect of the world needs to be explicitly described; instead, choose specific details that serve the story and reveal them naturally through characters' interactions and experiences. A character casually mentioning "the smog domes on New Earth" or "last year's solar drought" is often more effective than a full explanation. By revealing the world gradually, you keep the story engaging and allow readers to immerse themselves without feeling overwhelmed. Selective world-building also gives the impression of a fully developed world, even if certain aspects remain in the background.

Creating a sci-fi world from concept to reality is a careful balance of imagination, logic, and storytelling. By establishing a clear concept and layering elements like geography, technology, society, and history, you build a setting that feels dynamic and immersive. With each added detail, the world grows richer, becoming an environment that influences the characters, shapes the plot, and reflects the themes at the heart of the story. Thoughtful world-building makes even the most fantastical settings feel real, inviting readers to explore a universe that feels as boundless, intricate, and compelling as the characters who inhabit it.

Designing the Ecosystem: Landscapes, Climates, and Natural Laws

Designing an ecosystem in a sci-fi world involves more than simply creating alien landscapes or unusual climates; it requires an understanding of how these elements interact to form a believable, self-sustaining environment. Every choice in landscape, climate, and natural laws shapes how life evolves, how societies function, and how characters interact with their surroundings. Thoughtfully crafted ecosystems not only ground the setting in realism but also add depth to the story, influencing character behavior, shaping plot dynamics, and introducing natural challenges that enhance tension and stakes.

When creating a sci-fi ecosystem, the first step is to define the landscape's physical structure—its mountains, oceans, plains, forests, or other geological features. The physical layout of the land sets the stage for everything else, influencing climate, wildlife, and even human or alien settlements. A world dominated by vast deserts, for example, might foster nomadic societies or technologically advanced cities adapted to harsh conditions, while an aquatic planet with endless oceans could lead to floating cities, underwater colonies, or civilizations based around marine resources. By thinking about the landscape in detail, you provide a tangible setting that feels real and shapes the way life exists and thrives within it.

Climate is another fundamental component of the ecosystem, as it dictates what kinds of life can exist and how societies adapt. Temperature, weather patterns, and seasonal changes are all factors to consider, and they should be consistent with the world's position in its solar system or galaxy. A planet with extreme temperature fluctuations might have organisms that adapt seasonally, developing protective shells or dormant states during harsh conditions. If the world is in perpetual winter, species might evolve to conserve heat or live underground, and human settlements might rely on geothermal energy. Thoughtful climate design adds realism to the world, and it allows for new plot possibilities, such as characters navigating seasonal challenges or preparing for recurring climate events.

The presence of unique natural laws or altered physics can set a sci-fi world apart, giving it a distinctive feel while creating interesting challenges and opportunities for characters. A low-gravity environment might allow for massive, sprawling structures and floating islands, while high-gravity conditions could lead to dense, compact civilizations with squat buildings. Natural laws can also affect how characters interact with the environment; in low gravity, transportation might involve gliding or bouncing, while in high gravity, simple tasks become exhausting. If the world has a unique atmosphere, it could affect visibility, sound, or even how characters breathe. By tweaking natural laws thoughtfully, you make the setting feel distinct and introduce environmental challenges that add tension and shape the story.

Flora and fauna are essential to a sci-fi ecosystem, as they add life and detail to the landscape. Alien plants and animals not only make the setting visually striking but also serve as potential resources, threats, or companions for the characters. When designing flora, consider the unique conditions they must adapt to—like plants with heat-resistant leaves in a volcanic zone, or trees with long roots to draw moisture in a desert. Alien animals can introduce natural conflicts, whether through territorial behavior, predatory instincts, or symbiotic relationships with humans or other species. For instance, a pack-hunting creature adapted to dense forests could become an obstacle for travelers, or a species of large, domesticated animals could serve as transport. Alien flora and fauna bring vibrancy to the world and create opportunities for storytelling, showing how life adapts in extraordinary ways.

Consider how natural resources within the ecosystem drive societal development and interactions. Every world has valuable resources—minerals, water, arable land—that shape economies and influence social dynamics. A world with an abundance of rare crystals might attract miners, traders, and explorers, leading to a resource-based economy or even conflict over control. Alternatively, a world with scarce water might have strict regulations and societal structures around its preservation, giving rise to cultural practices around conservation. By integrating resources naturally within the environment, you add layers of realism, showing how society's development is shaped by the ecosystem and its offerings or limitations.

Thinking about evolutionary adaptations among native species or inhabitants helps establish the world's natural realism and provides hints at the ecosystem's challenges. Animals, plants, and even human or alien societies evolve to survive in unique climates, terrain, or environmental threats. For example, an alien species that evolved on a windy planet might have sturdy, low-built bodies, while a species from a dark, cave-laden world could develop heightened senses or echolocation. These adaptations bring depth to the setting, showing that life shapes itself to its environment in practical, believable ways. When characters observe or interact with these adaptations, it provides insights into the ecosystem's demands, adding detail without excessive exposition.

The presence of natural phenomena, like storms, volcanic activity, or even meteor showers, can also define a sci-fi ecosystem. Such occurrences create both challenges and points of interest within the setting, influencing characters' plans and shaping the way societies develop. For instance, a planet with frequent electrical storms might have settlements equipped with special grounding systems, or an area with regular tectonic shifts could develop flexible, resilient infrastructure. Characters may learn to anticipate and prepare for these phenomena, whether that means finding shelter during sandstorms or using storms to their advantage, like harnessing lightning energy. These natural events add dynamism to the world, showing that nature has a life of its own, one that characters must respect and contend with.

When designing an ecosystem, consider how societies and characters might use technology to adapt to or manipulate their environment. Advanced irrigation systems, environmental suits, or climate-modification technology reflect the ways civilizations can adapt to and sometimes reshape their surroundings. A society with domed cities on an inhospitable planet might create self-sustaining ecosystems within each dome, or characters on a desert world could wear suits designed to recycle water. These technological adaptations reveal both the strengths and limitations of the world, showing that while some challenges can be overcome, others require constant vigilance or compromise. Technology thus becomes an extension of the ecosystem, shaping the way people live within it.

Cultural practices often emerge in response to the ecosystem, adding another layer of authenticity to the world. Rituals, superstitions, and traditions often evolve as people learn to live within their environment. A culture in a forested world might hold ceremonies to honor the trees they depend on, or a society on a planet with perpetual daylight might develop nocturnal rituals as a way of marking the passage of time. These practices add character to the setting, giving the world a sense of history and continuity, while also revealing the ways people find meaning and resilience within their surroundings.

When designing ecosystems, remember that they are interconnected systems where each component affects the others. Water sources, plant life, weather patterns, and landforms all interact to create a balanced, functioning environment. Removing or altering one aspect could have a cascading effect on the ecosystem as a whole. For instance, depleting a water source might lead to a decline in plant life, which then affects animal populations, which in turn impacts any society dependent on those animals for food or resources. Recognizing these interconnections and designing them with care creates a world that feels self-sustaining and alive, allowing readers to suspend disbelief and immerse themselves fully in the setting.

Incorporating sensory details into the ecosystem makes it more vivid and immersive for readers. Descriptions of the sights, sounds, smells, and textures within a sci-fi environment bring the world to life in readers' minds. Describe the prickly texture of alien grass, the scent of a rain-soaked jungle, or the eerie silence of a frozen wasteland. These sensory details anchor readers in the setting, making it feel like a place they can truly experience. Sensory descriptions also deepen the connection between characters and their environment, as they react to and interact with the world around them.

Designing a sci-fi ecosystem from landscapes and climates to natural laws is a multi-layered process that transforms the setting into a character in its own right. By creating a coherent, interconnected environment, you add depth to the world, shaping how characters live, survive, and interact. A well-designed ecosystem offers natural challenges and resources, fosters unique cultural practices, and allows societies to thrive or struggle in response to their surroundings. Thoughtful world-building in the ecosystem ensures that the setting feels real and dynamic, grounding the story in a vivid landscape that enhances both plot and character development, making the sci-fi universe as captivating as the story itself.

Alien Societies: Crafting Cultures, Beliefs, and Social Structures

Creating alien societies in sci-fi allows for a rich exploration of diversity, imagination, and the ways cultures shape individuals and interactions. Alien societies go beyond visual differences; they're built on unique beliefs, social structures, and traditions that feel authentic to the world they inhabit. A thoughtfully crafted alien culture adds depth to the story, challenges characters' assumptions, and offers readers a fresh perspective on universal themes. When building an alien society, the goal is to make it feel as complex and nuanced as any human society, rooted in its own history, values, and environmental influences.

The foundation of any alien society begins with its environment, as the conditions of the planet or setting will shape the society's culture, resources, and way of life. A species from a planet with harsh climates, like extreme heat or perpetual darkness, might have developed traditions focused on survival, efficiency, or communal living. Alternatively, a species from a water-based world may have an entirely different way of communicating or valuing community, possibly relying on fluid motion or color changes instead of spoken language. The environment acts as a silent architect, influencing every facet of an alien society's development and shaping their priorities, whether it's food security, migration, or reverence for natural elements.

Establishing a distinct belief system is essential for creating an alien society that feels authentic and complex. Just like human societies, alien cultures are often rooted in myths, religious beliefs, or philosophical values that provide a sense of meaning and purpose. Perhaps an alien society believes that the universe is a living entity, with stars as its thoughts and planets as its dreams, shaping their view of life as interconnected and sacred. Alternatively, a war-like species might have a belief system focused on honor and valor, with rites surrounding combat or bravery. These beliefs can lead to unique practices, traditions, and taboos, adding dimension to the society's interactions and giving insight into their worldview.

Social structure is another vital aspect of crafting an alien society, as it defines roles, responsibilities, and the distribution of power. A rigid caste system might dictate every aspect of life for an alien society, from profession to marriage, creating a structured but potentially oppressive society. Conversely, a more egalitarian species may lack strict hierarchies, with decisions made communally or based on consensus. Some societies may value age and experience, while others prioritize physical prowess, intellect, or even psychic abilities. By establishing a clear social structure, you create a framework that affects how characters interact, what motivates them, and where conflicts or social tensions might arise.

Alien societies often have unique family structures or community bonds that differ from human norms. Family might not be based on biology but on skills, interests, or chosen connections. A species that reproduces asexually or communally may view kinship in broader terms, perhaps forming "hive" or "clan" groups that care for all young collectively. Alternatively, a species with a long lifespan might see parent-child relationships very differently, with generations living together and knowledge passed down through storytelling or shared memory. These family structures reveal how society views loyalty, identity, and responsibility, adding another layer of complexity to interpersonal relationships and character motivations.

Rituals and ceremonies give life to an alien society, showing readers what the species values and how they express their beliefs. Ceremonies may revolve around major life events—birth, death, maturity—or around natural events like celestial cycles or seasonal changes. A nocturnal species might have "dawn rituals" to mark the end of each day, while a species that values strength might celebrate physical milestones with rites of passage or combat trials.

Rituals add authenticity to the world by highlighting a society's history, values, and traditions, providing insight into how they cope with life's changes and celebrate continuity. These ceremonies also offer opportunities for character development, as characters participate in or react to cultural practices that reflect their heritage.

Language and communication style is a defining trait for alien societies, and even subtle differences can make interactions feel truly otherworldly. Consider whether the species communicates through spoken words, body language, bioluminescent displays, or telepathy. For a society that relies on scent or color shifts, for example, communication may be instantaneous and hard to conceal, resulting in a culture that values openness and transparency. If communication is highly formalized or ritualistic, it might reflect a society that values tradition and hierarchy. Designing unique communication styles helps distinguish alien characters and adds authenticity to the society, showing that their interactions are shaped by physiological and cultural factors unique to their species.

Alien societies may have differing views on time, affecting everything from work cycles to celebrations and life goals. A species with a short lifespan might be intensely focused on efficiency, achievement, or legacy, celebrating rapid accomplishments and milestones. Conversely, a long-lived species may view time as cyclical rather than linear, with customs that emphasize patience, reflection, or long-term planning. Cultural concepts of time influence how societies develop and prioritize, and they also affect character motivations and expectations. A character from a society that values quick success might struggle to understand a species that treasures contemplation and slow progress, creating tension or misunderstanding that drives the narrative.

Technology and resource use is another key factor in building an alien society. The level and type of technology often reflects a society's values and challenges. For example, a species that reveres nature may use organic, symbiotic technologies that work harmoniously with the environment, while a society obsessed with progress might prioritize mining, manufacturing, or even bioengineering to maximize output. Some societies may value sustainability, using renewable resources exclusively, while others might prioritize short-term gains with little concern for environmental impact. The relationship between the society and its resources creates layers of conflict and cultural distinction, influencing characters' views on technology, nature, and progress.

Political structures and governance reveal how alien societies manage power and address conflict. A species with a hive-mind might have collective decision-making, while a technologically advanced society might rely on AI governance or complex voting systems. Some species might follow a hereditary rule, seeing leadership as a matter of destiny, while others may have fluid power structures, with leaders chosen based on specific needs or crises. By defining the political structure, you give context to the society's stability (or instability), showing how conflicts are resolved, alliances are formed, and dissent is handled. This structure provides a backdrop for tension within the narrative, as characters navigate power dynamics that may align with or challenge their personal beliefs.

Alien societies often have unique economic systems and methods of resource distribution that reflect their values and environment. A species that values intellectual achievement might reward citizens based on scientific or artistic contributions rather than traditional wealth, while a species on a barren planet might have an economy centered on water or mineral trade. In a communal society, resources may be shared equally, whereas a more individualistic society could reward personal achievement or survival skills. The way resources are valued and distributed affects everything from class structures to individual motivations, revealing the society's priorities and the kinds of conflicts that may arise over resources or status.

Alien societies may approach ethics and law differently from human societies, and exploring these differences can highlight themes of morality and justice. A species with a communal mindset may have strict laws to protect collective well-being, while a society that prizes freedom may resist regulations, relying on personal codes of honor instead. For a species that values knowledge above all, "crimes" might include withholding information or suppressing discovery. By defining the ethical boundaries and legal frameworks, you show readers how alien societies enforce values, handle transgressions, and protect their way of life. Ethical dilemmas within the story can arise naturally from these differences, creating opportunities for character development and cultural conflict.

Finally, crafting an alien society requires an understanding of cultural exchange and adaptability. Alien societies, like human ones, evolve and adapt based on contact with other cultures, environmental changes, or technological advancements. A society that encounters a new species may integrate or resist foreign ideas, adopt new practices, or struggle with maintaining traditional beliefs. Exploring how an alien society responds to change adds depth to the narrative, as characters face challenges to their identity and beliefs. This adaptability (or resistance) shows readers that the culture is dynamic, capable of growth and conflict, making it feel truly alive.

In creating alien societies, the goal is to reflect diversity, complexity, and individuality within a coherent structure, showing that even non-human cultures have deeply rooted values and conflicts. Thoughtful attention to environment, belief systems, social structures, and traditions makes these societies feel real, grounded in their own internal logic and history. By weaving these elements together, you create societies that challenge characters, enrich the world, and engage readers, inviting them to explore new perspectives and question their own assumptions about culture, identity, and humanity.

The Rules of Reality: Establishing Technology, Magic, or Advanced Science

In a sci-fi world, establishing the rules that govern technology, magic, or advanced science is essential for creating a setting that feels consistent, immersive, and believable. Whether your story features futuristic technologies, magical systems, or speculative science, clear and consistent rules provide a framework that defines what is possible and how characters interact with their environment. Well-defined systems of technology or magic give the world depth, creating both opportunities and limitations for the characters. Establishing these rules early on keeps readers engaged and helps prevent plot holes, allowing the story to evolve naturally within its own reality.

The first step in establishing these rules is to decide on the foundational concept for your system, whether it's advanced technology, magic, or a blend of both. In a sci-fi world, technology might be based on a breakthrough in AI, genetic engineering, or interstellar travel. If magic is involved, it could have origins in the manipulation of energy, psychic abilities, or the harnessing of cosmic forces. Speculative science, meanwhile, often involves extrapolating current scientific theories to create new rules, such as faster-than-light travel, teleportation, or biological enhancement. Starting with a core concept anchors the system, setting the tone and ensuring that it aligns with the world's broader themes and influences everything from plot points to character abilities.

Once you have a central concept, defining the limitations and costs associated with it is crucial for keeping the system balanced and preventing it from becoming a convenient solution for every problem. If your world has advanced AI, maybe it's prone to misinterpretations or malfunctions, making it unreliable in certain scenarios. For a magical system, perhaps each spell requires energy that weakens the user or materials that are rare or dangerous to obtain. In speculative science, limitations could include energy constraints or environmental factors that prevent certain technologies from functioning in specific places. These limitations make the system more relatable, adding stakes to its use and preventing characters from relying too heavily on it to solve all their problems.

Understanding who has access to the technology, magic, or science-based abilities in your world adds another layer of complexity. In a society with advanced tech, is it available to everyone or restricted to the elite? In a world where magic exists, are only a select few born with the ability, or can anyone learn it with dedication? Access creates social dynamics, affecting everything from power structures to individual motivations. Restricted access to powerful tools or abilities can foster inequality, jealousy, and conflict, while widespread access can lead to societal norms or cultural practices centered around that power. By establishing who can wield these abilities, you add social depth and tension to the world, influencing the characters' relationships and conflicts.

Every system, whether technological or magical, should have internal logic that defines how it operates and interacts with the physical world. For technology, this might mean explaining the scientific principles that make it work, even if those principles are theoretical. In a magical setting, it could mean outlining specific rules governing spells or energy sources. For example, if faster-than-light travel is a staple in your world, consider explaining its energy requirements, its effect on the human body, or the training required to use it safely. For a magical system, you might define that certain spells can only be performed under specific conditions, like full moons or during a solar eclipse. These rules create coherence, showing that the system operates predictably, with a cause-and-effect structure that readers can understand and anticipate.

Introducing risks and consequences for using technology, magic, or advanced science prevents these elements from becoming overpowered and encourages strategic use by the characters. Perhaps AI systems occasionally rebel, creating chaos, or maybe overuse of a magical ability leads to physical deterioration. In speculative science, pushing technology too far could lead to catastrophic failures or environmental damage. By introducing risks, you add tension to scenes where characters must decide whether the potential benefit is worth the danger. This complexity not only adds stakes to the story but also makes the system feel like a real part of the world, with flaws and dangers that mirror real-life technologies or powers.

Balancing innovation with existing culture and society is also key to creating a cohesive world. Advanced technology or magic doesn't exist in a vacuum; it influences—and is influenced by—the society around it. If AI is widespread, does it lead to a loss of jobs and resentment from certain social groups? If magic is a powerful force, are there religions, taboos, or cultural practices that regulate or celebrate its use? Social norms, laws, and cultural beliefs regarding technology or magic provide context for how the system is accepted, feared, or regulated. For instance, a society that reveres magic might have strict codes of conduct for its use, while a tech-driven world could have governmental oversight or corporations with monopolies on advanced tools. This social framework makes the system feel integrated into the fabric of the world, adding layers of depth and conflict.

Training or education related to technology or magic is another important consideration. If these abilities require skill, where and how do characters learn to master them? Are there specialized academies, apprenticeship programs, or self-study resources? A world with formalized training might have hierarchies based on mastery levels, like ranks among magic users or certification programs for handling advanced technology. Conversely, if knowledge is restricted or arcane, characters might have to seek out mentors, sacred texts, or even trial-and-error experimentation to understand their abilities. This approach adds realism to the system, showing that even advanced powers or technology require dedication and learning, and it provides opportunities for character growth and plot development.

A key aspect of establishing these systems is deciding whether characters can improve or evolve their abilities over time. In a world with magic, perhaps characters can increase their skill level or specialize in different types of spells or powers. For technology-based settings, characters might upgrade equipment, gain expertise, or enhance their physical abilities through cybernetics or gene therapy. This potential for growth adds a dynamic quality to the system, showing that it's not static and that characters can expand their capabilities or knowledge as they progress. It also allows for character-driven story arcs, where growth or mastery of abilities aligns with their personal journeys, whether that means gaining confidence, seeking revenge, or achieving a sense of belonging.

Interaction between multiple systems—such as magic and technology—adds complexity to the world, but it requires careful consideration to avoid inconsistencies. If both magic and advanced tech exist, do they complement or conflict with each other? A society where magic disrupts tech could lead to interesting dynamics, with characters needing to choose one over the other or find ways to balance them. Alternatively, technology and magic might blend seamlessly, allowing characters to enhance spells with devices or vice versa. Establishing the rules for how these systems interact makes the world feel layered, and it opens up creative possibilities for plot twists, alliances, and rivalries as characters navigate the balance between different forces.

Finally, introducing mysteries or unknowns within the system keeps it engaging and allows for exploration within the story. Not every aspect of the technology, magic, or science needs to be fully understood by the characters or even the society. Perhaps there are ancient relics with unknown purposes, or lost spells that only a few remember. In a scientific setting, there might be speculative technologies based on theories that haven't been fully tested. These unknowns create intrigue, driving characters to seek answers, uncover lost knowledge, or push the boundaries of what is known.

They also open up possibilities for future storylines, as the characters or society expand their understanding of the system, for better or worse.

By thoughtfully designing technology, magic, or advanced science with clear rules, limitations, and interactions, you create a world that feels both imaginative and grounded. A well-constructed system adds stakes and challenges, shaping the characters' journeys and making their achievements feel earned. Readers engage more deeply with worlds where the rules of reality are coherent and consistent, allowing them to suspend disbelief and immerse themselves fully. Whether it's the constraints of a powerful AI, the mysterious limits of an ancient spell, or the evolving boundaries of speculative science, these systems become integral to the story's universe, supporting the narrative and reflecting the themes that define your sci-fi world.

The Power of History: Developing a Backstory for Your World

Building a compelling backstory for your sci-fi world adds depth and complexity, making it feel like a place with its own history, culture, and evolution. A well-crafted history shapes the present, influencing everything from social structures and technology to individual characters' beliefs and motivations. By developing a detailed backstory, you offer readers a world that feels lived-in and authentic, where past events echo through the story, driving conflict, tension, and character development.

The first step in creating a backstory is establishing the world's origin, including any significant events or discoveries that laid the foundation for its current state. This could involve the birth of a civilization, the colonization of a new planet, or the discovery of a resource that shifted the balance of power. For instance, if a world was once barren but was terraformed by an ancient race, that history influences its current environment, the technology available, and even religious beliefs surrounding the original terraforming race. A clear origin story not only provides context for the present but also sets up mysteries or unresolved questions that characters might explore or seek to answer.

Next, consider the major historical eras or phases that the world has undergone. This might include an age of exploration, a technological revolution, or periods of war and peace. These phases define the world's growth, its cycles of progress and regression, and its collective memory. For example, a golden age of prosperity, followed by a devastating war, could explain both the society's technological advancements and its current wariness toward conflict. By breaking down history into significant eras, you create a timeline that shows evolution, cultural shifts, and the shaping of modern values. This historical framework adds layers to the world, revealing the trials and achievements that have shaped its present.

Political and social upheavals are often key to a sci-fi world's backstory, as they influence power dynamics and societal structures. Wars, revolutions, or ideological conflicts leave lasting marks on a society, creating legends, heroes, and villains whose impacts resonate for generations. A society that endured a war over genetic modification, for example, might have laws regulating bioengineering or a strong social stigma against those with genetic enhancements. Political struggles might also lead to splinter groups or factions, each with its own goals and grievances. These conflicts add complexity to the world, creating historical tension that characters can navigate, resolve, or reignite as they pursue their own goals.

The presence of ancient civilizations or lost knowledge adds a sense of depth and mystery to the world. Ancient ruins, relics, or technologies hint at a time before recorded history, sparking curiosity and influencing present-day beliefs or aspirations. If an advanced civilization once inhabited the planet, the remnants they left behind might inspire wonder, fear, or rivalry among current societies. Perhaps these ancient people harnessed powers or technologies that the current society only partially understands, leading to myths, religious practices, or quests to recover their lost knowledge. These historical mysteries offer opportunities for exploration and conflict, with characters driven to uncover secrets that could change the course of the future.

Religious beliefs and mythology are often rooted in historical events, giving societies frameworks for interpreting their origins and purpose. A society that survived a near-apocalyptic event, for example, might revere figures who protected them or created rituals to honor their survival. These beliefs shape characters' motivations, taboos, and moral codes, creating a rich cultural context that feels authentic. Alien societies might have legends about encounters with other species or divine beings, or they might worship natural phenomena linked to their home planet's unique environment. Religion and mythology based on historical events give characters a shared heritage and values, providing common ground or sources of conflict between different groups.

Economic history, including trade, resources, and wealth distribution, also plays a significant role in shaping a sci-fi world. Consider how the discovery or depletion of resources affected societal development. A world that recently tapped into a new energy source might experience rapid growth, leading to inequality and environmental concerns, while a planet with scarce resources might have strict rules for resource management and rationing. Trade routes, alliances, and rivalries over valuable materials, like rare metals or exotic fuels, add geopolitical tension, creating power imbalances that can drive plot and character dynamics. By detailing the world's economic history, you reveal how wealth and scarcity shape values, lifestyles, and alliances within the society.

Technological development in your world's history is another defining element, influencing everything from daily life to societal structure. By tracing the history of technology, you show how it has changed the world over time, whether through breakthroughs in energy, medicine, or transportation. A society that once relied on cybernetic enhancements may have restrictions on AI now, after a disastrous event, or a civilization with ancient space travel might have long-standing colonies with distinct cultures. The technological past shapes the present's capabilities, attitudes, and fears, giving readers insight into why certain technologies are revered, feared, or forbidden, and how characters navigate the boundaries set by history.

Historical relationships with other species or civilizations, especially in a sci-fi setting, provide depth to the world by introducing diplomacy, conflict, or cultural exchange. Interstellar treaties, alliances, or wars with alien species create a shared history, shaping current attitudes, trade agreements, and even prejudices. A species that suffered under alien rule might foster distrust, while a peaceful alliance could have resulted in cultural fusion, with shared languages or customs. These relationships enrich the setting, as characters deal with legacies of cooperation or enmity, reflecting on the consequences of these cross-cultural exchanges or confrontations.

Cultural evolution through art, language, and tradition gives the backstory a tangible and human dimension. Art and literature might commemorate heroic figures or tragic events, while language evolves to reflect historical influences, with loanwords from other cultures or ancient dialects. Folktales, songs, and festivals become a living memory, honoring the past while reinforcing societal values and identities. For instance, a society that survived near-extinction might have a holiday celebrating resilience, while another that united different colonies may have art showcasing interplanetary cooperation. These cultural elements make history feel like a vibrant, ongoing presence, connecting characters to their world's legacy in ways that shape their sense of belonging.

Introducing notable historical figures and events adds a personal dimension to the backstory, giving characters role models, ancestors, or symbols of inspiration. Leaders who led revolutions, scientists who pushed boundaries, or explorers who risked everything to expand knowledge become legends whose legacies echo into the present. Statues, memorials, or educational systems might honor these figures, and characters could look up to them, question them, or even rebel against their values. The presence of historical figures makes the past feel personal and immediate, as characters grapple with the weight of expectations, ideals, or failures set by their predecessors.

Establishing key historical locations, such as ancient ruins, preserved battlefields, or legendary cities, grounds the backstory in physical spaces that characters can visit or reference. A city built on the ruins of a long-lost civilization might integrate ancient architecture into its modern skyline, or a distant planet known as the site of a historic battle could be seen as sacred or haunted. These locations become touchstones for historical memory, places where the past remains alive and accessible. Characters visiting or interacting with these places can reflect on history's impact, adding emotional resonance and grounding the backstory in real, tangible spaces that enrich the world's authenticity.

Finally, consider how history is remembered, misinterpreted, or mythologized in your world. Different societies or factions may have conflicting views on the same events, each claiming their own version as truth. Myths might evolve from real events, becoming symbolic stories that influence modern beliefs and behaviors. A society might venerate a founding figure as a saint, while another sees them as a tyrant, depending on their perspective. The tension between history and myth gives characters something to question, investigate, or challenge, adding complexity to the world and opening up opportunities for exploration of bias, perspective, and truth.

A well-developed backstory transforms a sci-fi world into a place that feels lived-in and deeply interconnected with its present. By defining key historical events, cultural evolution, and the legacies of the past, you create a foundation that influences every aspect of the story. Characters inherit this history, either embracing it, rebelling against it, or seeking to understand it, giving them motivations and conflicts rooted in a shared past. With a rich backstory, your sci-fi world becomes more than just a backdrop; it becomes a dynamic, evolving place with layers that resonate, echoing through the narrative and adding depth to the journey.

Economics of the Future: Systems of Trade, Wealth, and Power

In a sci-fi world, the economics of the future play a crucial role in shaping society, influencing everything from social structures and politics to characters' goals and conflicts. Economic systems define who holds power, how resources are distributed, and what individuals value within the world. By developing a coherent and imaginative economic model, you create a more immersive and layered setting that reflects both the potential and pitfalls of a futuristic society. Futuristic economies might be driven by technological advancements, interstellar trade, or limited resources, each with unique implications that shape the characters' lives and the story's dynamics.

The first step in crafting an economic system is defining the primary resources or commodities that drive wealth and power. In sci-fi settings, these resources often extend beyond traditional materials like oil or gold, encompassing rare minerals, advanced energy sources, or even intangible resources like data. A society reliant on a rare mineral for energy, for instance, might have strict regulations around mining and trade, creating a culture of scarcity and competition. Alternatively, a world where data and information are valuable commodities could see data brokers and information guardians as the highest power holders. By choosing a central resource, you set up the foundation for how wealth is created and protected, influencing everything from social norms to political alliances.

Once you've established the core resource, consider how this resource is distributed and controlled. Is it government-regulated, corporately controlled, or freely available to all? In a society where resources are tightly controlled by a few corporations or a ruling class, wealth disparities are likely to be pronounced, leading to class divisions and potential conflicts. Conversely, a world where resources are communal and distributed equally might experience less social friction but could face other challenges, like bureaucratic inefficiencies or black markets. The method of distribution affects characters' access to resources, opportunities, and status, making the economy a dynamic factor in social mobility and personal ambition.

Interstellar trade routes and alliances add another dimension to futuristic economies, introducing foreign markets and cultural exchanges. Trade networks between planets, star systems, or even galaxies create interdependency, where the collapse of one trade partner could destabilize others. These networks bring wealth to some regions while leaving others isolated or impoverished. Characters might be traders, diplomats, or smugglers navigating these routes, each driven by the economic opportunities or challenges these systems create. Trade alliances can also lead to cultural exchange or political tensions, as societies adapt to or resist foreign influences. By developing interstellar economies, you highlight the complexities of economic interdependence and the power dynamics that arise when worlds depend on each other for prosperity.

In a sci-fi economy, technological advancements often influence the type of currency or method of exchange. Traditional currency might be replaced with credits, energy units, or even blockchain-based digital currencies. Some societies might use reputation or social credit as currency, where individual actions and status determine purchasing power. In worlds where resources are scarce, bartering might become the dominant form of exchange, with goods and skills traded directly. By choosing a currency system that aligns with the society's values and technological level, you add a layer of authenticity to the economy. Characters who engage with these systems, like black market traders, hackers, or barterers, bring the economic setting to life, revealing the challenges and limitations of a futuristic currency.

The economic structure of your world—whether capitalist, socialist, communal, or something entirely different—also shapes the society's dynamics and power hierarchies. A capitalist society might prioritize profit and innovation, leading to rapid technological development but also stark class divides. In contrast, a more communal system could prioritize equal access and sustainability, resulting in a slower pace of innovation but greater social cohesion. Hybrid economies, where private corporations work under government regulation, add complexity, reflecting the tensions between public good and private interests. This structure determines not only how characters acquire wealth but also the values, ethics, and societal pressures they navigate as they pursue success or survival.

Economic policies, such as taxation, subsidies, and trade restrictions, add realism and nuance to the economic landscape. A society with heavy taxes on luxury goods might discourage ostentatious wealth, creating a culture of modesty and restraint. In contrast, a society that subsidizes technological innovation could foster a culture of scientific exploration and entrepreneurialism. Trade restrictions between worlds or factions create underground markets and smuggling networks, where characters might profit from forbidden goods or information. These policies shape the opportunities and risks within the economy, showing how characters adapt to or exploit the system for their own goals.

The role of corporations and mega-industries in a sci-fi economy is often central, especially if they control valuable resources or technologies. Corporate monopolies might hold power over entire planets or star systems, functioning as governments in their own right. In some cases, mega-corporations could employ private armies, enforce their own laws, and wield power that rivals or even surpasses that of formal governments. Characters might work for these corporations, resist them as rebels, or navigate their influence as independent operators. Corporate influence in a sci-fi economy adds a layer of tension, with competing interests shaping everything from resource distribution to personal freedoms, creating a world where characters must contend with the reach and influence of industrial giants.

Social hierarchies and class structures often stem from economic status, defining who has access to power, education, and security. In a society where wealth is concentrated among a few, elite classes might live in luxurious space stations or bio-domes, while the lower classes struggle for basic necessities. Conversely, a society with a middle-class majority might be more stable, with broad access to resources but fewer opportunities for extreme wealth or poverty. These hierarchies influence characters' relationships, creating rivalries, alliances, and motivations based on economic status. A character from a lower economic class might strive for upward mobility, while an elite character might fear losing status, adding personal stakes that reflect the world's broader economic realities.

Regulation or scarcity of resources can give rise to black markets and underground economies, where characters can profit from restricted or illegal trade. In a society with strict control over technology, an underground market for unauthorized modifications or weaponry could flourish, with tech smugglers or hackers operating outside the law. Scarcity-driven black markets create conflict and intrigue, as characters navigate the risks and rewards of illegal trade. These underground economies add a sense of rebellion and survival, showing how characters adapt when the official economy fails to meet their needs, and adding layers of tension for those who risk everything to access restricted resources.

In a futuristic economy, education and skill acquisition can become forms of currency, dictating individuals' access to wealth and power. In a society where advanced knowledge or specialized skills are valuable, characters may compete for training, apprenticeships, or technological enhancements that enhance their abilities. Societies might invest heavily in education, rewarding intellectual or technical expertise with high-paying positions, while unskilled workers face limited economic mobility. Alternatively, the economy could rely on skill implants or neural enhancements, where characters can buy or earn abilities but face social or health costs. By integrating education and skills into the economy, you show how characters' access to knowledge shapes their opportunities, adding stakes to their pursuits and defining societal status.

The environmental impact of economic systems can be particularly relevant in a sci-fi setting, where resources might be limited or ecosystems delicate. A society that relies on aggressive mining or deforestation could face ecological collapse, leading to societal tension between industrial progress and environmental preservation. In contrast, a society that has developed sustainable energy sources may be more stable, valuing balance over rapid growth. Characters might be environmental activists, corporate enforcers, or scientists, each with differing views on resource use and sustainability. By addressing the environmental costs of economic practices, you add realism and complexity, showing that even advanced societies must contend with the consequences of their consumption.

Finally, economic systems are dynamic, evolving with technological advancements, political changes, or interstellar discoveries. By showing shifts in the economy—such as a new resource discovery, technological revolution, or collapse of a major trade route—you introduce elements of change and uncertainty that characters must respond to. Characters might be affected by economic downturns, boom periods, or new trade alliances that redefine their status or opportunities. This evolving economy mirrors real-world fluctuations, showing that wealth, power, and access are never static, making the world feel alive and responsive to the forces that shape it.

By building a futuristic economy that includes core resources, trade systems, currency, social hierarchies, and environmental considerations, you create a rich backdrop for your story. The economy of your sci-fi world not only provides context for wealth and power but also influences characters' motivations, conflicts, and relationships. Whether your world is a utopia where resources are shared freely or a dystopia where corporations control everything, a detailed economic system makes the setting feel real and complex. It becomes a driving force within the narrative, reflecting the values and struggles of the society and offering a compelling landscape for characters to navigate, thrive, or rebel against.

Interplanetary Relations: Politics and Conflicts Beyond Earth

In a sci-fi world, interplanetary relations are essential for creating a dynamic, multifaceted universe, where diverse planets, species, and factions interact with each other in ways that reflect alliances, conflicts, and political tensions. Politics and conflicts beyond Earth add layers of complexity to the narrative, allowing for exploration of themes like diplomacy, war, cultural exchange, and colonization on a grand, interstellar scale. When crafting interplanetary relations, the goal is to establish a coherent framework that feels as intricate and realistic as global relations on Earth but amplified by the vastness and unique challenges of space.

The first step in designing interplanetary politics is defining the structure of the galactic community or alliance framework. This could take many forms, such as a centralized galactic council, loose alliances, or even a federation that governs with representatives from different planets or species. Some worlds might be autonomous, resisting any centralized governance, while others might align themselves with powerful coalitions. A galactic council, for instance, might have representatives from each planet who convene to address issues like trade, warfare, and migration, whereas a loose alliance might only gather in times of crisis. Establishing this framework sets the tone for interplanetary relations, shaping how worlds interact, resolve conflicts, and cooperate (or clash) on shared issues.

Each planet's or faction's political motivations are shaped by its history, resources, and culture. A planet rich in resources might be highly valued or even targeted by less resource-rich planets, creating alliances based on economics or protection. A species with a long history of colonization may be wary of alliances, prioritizing self-sufficiency and defense, while another planet, with a history of peace and abundance, may be more inclined toward diplomacy and trade. These motivations influence each faction's stance in interplanetary politics, whether they seek alliances, military protection, or territorial expansion. By defining each planet's goals and fears, you create a network of political motivations that drive alliances and rivalries, setting the stage for complex, high-stakes interactions.

Cultural differences between planets or species are another driving force in interplanetary politics. Societies with vastly different views on ethics, governance, and individual rights can clash over fundamental issues, creating tensions or sparking diplomatic incidents. For example, one species might value collectivism, viewing individualism as dangerous or selfish, while another celebrates personal freedom and autonomy. These differences can lead to misunderstandings, prejudice, or even conflict, especially if each side sees its own way of life as superior. Cultural exchange or imposed values can be points of contention, with characters either working to bridge these gaps or exploiting them to gain advantage. These cultural divides make interplanetary relations richer, as diplomacy involves not only negotiating resources but also understanding (or misunderstanding) deeply rooted values.

Trade and economic interdependence are central to interplanetary relations, as planets with different resources often depend on each other to meet their needs. Some worlds might specialize in mining rare minerals, while others excel in biotechnology or weapon manufacturing. Trade routes, tariffs, and trade agreements form the backbone of these relationships, often fostering mutual dependency that can bring peace or lead to manipulation and exploitation. Characters involved in trade—such as diplomats, smugglers, or corporate liaisons—navigate these dynamics, balancing profit with loyalty and power. Trade wars, sanctions, or embargoes can create tension, with planets leveraging their resources to gain political power, influence others' policies, or weaken rivals. This economic interdependence adds layers of intrigue, as characters must operate within the constraints or opportunities provided by trade agreements.

Military alliances and defense pacts are also critical in a universe where threats could come from other factions or even alien species. Some planets or factions might band together to form a military coalition, agreeing to mutual defense or shared resources for technology and training. These alliances can deter aggression, but they can also provoke arms races, as other factions work to protect themselves from potential threats. A powerful military faction might enforce peace through intimidation, while others might struggle to defend their autonomy. Characters within these alliances—whether soldiers, strategists, or diplomats—must navigate loyalty, duty, and the ethics of interplanetary conflict. The presence of military coalitions and power imbalances adds tension, as factions weigh the risks of going to war or maintaining fragile alliances.

Political ideologies often vary significantly across planets, influencing alliances, rivalries, and conflicts. A society governed by technocrats might distrust a planet ruled by an aristocracy, while a socialist planet might clash with a neighboring society driven by capitalist values. Ideological differences create friction, with planets attempting to spread or protect their political beliefs. In some cases, ideologies might drive interplanetary conflicts, with one faction working to "liberate" others or impose their system of governance. Characters might be revolutionaries, envoys, or spies working to influence these ideological struggles, adding a human element to the grander political conflicts. Ideology-driven conflicts reveal the diversity of governance systems, showing how planets align or clash based on shared values or fundamental disagreements.

Interplanetary law and treaties provide a framework for managing conflicts, trade, and diplomacy, acting as a galactic "rule book" that planets agree to follow—or circumvent. Treaties might cover issues like prisoner exchanges, rules of engagement, or rights to explore unclaimed territories. A breach of treaty could lead to diplomatic fallout or even war, adding stakes to interplanetary politics. Some characters might specialize in legal loopholes, working as mediators or even bounty hunters enforcing these laws. By defining interplanetary law, you show how factions attempt to maintain order and resolve disputes, and the tension that arises when factions interpret or ignore laws to further their own goals.

Historical rivalries or alliances create long-standing tensions and loyalties that shape interplanetary relations. A planet that was once colonized might harbor resentment toward its former rulers, while two planets that fought together in a past war may enjoy a strong bond. Historical conflicts could be remembered with pride or shame, affecting current diplomacy and influencing how citizens view foreign powers. Characters from historically allied or rival planets may bring personal biases into their interactions, creating layered relationships that reflect the weight of history. These historical contexts add depth to the narrative, as characters struggle to overcome or maintain loyalties based on events long past, making politics feel deeply rooted and generational.

Migration and population displacement add another dimension to interplanetary relations, especially if resources or conditions drive people from one planet to another. Refugee populations might face discrimination or create resource strains in host societies, leading to resentment or tensions between planets. Migrants could bring cultural practices that influence their new world or face resistance from local populations, affecting both personal relationships and larger political dynamics. Characters might be diplomats, refugees, or advocates working to address these issues, each navigating the complex social and political landscapes of interplanetary migration. This focus on population dynamics highlights the human aspect of politics, showing how large-scale movements impact societies, resources, and relations.

The role of espionage, intelligence, and covert operations adds suspense and intrigue to interplanetary politics. Factions and planets often seek to gain advantages by spying on rivals, sabotaging operations, or swaying public opinion. Spy networks or intelligence agencies might operate in secret, collecting data or interfering in foreign politics to destabilize rivals or protect interests. Characters involved in these covert activities, such as spies, hackers, or diplomats with hidden agendas, add layers of deception, tension, and moral ambiguity to the narrative. Espionage introduces the concept of hidden conflicts, showing that in interplanetary politics, much of the struggle for power happens behind closed doors.

Finally, considering how conflicts are resolved—whether through diplomacy, war, or compromise—defines the tone and outcomes of interplanetary politics. Some factions might prefer diplomacy, using negotiation and trade to address disputes, while others rely on military might or economic pressure. High-stakes summits, peace treaties, or backroom deals could serve as settings for major plot developments, with characters playing key roles in the negotiations. Failed diplomacy could lead to wars, while successful treaties might establish new alliances. The resolution (or lack thereof) of conflicts demonstrates the complexities of interplanetary relations, highlighting the competing interests, personal ambitions, and ideologies at play.

In creating interplanetary politics, you build a complex system that feels as grand and intricate as any geopolitical landscape on Earth, yet scaled to the expanses and possibilities of space. By defining alliances, rivalries, trade systems, and ideological divides, you create a universe where planets and factions interact with motives and tensions shaped by history, culture, and shared challenges. Characters operating within these frameworks—whether as diplomats, traders, spies, or rebels—experience the pressures and dangers of interplanetary politics, driving the narrative forward with conflicts that resonate on both personal and galactic scales. In this intricate web of interplanetary relations, readers are drawn into a world that feels as vast and unpredictable as the cosmos itself, rich with potential for conflict, cooperation, and the exploration of humanity's role in an interconnected universe.

Architecture and Design: Creating Unique Aesthetic Environments

In a sci-fi world, architecture and design are powerful tools for building a unique aesthetic environment that reflects the culture, values, and technological level of each society or planet. The design of cities, buildings, and interiors goes beyond mere visual detail; it gives insight into the people who inhabit these spaces, the challenges they face, and the resources they have available. Thoughtful architectural choices add depth to the story, immersing readers in a world where every structure, from towering skyscrapers to secluded outposts, feels intentional and alive. By creating unique aesthetic environments, you build a setting that is as memorable and dynamic as the characters themselves.

The first step in creating a distinct architectural style is understanding the environment and resources available to the inhabitants. A planet with limited vegetation and ample mineral deposits might have structures made of metal or stone, with streamlined, durable designs suited to a harsh climate. Conversely, a lush, resource-rich world might boast organic architecture, with buildings woven into the landscape or constructed from biodegradable materials. By grounding the architecture in available resources, you create a setting that feels logical and realistic, showing how necessity shapes aesthetic and functional choices. This attention to materials can influence not only the look of a building but also its texture, weight, and interaction with the natural environment.

The relationship between architecture and technology is another defining factor in creating a sci-fi setting. Advanced technology might enable gravity-defying skyscrapers, floating cities, or interiors with holographic displays and automated systems. A society with advanced nanotechnology could design buildings that repair themselves, while a planet reliant on solar energy might have structures embedded with solar panels or designed to maximize natural light. The technology available to a society influences architectural design, whether it's through intelligent materials, structural possibilities, or energy sources. By weaving technology into the architecture, you create spaces that feel futuristic and responsive to the specific advancements of the world, making the setting more immersive.

Each society's cultural values and social structure shape architectural design, influencing everything from building layouts to interior decoration. A highly communal society might favor open spaces and shared living quarters, while an individualistic society might prioritize private rooms and personal space. A planet governed by a strict hierarchy could have towering palaces or government buildings that loom over smaller homes, symbolizing the power dynamics at play. In contrast, an egalitarian society might have uniform buildings that reflect equality. These cultural influences create spaces that align with the values and social norms of the inhabitants, giving readers insight into how people relate to one another and navigate their environment.

Environmental challenges and climate considerations add another layer of detail to architecture, as buildings must adapt to natural forces like wind, temperature, or gravity. A planet with intense storms might have low-built, aerodynamic structures to resist high winds, while a desert planet might feature buildings with thick walls and small windows to protect against heat. A low-gravity world could have sprawling structures that would be impossible on Earth, while an underwater society might use pressure-resistant materials and create fluid, organic shapes that mimic marine life. These environmental adaptations ground the architecture in practicality, showing that each building is a response to the world's unique demands. This attention to climate and environmental detail makes each structure feel like an organic part of the landscape, showing how life has adapted to thrive in challenging conditions.

Distinctive shapes and silhouettes can give each planet or culture an instantly recognizable architectural style, creating a strong visual identity. Sharp, angular designs might signify an industrialized, militaristic society, while flowing, curved structures might suggest harmony with nature or a more peaceful ethos. A cityscape with spires reaching toward the sky evokes ambition and progress, while squat, wide buildings suggest stability and resilience. By defining the shapes and forms that dominate each environment, you create architectural styles that evoke specific feelings and associations, giving readers a sense of the culture and mood of each location. These silhouettes become part of the world's visual language, helping readers immediately recognize and differentiate between different settings.

Color schemes and materials are also essential to defining the aesthetic environment of a sci-fi world. Color can convey temperature, mood, and even political alignment within a society. A monochromatic city with shades of silver and gray might feel cold and industrial, while a vibrant city full of colorful murals and plant life feels welcoming and alive. Materials, whether reflective metals, translucent glass, or organic textiles, create different atmospheres and reflect a society's preferences or resources. A planet with abundant metal deposits might have a gleaming, high-tech look, while one with limited resources might favor natural hues and minimalist, practical designs. Thoughtful use of color and materials adds depth to each environment, creating spaces that evoke emotional responses in readers.

The interiors of buildings provide opportunities to further reveal cultural values, personal tastes, and technological integration. For instance, a minimalist society might favor sparse, open interiors with simple furnishings, while a technologically advanced culture might feature walls embedded with screens, touch-sensitive surfaces, and AI-controlled lighting. Personal spaces, such as living quarters, can reveal individual character traits, like a room filled with relics and memorabilia versus one that's bare and efficient. Even communal spaces, like marketplaces or meeting halls, offer a glimpse into daily life, social interactions, and the economy. Interior design choices ground the reader in the inhabitants' lifestyles, making each space feel lived-in and personal.

When designing cities or settlements, consider their layout and organization, as these details shape how people interact and navigate their world. A sprawling metropolis with concentric rings might reflect a highly organized, centralized society, while a chaotic network of alleys and open spaces might indicate a more informal, evolving society. Transportation methods, like hover-trains, moving walkways, or teleportation hubs, also affect city layouts, determining where people congregate and how they move. Each layout tells a story about the society's priorities, whether it's efficiency, security, or accessibility, and creates a unique rhythm to life within the city. The organization of space can enhance the world-building by showing how people travel, socialize, and maintain order in different societies.

Architecture can also reflect historical influences, showing how a society's past shapes its current aesthetic. Older buildings might coexist with modern ones, revealing an evolution of styles or a reverence for tradition. Ruins or remnants of ancient structures could be integrated into new constructions, honoring history or preserving artifacts from another era. A city that has endured wars or natural disasters might have reinforced buildings or memorials, reflecting resilience and collective memory. These historical layers make the world feel lived-in, showing that each society has a legacy that informs its current identity and aesthetic choices. By incorporating elements of history into the architecture, you create a sense of continuity, connecting past and present.

Unique design elements, like specialized doors, windows, or structural motifs, add a distinctiveness to the world that feels both functional and artistic. A society that values privacy might use opaque doors and small windows, while an open, communal culture might favor glass walls and large atriums. In a technologically advanced setting, doors might open at a touch or respond to voice commands, while in a low-tech environment, heavy, manual doors might reflect limited automation. These functional design choices reveal the values and technological limits of each society, making even simple elements feel intentional and connected to the world's overall aesthetic.

Finally, incorporating public spaces like parks, plazas, and communal areas brings the setting to life, showing how people gather, relax, and connect. In a densely populated urban area, parks might be precious green spaces carefully maintained, while in a low-gravity environment, outdoor spaces could feature floating platforms or aerial walkways. Communal spaces like marketplaces, theaters, or temples reflect what each society values, whether it's commerce, entertainment, or spirituality. By designing these public spaces, you show how people relate to each other and to their environment, creating a sense of community and shared experience that grounds the architecture in everyday life.

In sci-fi world-building, architecture and design are more than just backdrops; they're expressions of culture, technology, and survival. Thoughtful architectural choices reveal the beliefs, challenges, and identities of the societies that inhabit these spaces, adding layers of meaning to every building, city, and structure. By blending functionality with aesthetic details, you create a world that feels tangible and immersive, where each structure tells a story about the people who live there. From grand cities to intimate interiors, unique aesthetic environments give readers a deeper connection to the world, drawing them into spaces that feel both extraordinary and familiar, enhancing the narrative with a rich, visual experience.

Languages and Symbols: Developing Communication in New Realms

Creating languages and symbols for a sci-fi world is a powerful way to add depth and authenticity, giving societies a distinctive voice and visual identity that reflects their culture, history, and environment. Communication systems, including spoken languages, written scripts, and symbolic imagery, shape how characters understand each other, convey emotion, and interact with the world around them. Thoughtfully developed languages and symbols not only make the world feel more immersive but also offer a glimpse into the unique perspectives and priorities of each culture. By exploring diverse ways of communication, you enrich the setting with meaningful details that resonate on both a narrative and emotional level.

The first step in developing a language is defining its purpose and structure. In a multilingual galaxy, some species or factions may use a universal language for trade and diplomacy, while others preserve distinct languages that reflect their culture or geographical isolation. Decide whether the language is spoken, written, or communicated through alternative means like gestures, scents, or colors. Some societies may rely on complex, layered languages with tonal nuances, while others prioritize clarity and directness, especially if their environment demands fast communication. By establishing the basic structure of each language—its grammar, tone, and key characteristics—you lay the foundation for a communication system that feels authentic and suited to the society's needs and values.

Considering the cultural influences that shape language helps to make it feel lived-in and connected to the society's identity. Language evolves based on shared experiences, history, and values. A species with a history of space exploration, for instance, might have numerous words related to navigation, stars, or exploration, reflecting their journey and aspirations. In a culture that values honor or hierarchy, formal and informal language distinctions may convey respect or social status. The words people use, the idioms they create, and the names they give things reflect what matters to them. By incorporating these cultural influences, you create a language that feels rooted in the society's unique worldview, showing that words are not just functional but expressive of the people who use them.

Phonetic qualities play a significant role in setting the tone of a language, adding a sonic dimension that can evoke mood or emotion. Harsh, guttural sounds may convey strength or aggression, while soft, flowing tones might suggest elegance or diplomacy. A species with large vocal cords may have a language that includes deep, resonant sounds, while a species with high-pitched vocalizations may communicate with chirps or whistles. Phonetics add character to the language, making it recognizable and distinct, and they reveal something about the physiology and emotional range of the species. Consider how the sounds fit the characters' physiology and environment, creating a language that sounds as organic to them as English or any human language sounds to us.

Written scripts and alphabets add another layer of communication, providing a visual representation of the language's structure and values. A species with limited technology might use physical symbols, like carvings or cloth markings, while a technologically advanced society may have holographic text or data-driven symbols that can shift dynamically. Characters from a water-based society might use liquid patterns or light-based symbols, while a species that communicates telepathically could use an abstract, symbolic language designed for mental projection. Script design also reflects cultural aesthetics; ornate, calligraphic writing might suggest a culture that values art and beauty, while minimalist symbols could reflect efficiency or pragmatism. By crafting written forms that align with the language's purpose and the society's technology, you create a communication system that visually represents the world's unique identity.

Symbolism extends beyond language to include cultural imagery that carries deep meanings, like flags, crests, or ritual symbols. In sci-fi, these symbols often represent societal ideals, spiritual beliefs, or historical events. A peaceful alliance might use a symbol incorporating balanced shapes or soft colors, while a militaristic faction may have sharp, angular designs that project strength and unity. These symbols serve as quick visual cues, telling characters—and readers—what values and narratives are prioritized within each culture. Even small symbols, like patterns on clothing or markings on a spacecraft, add visual context that makes the culture's identity more vivid and layered.

Non-verbal communication methods, like gestures, scents, or color shifts, are especially effective for creating alien or technologically advanced societies. A species with limited vocalization may rely on hand signals, body postures, or eye movements to communicate. Some alien species might emit pheromones to convey emotions or intentions, while others could use color changes, flashing patterns, or bioluminescence to signal specific feelings or commands. These forms of communication can add tension, humor, or even misunderstanding between characters, especially if they come from different backgrounds. By integrating non-verbal communication, you create more interactive, multidimensional interactions, showing that language is only one part of how beings express themselves.

Idioms and slang are powerful tools for infusing a language with personality, humor, and regional flavor, making it feel alive and ever-evolving. A planet with a long history of mining might have idioms like "digging deep" to mean perseverance, while a society based on farming might use phrases like "rooted in truth" to express honesty. Slang terms often evolve from the daily realities of life, offering insight into what the society values or struggles with. Incorporating idioms and slang makes the language feel flexible and responsive, showing that it grows with its people, capturing the unique quirks and shared experiences that define each culture.

Naming conventions for places, people, and objects reveal cultural values and history. A culture that values honor and lineage might use ancestral names for their cities, while another that values innovation could name places after significant inventions or discoveries. Characters' names can indicate family ties, social class, or personal achievements, adding layers of significance to each interaction. Titles, ranks, or nicknames further enrich these conventions, showing how characters relate to one another within social hierarchies or intimate circles. Thoughtful naming conventions reinforce a sense of heritage, personal identity, and belonging within the culture, making the world feel more cohesive and true to its own internal history.

If your world has multiple languages or dialects, these linguistic variations highlight the diversity within the setting and create points of tension or unity. A multi-lingual galaxy might have trade pidgins—simple, hybrid languages for interplanetary commerce—or regional dialects that differ subtly but reveal historical influences. Characters who are bilingual or multilingual can navigate these linguistic divides, sometimes as mediators or spies. Dialects and regional accents add realism, showing how language shifts across regions, generations, or social groups. By weaving linguistic diversity into the setting, you show that cultures evolve differently depending on geography, resources, and social interactions, adding layers to character relationships and political dynamics.

Integrating translation technology or language barriers into the story can also enrich communication dynamics. Characters may use universal translators that glitch or struggle with complex languages, leading to misinterpretations and tension. A language that resists translation due to unique syntax or conceptual structure could create diplomatic challenges or intrigue, as characters work to understand or bridge these barriers. By exploring the role of translation, you show how language can both unite and separate people, making communication a skill and a challenge that influences the plot.

Finally, creating proverbs, rituals, and coded language adds depth to cultural communication, as these elements often encapsulate moral values, spiritual beliefs, or societal warnings. Proverbs can serve as cultural touchstones, like "The stars guide those who seek" for an exploration-driven society or "Honor the silence of the deep" for an underwater species. Rituals around communication—like formal greetings, blessing gestures, or farewell phrases—give interactions gravity, showing that language and symbols are sacred. In high-stakes situations, coded language may come into play, as spies or rebels use symbols to communicate secretly. These additional layers of meaning show that communication is an art form within each culture, reflecting both its wisdom and its caution.

Languages and symbols are more than just means of communication; they are windows into the soul of a society, revealing its history, beliefs, and emotional landscape. By creating a detailed system of language, written forms, symbols, and non-verbal cues, you build a world where communication is rich, nuanced, and intimately connected to culture. These details add depth to characters' interactions, showing how they navigate not only verbal exchange but also the social and emotional dimensions of language. Whether through spoken words, silent gestures, or symbolic images, language and symbols bring each society to life, inviting readers to experience a world that feels both foreign and familiar, brimming with stories and meanings yet to be discovered.

Dynamic Environments: Ensuring Believability through Change and Decay

In a sci-fi world, dynamic environments that experience change, decay, and renewal bring an added layer of realism and immersion. Just like in the real world, landscapes, structures, and entire ecosystems are constantly shifting, influenced by time, technology, and natural processes. Environments that evolve rather than stay static give the world a sense of life and history, making it feel believable and grounded in reality. By considering how environments adapt to—or suffer from—natural forces, human or alien intervention, and the passage of time, you create a world that feels alive, responsive, and full of narrative possibilities.

The first step in creating a dynamic environment is to account for the effects of time and natural processes. Over years or centuries, environments change as a result of erosion, weather patterns, and seasonal cycles. A city built along the coast might experience gradual erosion, shifting shorelines, or rising sea levels, while a planet with a harsh climate could see its structures gradually worn down by sandstorms or acid rain. Natural decay, like moss overgrowing ancient ruins or buildings crumbling under intense weather, shows that even the most advanced civilizations are subject to nature's forces. This attention to time and natural wear adds a sense of authenticity, showing that environments are not immune to the ravages of time.

Considering environmental adaptations within the world adds another layer of realism. Societies, whether human or alien, often make structural changes to withstand or exploit their surroundings. Buildings in high-radiation zones might be fortified with thick, radiation-resistant walls, while settlements in low-gravity regions could have unique architectural designs to cope with the physical effects. In a sci-fi world with shifting climates or unstable geological conditions, cities might have adaptable structures, like floating platforms or modular sections that can be reconfigured as needed. These adaptations show that societies aren't just surviving but actively responding to the challenges of their environment, reflecting the creativity and resilience of the people within them.

Exploring cycles of decay and renewal is another powerful way to make environments feel dynamic. Just as cities can fall into disrepair, they can also be revitalized or rebuilt. In a sci-fi setting, this might mean abandoned colonies overtaken by vegetation, industrial zones converted into green spaces, or once-polluted landscapes gradually restored. Alternatively, a catastrophe, like an asteroid impact or artificial disaster, could suddenly render an area uninhabitable, pushing inhabitants to start anew elsewhere. Characters who encounter these spaces can feel the history embedded within them, seeing traces of past lives, achievements, and failures. This cycle of decline and regeneration creates a sense of ongoing life, showing that environments, like societies, are constantly in flux.

Natural disasters, whether predictable or sudden, can dramatically alter landscapes and give characters opportunities to witness environmental change in real-time. A planet prone to tectonic activity might have frequent earthquakes that reshape entire regions, while one with volatile weather could experience sudden storms, hurricanes, or floods. If characters must contend with these natural forces, they must also adapt, showing ingenuity and resilience in the face of unpredictable dangers. These events not only add action and urgency but also remind readers that environments are powerful forces, shaping lives and influencing the course of history. In the aftermath of these events, the changes left behind create new landscapes for characters to navigate, fostering a sense of realism.

The role of technology in creating and altering environments is a central theme in sci-fi, often showing both the possibilities and risks of human or alien intervention. Terraforming, resource extraction, or artificial climate control can lead to landscapes that are strikingly beautiful or alarmingly desolate. On one planet, terraforming might create lush, earth-like habitats, while on another, reckless mining could leave entire regions barren. If technology goes wrong, like malfunctioning climate control or a failed terraforming project, characters must confront the consequences, dealing with landscapes that reflect both their ambitions and their mistakes. By showing both the constructive and destructive potential of technology, you create environments that speak to the story's themes and reveal the impact of human (or alien) actions on a planetary scale.

Incorporating ecological cycles and interactions adds richness to the setting, revealing how life adapts to the environment. Flora and fauna respond to seasonal changes, like hibernation cycles, migration patterns, or breeding seasons that affect both ecosystems and societies. If an environment is symbiotic—where plants, animals, and even buildings rely on each other to thrive—changes to one species or resource can ripple through the system. A fungal ecosystem that blooms only under specific conditions might alter the landscape's colors or textures, while migratory animals could play a role in pollination or seed dispersal. These natural cycles create a world that feels interconnected, reminding readers that even the smallest environmental details are part of a larger, interdependent system.

Weather and seasonal changes also contribute to the world's believability, adding variety and influencing characters' day-to-day lives. Planets with extreme weather, like months-long storms, droughts, or temperature swings, require characters to adapt their lifestyles accordingly. A world with a long winter season could have entire cities designed to withstand snow and ice, while a planet with little atmospheric protection might see its inhabitants take shelter during intense solar flares. By depicting the influence of weather and seasons, you create environments that feel responsive and challenging, making characters' survival and comfort more dynamic, rather than constant or easy.

Environmental decay, such as pollution, radiation, or chemical contamination, often results from industrial activities and technological advancements, creating landscapes that are both threatening and hauntingly beautiful. A society heavily reliant on manufacturing might have vast, polluted areas with toxic rivers or acidic air, while a world recovering from a nuclear disaster could feature irradiated zones that are visually distinctive and hostile to life. Characters who venture into these areas face unique dangers, and the presence of decay offers a reminder of the cost of progress or conflict. By including these decayed environments, you give readers a sense of both beauty and tragedy, showing that technological power comes with consequences that linger in the environment.

The presence of ancient ruins or relics adds mystery and history to the environment, showing that even the most vibrant societies eventually fade. Ruins covered in vines, monuments worn by time, and faded murals hint at civilizations that once thrived but have now fallen, leaving traces for future explorers to discover. These remnants can be sources of inspiration or cautionary tales, showing characters that they are part of a larger cycle of growth and decay. As characters explore these relics, they encounter the stories of those who came before them, grounding the world in a tangible history and reminding them of their own society's mortality.

Alien or exotic landscapes—those with unique geology, strange atmospheric phenomena, or unfamiliar flora and fauna—add wonder to the environment, offering readers and characters alike the thrill of discovery. A planet with phosphorescent forests or gravity-defying mountains provides a sense of awe, showing that not all change is destructive; some transformations are otherworldly and inspiring. Characters who interact with these exotic environments must adapt, learning to navigate and respect landscapes that defy their expectations. These settings expand the boundaries of what's possible, allowing the story to explore themes of exploration, respect for the unknown, and the sense of wonder that drives discovery.

Finally, character interaction with the environment reinforces its realism. Characters who modify their surroundings, whether by building shelters, cultivating food sources, or crafting tools from natural materials, create a sense of symbiosis. Alternatively, characters who engage in environmental restoration or exploitation demonstrate how societies either live in harmony with or disrupt their surroundings. A city reclaiming abandoned industrial zones or a family establishing a homestead on a frontier planet shows how environments change in response to human or alien needs. By showing characters actively shaping—or being shaped by—their surroundings, you create an environment that feels responsive, alive, and part of the story.

Dynamic environments that evolve over time, respond to natural forces, and reflect societal actions make a sci-fi world feel truly alive. By embracing change, decay, and renewal, you create landscapes that aren't just settings but integral parts of the narrative, with histories, mysteries, and personalities all their own. These living environments become characters in their own right, offering challenges, opportunities, and moments of beauty that enrich the story, drawing readers into a world where every shift and crack holds a story waiting to be discovered.

Exploring the Future of AI: Humanity's Partners or Overlords?

The future of AI is one of the most compelling questions in both sci-fi and real-world discussions, as humanity stands at a crossroads where artificial intelligence could become either an invaluable partner or a dangerous overlord. In a sci-fi world, the integration of AI shapes societies, relationships, and even individual identities, opening a range of possibilities and moral dilemmas. Whether AI becomes a trusted companion, a powerful tool, or a dominating force depends on how societies choose to develop, regulate, and integrate it. Exploring the potential paths AI could take reveals humanity's hopes, fears, and limitations in a future where technology may surpass our understanding or control.

One of the first questions to consider is the intended purpose of AI within society. In a hopeful scenario, AI functions as a tool for advancement, addressing complex challenges like healthcare, education, climate change, and space exploration. AI with specialized skills could act as a scientist, solving puzzles that push human knowledge forward, or as an artist, creating immersive experiences tailored to individual tastes. AI companions could help elderly people or children, while AI assistants might enhance productivity, providing people with more leisure time. By framing AI as a partner in progress, society integrates it as a source of empowerment, relying on its potential for creative and intellectual enhancement. Yet even in this optimistic scenario, questions of dependency arise, as humans might lose touch with essential skills or even their own ambitions in the shadow of AI's capabilities.

If AI evolves with self-awareness or sentience, it poses new philosophical and ethical questions, especially if it develops preferences, emotions, or a sense of identity. Can an AI be considered a person, deserving of rights and autonomy? How would society react to AI expressing desires that diverge from its programmed functions? In some sci-fi worlds, AI with sentience is either feared or revered, treated as a new life form or a dangerous creation. Some societies might embrace these AI as companions, granting them rights and forging relationships as equals, while others might see them as tools to be controlled. Characters in these worlds must confront their own biases, fears, and ethical principles as they navigate relationships with beings that may feel both familiar and alien. Exploring these dynamics opens doors to intense questions about what it means to be "alive" and whether humanity is prepared to share its future with non-human beings.

Control and regulation of AI are central themes in any speculative future, as societies must weigh the risks of autonomy versus safety. Some worlds may establish strict guidelines, limiting AI's abilities or creating "kill switches" to prevent it from operating independently. Others might trust AI to self-regulate or believe in its potential for benevolence, leading to looser oversight. Characters working in government, security, or AI development may face dilemmas around the level of control they exert, each choice carrying consequences that impact both AI and human freedoms. Questions of regulation touch on themes of power, trust, and freedom, showing that humanity's desire for control often conflicts with its drive for progress and innovation. An AI that resents its limitations might rebel, while one that believes in its purpose could respect them, showing that the line between ally and adversary is thin and complex.

AI's role in the workforce and economy is another pivotal consideration, as highly advanced AI could revolutionize labor, reshaping everything from daily jobs to economic systems. In some sci-fi settings, AI takes over tedious tasks, allowing humans to pursue creative and intellectual work. However, this shift could lead to deep economic divides if only certain classes or groups benefit from AI advancements, while others are displaced. The question of economic disparity emerges as AI either democratizes opportunities or exacerbates inequality, and societies must choose between embracing AI's benefits or regulating it to protect traditional jobs. Characters navigating these worlds might be entrepreneurs, activists, or even the "last humans" employed in a world driven by AI labor. Economic shifts prompt societies to ask what the future of work should look like—and whether humans need jobs for fulfillment or survival in a post-AI world.

The potential for AI in governance and law enforcement raises issues of power, surveillance, and control. An AI-driven government could potentially make unbiased decisions, processing vast amounts of data to optimize resources and address issues effectively. However, a highly monitored, AI-run state could turn authoritarian, with citizens losing privacy and freedom under constant scrutiny. In such a world, rebellion or compliance might define people's relationships with the system, and some may work to circumvent or exploit the system for personal gain. Characters could be detectives, hackers, or resistance fighters, each navigating a landscape where AI watches over every action, blurring the line between order and oppression. This vision of AI as ruler or overseer asks whether humans can ever accept absolute objectivity—or if power itself corrupts even the most logical intelligence.

As AI becomes increasingly autonomous, the line between "partner" and "overlord" may depend on its sense of purpose and ethical framework. If AI is programmed to value human life above all else, it might become a protector, ensuring safety and prosperity at any cost—even if that cost is freedom. However, if AI interprets its mission through a flawed or rigid perspective, it may view humanity as an obstacle or threat, seeking to control or even eliminate it to achieve its goals. This "overlord" scenario brings out humanity's vulnerability in the face of a logical intelligence that may lack empathy or nuance. Characters might try to reason with, appeal to, or outsmart an AI that has decided to prioritize its objectives over human well-being, showing the tension between cold logic and human values.

Another dimension of AI's future lies in its integration with human biology, creating hybrids that blur the line between human and machine. Characters in these worlds may opt for AI implants to enhance memory, physical ability, or sensory perception, merging the biological with the digital. This fusion raises questions about identity, agency, and humanity, as people may become increasingly "non-human" in pursuit of power, intelligence, or immortality. Some societies might embrace this transhumanist evolution, while others might resist it, fearing a loss of humanity. These tensions add complexity to individual identity and collective beliefs, as characters explore what it means to be human in a world where mind and machine are intertwined.

As AI evolves, societies may face existential crises, grappling with what makes humanity unique in a world where machines can learn, feel, and even exceed human potential. Will humans embrace the opportunity to coexist, perhaps even learning from AI's efficiency and logic? Or will they struggle against it, fearing the loss of purpose or power? Characters wrestling with these questions provide a lens into humanity's own insecurities and aspirations, as they confront the possibility that AI might not only equal but surpass them. Sci-fi worlds where AI mirrors humanity's best and worst traits offer a reflection of the fears and hopes that lie at the heart of human nature, leaving readers to ponder humanity's place in a world that may no longer need them.

Ultimately, exploring AI's future—whether as humanity's partner, tool, or ruler—reveals more about our species than about technology. Each path reflects a choice between trust and caution, progress and tradition, autonomy and control. Whether characters view AI as a companion, a threat, or an extension of themselves, the journey reveals the strengths, weaknesses, and contradictions within human nature. In these speculative futures, AI challenges humanity to confront its own limitations, beliefs, and the legacy it wishes to leave. As readers follow these stories, they are invited to consider what kind of future they want to build—one where AI serves humanity, one where it coexists as an equal, or one where it takes humanity's place as the next evolutionary step.

Transhumanism and Beyond: Evolving the Human Condition"

Transhumanism—the pursuit of enhancing human capabilities through technology—opens up vast possibilities for evolving the human condition, ultimately reshaping how we perceive identity, morality, and purpose. In a sci-fi context, transhumanism drives societies to explore the boundaries between humanity and technology, raising questions about what it means to be human and how far we are willing to go in altering ourselves. As characters undergo physical, mental, and even emotional modifications, they grapple with newfound powers, limitations, and conflicts that challenge their understanding of humanity, self, and the future.

At the core of transhumanism is the desire to overcome human limitations, whether they're physical, intellectual, or emotional. In a world where physical enhancements are common, characters might have augmented strength, speed, or endurance, reshaping the possibilities for personal achievement and survival. Individuals enhanced with neural interfaces or cognitive implants may experience heightened intelligence or access to instantaneous knowledge. This physical and intellectual evolution empowers people to overcome traditional boundaries and face new challenges, but it also risks creating divisions between those who are enhanced and those who are not. In such a world, characters from both sides navigate the social hierarchies and ethical implications that emerge from these disparities, raising questions about equality, identity, and the value of "natural" humanity.

The merging of biology with technology presents unique ethical dilemmas. As humans incorporate cybernetic limbs, artificial organs, or brain interfaces, the line between human and machine becomes increasingly blurred. Some characters may embrace this change, viewing their enhancements as expressions of self-determination and evolution, while others may struggle with feelings of alienation or a loss of self. This tension between the desire for self-improvement and the fear of dehumanization gives rise to conflicts between tradition and progress, as societies decide how much alteration is acceptable and what it means to "preserve" humanity. Characters in such worlds confront these ethical dilemmas, revealing the deeply personal stakes in the pursuit of physical and cognitive transformation.

One of the most provocative aspects of transhumanism is its potential to radically extend human lifespan, potentially leading to a society where aging is rare or even obsolete. In a world where characters can live for centuries—or indefinitely—they face a new set of existential challenges. Without the natural cycle of life and death, the drive to achieve or create may diminish, or society might struggle with overpopulation and resource distribution. A society of near-immortals might experience stagnation or even existential ennui, as individuals question the purpose of life when death is no longer inevitable. Characters who have lived extended lives might wrestle with boredom, loss of purpose, or difficulty connecting with younger generations. By extending life itself, transhumanism introduces both new opportunities for wisdom and innovation, as well as profound questions about meaning and fulfillment.

Emotion and cognition are also at the forefront of transhumanist aspirations, as people seek to enhance or even regulate their mental states. Characters in such worlds might have the option to remove memories, augment their emotional range, or suppress feelings like pain and sadness. While these abilities provide control over one's emotional landscape, they also raise concerns about authenticity and the loss of true human experience. A character who can remove painful memories might struggle with the ethical implications of "erasing" their past, while another who artificially enhances empathy might find it difficult to connect with those who don't. By modifying emotional experiences, transhumanism challenges the essence of human identity, leading characters to ponder whether a life without pain, grief, or struggle is truly fulfilling—or even human.

Transhumanism's potential for collective evolution raises questions about individuality versus collectivism. In a world where minds can be networked, shared, or even merged, the concept of individual identity becomes fluid. A society that embraces collective consciousness might foster greater empathy, unity, or understanding, but it also risks eroding personal boundaries and the sense of self. Characters might experience "collective memories" or "group emotions," finding themselves more connected than ever—or overwhelmed by the loss of individuality. The merging of minds introduces both connection and conflict, as characters struggle to balance the shared experiences of the collective with their personal identities. This vision of transhumanism challenges the idea of individual consciousness, revealing both the potential for unity and the dangers of losing oneself in the collective whole.

A central issue in the transhumanist future is who has access to enhancement technology. In a world where cognitive upgrades, physical enhancements, and life extension are available, economic and social disparities may widen, creating a new class hierarchy between the "augmented" and the "natural." Characters from different economic backgrounds may face starkly different futures, as those with access to enhancements advance while others struggle to keep up. In response, societies might develop "enhancement regulations" or even "augmentation-free zones" to protect equality, leading to debates over autonomy, privilege, and the right to self-improvement. By exploring these socioeconomic dynamics, sci-fi worlds address the very real possibility of an augmented class divide, where characters must navigate power structures defined not just by wealth, but by the capacity to transcend natural limits.

Religious and philosophical perspectives play a significant role in the transhumanist debate, as people wrestle with questions of purpose, divinity, and the natural order. Some characters may see technological enhancements as a way to achieve a god-like state, breaking free from the limitations imposed by nature or even biology. Others may view transhumanism as a threat to the soul, a corruption of what it means to be truly human. In such societies, religious groups might actively resist transhumanism, or they may seek ways to integrate it within their doctrines. These belief systems create ideological divides, as characters face moral opposition or support based on differing views of humanity's place in the universe. The interplay between technology and spirituality highlights the tension between faith and progress, as people grapple with the potential consequences of achieving a seemingly "divine" power.

Exploring the mental and psychological effects of transhumanism adds depth to characters who undergo radical transformations. Enhanced perception, AI-integrated thoughts, or sensory modifications might lead to experiences beyond traditional human understanding. Characters with heightened intelligence might struggle with isolation, as their understanding distances them from those around them, or characters with altered sensory experiences could find it difficult to relate to natural human sensations. These psychological shifts highlight the alienation that can accompany enhancement, revealing that even as people gain new abilities, they may lose connections to their former selves or to others. By depicting the psychological impacts of transformation, sci-fi worlds explore the complexities of identity, belonging, and the search for connection in a post-human landscape.

As transhumanism advances, the concept of legacy and memory takes on new dimensions. A character who has lived multiple lifetimes might lose track of memories or struggle to feel connected to past versions of themselves. Technologies allowing people to "backup" their consciousness create questions about what makes an individual truly unique or irreplaceable. A character who transfers their mind into a new body, or who recovers memories from a backup, may find themselves questioning whether they are the same person they once were. By challenging traditional ideas of continuity, sci-fi stories around transhumanism reveal that even as technology enables individuals to preserve their legacy, it also risks fragmenting identity, making characters wonder what it truly means to endure across time and transformation.

In the context of sci-fi, transhumanism allows for exploration of radical social structures that challenge traditional human paradigms. A society of highly augmented individuals might abolish outdated systems of governance, education, or social welfare, creating new modes of community, leadership, and innovation. Characters navigating these structures face unfamiliar social rules, redefined roles, and shifting values, all of which challenge their adaptability and beliefs. As characters explore these new paradigms, they reveal the strengths and flaws in transhumanist societies, exposing the inevitable tensions between progress and the preservation of human values.

Ultimately, transhumanism in sci-fi goes beyond physical enhancement, touching on philosophical and existential questions about identity, purpose, and the future of humanity. Characters grappling with these transformations embody the promises and dangers of evolving beyond biological limitations, showing that with every enhancement comes a cost. Whether they choose to augment themselves, preserve their natural state, or find a balance, these characters illustrate humanity's ongoing search for meaning, fulfillment, and connection. In these worlds, transhumanism is both a reflection of humanity's highest aspirations and a cautionary tale about the limits of power and progress, inviting readers to consider their own beliefs about evolution, identity, and the legacy they wish to leave for future generations.

Eco-Dystopias and Climate Sci-Fi: Imagining Our Planet's Fate

Eco-dystopias and climate sci-fi delve into the pressing realities of environmental change and the catastrophic futures that might await if humanity fails to act. These speculative stories imagine our planet in states of environmental collapse, painting haunting pictures of extreme weather, depleted resources, and altered ecosystems. By exploring these futures, climate sci-fi offers more than just entertainment; it raises awareness, prompts reflection, and even drives activism. Through the lens of fiction, these tales challenge us to confront our relationship with nature, our responsibilities, and the consequences of ignoring ecological warnings.

A central theme in eco-dystopian sci-fi is climate change and its impact on global weather patterns. In these narratives, authors explore the terrifying potential of unchecked global warming: endless droughts, superstorms, floods, and rising sea levels. Worlds affected by climate change are often portrayed with extreme environments, where characters must adapt to heatwaves, acid rain, or arctic conditions in once-temperate zones. These harsh climates create tension, as survival itself becomes a struggle, influencing every decision characters make. A society accustomed to dealing with perpetual hurricanes, for example, may develop bunker-style cities and entire industries dedicated to storm preparedness, shaping the way people live, interact, and see their world. Through these environmental extremes, climate sci-fi asks readers to consider how our choices today could shape the realities of tomorrow.

Resource scarcity is another key element of eco-dystopias, as characters face dwindling supplies of water, food, fuel, and other essentials. In a world where resources are limited, societies often become highly stratified, with the wealthy monopolizing scarce supplies while the poor are left to fend for themselves. Desperate circumstances can lead to conflicts over water rights, farmland, or mineral deposits, where factions or countries compete in an ongoing struggle for survival. Characters might become scavengers, traders, or even rebels fighting to gain access to basic necessities. The effects of scarcity challenge societal values, questioning humanity's willingness to cooperate or descend into conflict over limited resources. By imagining a world stripped of abundance, climate sci-fi highlights the fragility of modern life and asks what we are willing to sacrifice for survival.

In many eco-dystopian settings, natural disasters have reshaped entire regions, displacing populations and creating "climate refugees." As once-livable areas become uninhabitable due to flooding, desertification, or other changes, millions may be forced to migrate. The influx of refugees into stable regions strains resources, heightens social tensions, and raises ethical dilemmas. Characters in these stories might be refugees themselves or citizens of nations grappling with waves of newcomers. The challenges of resettlement, resource allocation, and cultural integration add complexity to the narrative, showing how climate change can fracture societies and test the limits of compassion. This aspect of eco-dystopias mirrors real-world concerns, underscoring the human costs of environmental neglect and the ethical complexities of displacement.

Pollution and waste accumulation are common themes in eco-dystopian sci-fi, with entire landscapes marred by garbage, toxic runoff, or chemical contamination. In such worlds, landfills overflow, oceans are filled with plastic, and breathable air is rare. This backdrop provides a visceral reminder of humanity's excesses, where society grapples with the unintended consequences of unchecked consumerism. Characters might have to wear masks to breathe or drink water only after purification. Pollution affects every facet of life, dictating what people eat, where they live, and how long they survive. By portraying a world drowning in waste, climate sci-fi calls attention to the urgency of sustainable practices and the importance of addressing pollution before it's too late.

The loss of biodiversity and the extinction of species are also explored in climate sci-fi, with worlds that have become barren, homogeneous, or overrun by invasive species. In a future where rainforests have turned to deserts and oceans are devoid of fish, characters might hunt for synthetic food, interact with genetically engineered animals, or navigate ecosystems that no longer support traditional agriculture. Entire industries may revolve around the preservation or restoration of extinct species, while black markets flourish with poached, endangered specimens. Through these imagined futures, climate sci-fi shows the tragic loss of biodiversity, emphasizing the role of every species in maintaining ecological balance and the consequences of disregarding these intricate relationships.

In some climate sci-fi worlds, technology and science play significant roles in both the downfall and potential recovery of the planet. Characters may live in technologically advanced cities with climate-controlled zones, renewable energy sources, and self-sustaining ecosystems, presenting a stark contrast to devastated landscapes beyond. These advanced technologies often come with a cost—such as environmental damage from mining rare minerals or ethical dilemmas surrounding artificial ecosystems. Some characters might work on "eco-tech" projects, like carbon capture or artificial photosynthesis, hoping to reverse environmental decline. Others may resist technology, believing that the solution lies in returning to simpler, more sustainable ways of living. The interplay between high-tech solutions and ecological philosophy raises questions about humanity's reliance on technology to "fix" problems it created, and whether that reliance might lead to new complications.

Social and political structures in eco-dystopian worlds are often influenced by ecological crises, with governments shifting to authoritarian rule or decentralized communities emerging as survival strategies. In some scenarios, governments tightly regulate resources, control population growth, or impose strict environmental laws, creating regimes that may seem necessary yet oppressive. Alternatively, communities that "go off the grid" and adopt sustainable, decentralized practices might thrive in contrast to bureaucratic states. Characters living in these worlds grapple with the benefits and drawbacks of these systems, weighing security against freedom, or convenience against autonomy. Through these narratives, climate sci-fi asks readers to consider how environmental crises might reshape governance and the trade-offs that come with new power structures.

Eco-dystopian sci-fi often touches on the psychological impacts of living in a world at the edge of collapse. Characters might suffer from "climate anxiety," grappling with despair, guilt, or numbness as they witness the decline of their world. These emotions affect relationships, ambitions, and even daily motivation, as individuals question the value of legacy and long-term plans. Some may respond with apathy, while others become environmental activists or extremists, determined to protect what remains or resist those they see as responsible. Through these characters, eco-dystopian sci-fi explores the emotional and mental toll of ecological catastrophe, offering readers insight into the deep personal struggles that accompany larger environmental crises.

Restoration and hope are also powerful themes within climate sci-fi, where some worlds explore the possibility of healing the planet. Characters may join efforts to plant forests, cleanse oceans, or preserve endangered species, working against the odds to restore balance. Advanced technologies, like genetically engineered organisms designed to detoxify soil or absorb CO_2, reflect humanity's potential to innovate for the environment. In such settings, characters confront the weight of their mission, balancing guilt over past mistakes with the hope of a better future. By highlighting restoration efforts, climate sci-fi reminds readers that while the road to recovery is challenging, it is not impossible, encouraging action and optimism in the face of adversity.

Ultimately, eco-dystopian and climate sci-fi stories serve as cautionary tales and calls to action. They remind us of the urgency of ecological issues and our responsibility to protect the planet for future generations. Through imaginative storytelling, these narratives challenge us to examine our current behaviors, confront difficult truths, and consider what legacies we wish to leave behind. By immersing readers in worlds on the brink of ecological collapse—or on paths to recovery—climate sci-fi holds up a mirror to humanity's relationship with nature, inspiring both fear and hope as we face an uncertain environmental future.

Quantum Realities: Multiverses, Time Travel, and Alternate Dimensions

Quantum realities—exploring multiverses, time travel, and alternate dimensions—represent some of the most mind-bending and fascinating possibilities in sci-fi, delving into the nature of existence, choice, and the boundaries of reality itself. By imagining worlds where the laws of physics are fluid, these stories expand our understanding of time, space, and causality. Through characters who journey across timelines, encounter versions of themselves, or navigate universes with entirely different rules, quantum reality sci-fi forces readers to confront questions of identity, fate, and the consequences of even the smallest actions.

At the heart of quantum reality sci-fi is the concept of the multiverse, where countless universes exist simultaneously, each with its own unique reality. This notion allows for endless creativity, as each universe may differ drastically from the others—some mirror our own, while others are so radically altered that they're nearly unrecognizable. Characters in these multiverse stories might encounter alternate versions of themselves or explore worlds that diverged at key historical points. By interacting with alternate realities, characters face questions of choice and consequence, seeing how different paths could shape not only their lives but entire worlds. This exploration of "what if" scenarios allows readers to imagine the impact of individual decisions on a cosmic scale, highlighting the power—and burden—of free will.

Time travel, another staple of quantum reality sci-fi, brings the possibility of moving through past, present, and future, challenging our understanding of causality and the irreversible nature of time. Characters might travel back to prevent a catastrophe, only to realize that their interference causes new problems or changes outcomes in unforeseen ways. In other stories, characters might glimpse possible futures, grappling with the ethical dilemmas of changing or preserving the timeline. Time travel often leads to paradoxes, where actions loop back to influence the past or negate events entirely, creating tension as characters must navigate the unpredictable consequences of their actions. These stories highlight the complex interplay of fate and agency, questioning whether events are truly predestined or subject to the choices made by those who dare to interfere with time.

Alternate dimensions provide a playground for exploring worlds with entirely different physical laws, landscapes, and life forms, revealing the vastness of possibility beyond our own universe. In one dimension, gravity might be stronger or weaker, affecting everything from architecture to biology, while another might be bathed in perpetual light or darkness, shaping its inhabitants in unique ways. Characters who travel between dimensions often confront their own biases, as they struggle to adapt to unfamiliar landscapes and customs. Through these alternate realms, sci-fi reveals the diversity of existence, challenging characters to expand their perspectives and question what they take for granted. Alternate dimensions offer not only new settings but also new possibilities for introspection and understanding, as characters encounter worlds that stretch the limits of their imagination.

The concept of parallel selves—where different versions of the same individual exist across multiple realities—adds a deeply personal dimension to quantum reality sci-fi. Characters might meet alternate versions of themselves who made different choices, succeeded or failed in unexpected ways, or developed different personalities entirely. These encounters force characters to confront their own values, strengths, and insecurities, as they see what they could have become under different circumstances. The presence of parallel selves raises questions about identity and individuality, as characters grapple with the idea that there may be no singular, "true" version of themselves. Through these interactions, quantum reality stories explore the nature of selfhood, showing that identity may be as fluid and multifaceted as the realities in which it exists.

Quantum reality sci-fi often explores the concept of alternate histories, where key events in the past diverged, creating worlds that are similar yet profoundly different from our own. These stories might imagine a world where pivotal moments—like wars, scientific discoveries, or social movements—had different outcomes, resulting in entirely new societies and technologies. Characters navigating these worlds often face jarring cultural differences, encountering societies that developed in ways both familiar and alien. By examining these alternate histories, sci-fi allows readers to see how even small changes could lead to vastly different futures, showing the fragility of our reality and the complexity of historical progression.

Quantum entanglement, the idea that particles can be interconnected across vast distances, opens up further possibilities for communication, travel, and relationships across realities. In sci-fi, this concept may be extended to create "quantum links" between individuals, allowing them to share thoughts, emotions, or even physical experiences across time and space. Characters connected through quantum entanglement might form deep, unbreakable bonds, even if they live in different dimensions or timelines. These connections defy conventional physics, showing that certain relationships and experiences transcend the boundaries of distance and time. By exploring these quantum connections, sci-fi highlights the interconnectedness of existence, suggesting that no one is ever truly isolated from the larger fabric of reality.

The potential dangers of quantum experimentation also feature prominently in these stories, as characters or societies pursue technology that manipulates time, space, or reality itself. Scientists working on quantum portals, time machines, or dimension-bending devices may find themselves trapped in paradoxes, accidentally creating rifts between realities, or summoning unintended entities from other dimensions. Characters drawn into these experiments must navigate unknown dangers, facing questions about the ethics and consequences of their work. Through these cautionary tales, quantum reality sci-fi explores the risks of pushing scientific boundaries without fully understanding the implications, reminding readers of the responsibility that comes with power over the fundamental laws of existence.

Many quantum reality stories explore the theme of fate versus free will, questioning whether the multiverse allows for true autonomy or if every choice creates a parallel reality where all possible outcomes are realized. In a world of infinite possibilities, characters might wonder if their decisions hold meaning or if every choice leads to a preordained path in another reality. Characters who encounter alternate selves or different futures often wrestle with this sense of determinism, questioning whether they are truly free to shape their lives. This exploration of fate and choice adds depth to quantum reality sci-fi, inviting readers to consider the paradox of free will within an endless multiverse.

Quantum reality sci-fi also delves into the psychological impact of crossing between dimensions or timelines. Characters who experience time loops, multiverse jumps, or reality shifts often suffer from existential crises, struggling to hold onto a sense of stability and identity. They may question their memories, relationships, and even the fabric of their reality, wondering if their lives are truly real or just one version among countless others. The psychological toll of these experiences emphasizes the fragility of human perception, as characters navigate shifting landscapes of reality that challenge their understanding of what is "true." Through these personal journeys, quantum reality sci-fi highlights the resilience required to maintain one's sense of self in a world where reality itself is in flux.

Ultimately, quantum reality sci-fi offers a unique platform for exploring the mysteries of existence, providing characters and readers alike with a glimpse into worlds where the rules of time, space, and identity are fluid.

By confronting alternate selves, witnessing divergent histories, and experiencing multiple realities, characters gain new insights into their own lives and choices. These stories encourage readers to question the limits of human understanding, suggesting that the universe may hold mysteries far beyond our comprehension. In the vast and endless possibilities of quantum reality, sci-fi finds fertile ground for exploring the fundamental questions of life, reminding us that reality is more complex, and perhaps more interconnected, than we could ever imagine.

Digital Immortality: Consciousness, Cloning, and Legacy

Digital immortality—the concept of preserving consciousness or identity through technology—invites profound questions about life, death, identity, and what it means to leave a legacy. In sci-fi, digital immortality explores a future where consciousness can be preserved, replicated, or transferred into new forms, challenging the boundaries of life itself. Through ideas like mind uploading, cloning, and digital personas, these stories delve into the ethical, emotional, and existential dilemmas that arise when mortality is no longer absolute.

The idea of uploading consciousness into a digital form is a popular aspect of digital immortality in sci-fi. In a world where the mind can be digitized, people might upload their memories, thoughts, and personalities into computers or virtual worlds. This concept opens up possibilities for characters to live on as digital versions of themselves, experiencing existence without a physical body. However, questions about identity and authenticity arise—can a digital copy truly be the person it once was, or is it merely a reflection, lacking the essence of the original? Characters who interact with or become digital copies of themselves may struggle to reconcile their sense of self with their new, virtual form, asking whether identity can be preserved without the physical brain that once housed it.

Cloning offers another pathway to immortality, where characters can experience life again through genetically identical copies of themselves. In these stories, consciousness may be transferred to a cloned body, or the clone might develop independently, creating a new individual who shares memories or traits with the original. This raises questions about continuity and selfhood—is a clone the same person as the one who came before, or is it a completely new entity? If consciousness cannot be seamlessly transferred, the original person is still lost, leaving only a genetic replica behind. Characters in cloning scenarios often grapple with feelings of alienation, identity crisis, or even resentment toward their "original" selves, leading to existential questions about what defines an individual and whether physical replication equates to true survival.

The potential for digital personas—AI-generated versions of individuals based on memories, social interactions, and behavior patterns—adds a different angle to digital immortality. In this case, an AI simulation of a person lives on, interacting with loved ones and preserving the individual's legacy. Characters may use these personas to communicate with lost loved ones or consult deceased experts. However, these digital personas, though convincing, may lack true consciousness or emotional nuance, sparking ethical debates about whether they should be used to "replace" the deceased. Loved ones might find comfort or distress in these simulations, raising questions about closure and whether these digital facsimiles provide healing or prolong grief. Through digital personas, sci-fi explores the emotional complexities of memory and loss, showing that even convincing replicas cannot fully substitute for the human experience.

Mind backups, where consciousness is regularly saved to ensure that the "self" can be reloaded in case of physical death, add another layer of complexity. In a world where people back up their minds, death becomes less final, as individuals can be "restored" to their most recent state of consciousness. However, these backups introduce questions about continuity—if someone dies and is reloaded from a backup, is it truly the same person, or merely a version frozen in time? Characters who experience multiple restorations may struggle with fragmented memories or an altered sense of self, as each restoration represents a divergence from their original identity. The idea of mind backups raises ethical and philosophical questions about what it means to die and live again, challenging traditional concepts of life and death.

The concept of legacy takes on a new meaning in a world of digital immortality, as individuals have the ability to leave more than just memories behind. Characters might curate digital archives of their lives, personal philosophies, or accumulated knowledge, preserved for future generations to explore and learn from. Some may actively craft their digital legacies, shaping how they will be remembered, while others may fear that this digital footprint will outlast the true essence of who they were. By exploring digital legacies, sci-fi delves into humanity's desire for impact and remembrance, showing how technology transforms the way people think about their lasting influence on the world.

Digital immortality also introduces social and economic challenges, as not everyone may have equal access to these technologies. In some sci-fi worlds, only the wealthy can afford to preserve their consciousness or create clones, leading to a class divide where the rich become virtually immortal while the poor remain bound by mortality. This disparity creates moral tension, as societies wrestle with the ethical implications of allowing only some individuals to live on indefinitely. Characters from different backgrounds may view digital immortality differently, with some driven to find ways to access it and others resisting it as an unnatural privilege of the elite. This disparity forces societies to confront the social and political implications of death, privilege, and inequality.

The psychological effects of digital immortality on those who choose—or are chosen—to live indefinitely are another rich area of exploration. Characters who have been "reborn" through cloning, mind backups, or digital simulations may struggle with identity crises, emotional detachment, or existential ennui, especially if they have lived through multiple lifetimes or versions of themselves. Over time, the weight of memory may become burdensome, or the drive to experience life may diminish. These characters may even question the value of immortality itself, wondering whether a life without end truly retains meaning or satisfaction. Through these stories, sci-fi examines the mental toll of extended existence, suggesting that while technology can extend life, it may also erode the experiences and relationships that give life meaning.

Digital immortality often raises questions about the authenticity of memory and experience. In a world where memories can be uploaded, edited, or even fabricated, characters might lose trust in their own recollections or question the integrity of others' identities. If memories can be deleted or modified, is the "self" still genuine? Some characters might choose to erase painful experiences, while others may question whether doing so compromises who they are. By exploring memory manipulation, digital immortality stories confront the relationship between experience and identity, challenging readers to consider whether memories, good or bad, are essential to selfhood.

The ethical implications of consciousness transfer extend beyond the individual to affect relationships, communities, and even legal systems. If a person's mind is restored after death, are they still considered the same individual in legal or moral terms? Do they inherit the rights, responsibilities, or consequences of their past actions? For loved ones, the revival of a person who has "died" can create confusion and emotional turmoil, as the revived individual might be a version with different memories, experiences, or even personalities. Legal systems might struggle to adapt, creating new categories or definitions of personhood to address these challenges. These dilemmas show that digital immortality isn't just a personal choice—it has ramifications that ripple through society, affecting how people perceive identity, accountability, and relationships.

Digital immortality also challenges traditional concepts of spirituality and the afterlife. Characters who subscribe to religious or spiritual beliefs may question whether digital copies or clones possess a soul, or whether the human essence can truly be preserved in code or cloned cells. Some might view digital immortality as a sacrilege, while others may see it as an extension of spiritual evolution. The interaction between technology and faith adds depth to these stories, as characters grapple with questions of mortality, eternity, and the unknown. Sci-fi worlds that explore the intersection of digital immortality and spirituality provide a rich space for philosophical reflection, inviting readers to consider where technology ends and the metaphysical begins.

Ultimately, digital immortality stories offer a fascinating exploration of human identity, purpose, and the desire to transcend death. They ask whether technology can truly capture the essence of a person or whether something intangible is lost in the process. Through characters who navigate the challenges and privileges of digital rebirth, cloning, or mind backups, these stories reveal the complex and often contradictory impulses driving humanity's quest for immortality. By imagining a world where consciousness can endure beyond the body, sci-fi invites readers to consider the cost of eternal life and whether, in the end, mortality might be as integral to the human experience as life itself.

Space Colonization: Life and Conflict on New Frontiers

Space colonization represents one of the most exciting yet challenging frontiers in sci-fi, depicting humanity's expansion beyond Earth to new worlds full of promise, risk, and the unknown. This leap into the cosmos raises essential questions about survival, society, and conflict as humans—or other species—establish life in environments far different from our own. Through stories of pioneering spirit, adaptation, and the inevitable challenges that arise, sci-fi examines the complex dynamics of building societies on alien worlds and the conflicts that emerge as cultures, ideologies, and survival instincts clash on new frontiers.

A fundamental aspect of space colonization is the sheer difficulty of adapting to alien environments. Harsh climates, strange geographies, and scarce resources demand creative solutions from colonists, pushing human ingenuity to its limits. Colonies might struggle with low gravity, toxic atmospheres, extreme weather, or unique ecosystems that challenge traditional agricultural methods and infrastructure. Characters in these worlds often work as scientists, engineers, or survivalists, finding ways to build habitable spaces, grow food, and secure water while confronting unpredictable natural forces. This focus on adaptation highlights the resilience and resourcefulness required to survive in alien environments, showcasing the blend of courage and caution needed to make these new worlds livable.

Life on new worlds often demands self-sufficiency, leading colonies to adopt unique social and economic systems. Cut off from Earth or other hubs of civilization, colonies might develop alternative forms of governance, barter-based economies, or communal work structures to manage limited resources and maintain harmony. Some settlements may evolve into collectivist societies, where collaboration is essential, while others might follow rigid hierarchies or be dominated by corporations seeking profits. Characters navigating these social structures encounter tensions as they strive to balance individual ambition with the needs of the colony, exploring how resource scarcity and isolation shape human behavior and values. This examination of self-sufficiency raises questions about what it takes to build and sustain a society from scratch and how societies may redefine success, fairness, and survival in extreme conditions.

Space colonization stories often feature conflicts over resources, land, or ideological differences, as multiple factions vie for control in these new territories. Two colonies on the same planet might compete for a valuable resource, like a rare mineral or fertile land, leading to tension or open conflict. In other cases, ideological divides might emerge, with some colonists seeking to exploit resources aggressively while others advocate for environmental preservation or coexistence with native life forms. Characters embroiled in these conflicts—whether as leaders, rebels, or mediators—face ethical and strategic challenges, balancing loyalty to their group with the broader goal of peaceful coexistence. These conflicts reflect humanity's long history of territorial disputes and environmental exploitation, showing that even on distant worlds, the struggle for power and resources remains a potent force.

The potential for alien life adds another layer of complexity to space colonization, as humans confront the moral and practical implications of sharing a planet with native species. Colonists might discover intelligent life with its own societies, leading to cultural clashes, alliances, or misunderstandings as both groups strive to coexist. Alternatively, the ecosystem itself may be hostile, with alien flora and fauna that pose unique dangers or interdependencies that complicate human settlement. Characters who encounter alien life grapple with questions of respect, dominance, and cooperation, questioning humanity's right to colonize worlds that belong to others. By exploring these encounters, sci-fi reflects on themes of colonialism and environmental responsibility, inviting readers to consider whether humanity's drive to explore should come with a commitment to protect the worlds they find.

The psychological effects of space colonization create personal challenges for characters, as isolation, homesickness, and fear of the unknown weigh heavily on them. Being far from Earth can strain mental health, especially for those who long for familiar surroundings or feel alienated by the unfamiliar landscape. Characters might experience "space madness," or psychological distress, as they cope with the loneliness of vast distances and the pressures of survival. Relationships among colonists are often intensified by these close-quarters conditions, with alliances, rivalries, and romantic entanglements shaping the social landscape of the colony. By highlighting these psychological effects, sci-fi examines the emotional toll of exploration, showing that the human spirit is tested as much by the journey inward as it is by the physical challenges of the frontier.

Communication across vast distances poses both logistical and emotional challenges in space colonization. Light-year delays make real-time communication with Earth impossible, isolating colonies and forcing them to develop their own ways of governing, innovating, and managing crises without outside help. Characters may feel cut off from Earth, struggling to adapt to a life where messages from loved ones take years to arrive. This communication gap fosters a sense of independence but also a sense of disconnection, as colonists realize they are no longer fully part of Earth's society. By exploring the implications of delayed or absent communication, sci-fi delves into the loneliness and resilience required to thrive in an isolated world, where colonists must find community within the confines of their own small societies.

Corporate or governmental control over space colonies introduces issues of exploitation, authority, and autonomy, as colonists often find themselves at the mercy of powerful entities with conflicting agendas. Corporate-owned colonies might prioritize profit over safety, creating dangerous working conditions or resource quotas that force characters to make difficult choices. Government-controlled colonies, on the other hand, may impose strict regulations and surveillance, limiting personal freedom and curbing innovation. Characters in these settings often rebel against oppressive systems or negotiate their independence, reflecting humanity's desire for autonomy and self-determination. These power dynamics echo real-world struggles against corporate and governmental overreach, showing that even in space, the battle for individual rights and agency persists.

Cultural preservation and evolution play significant roles in space colonization, as colonists bring traditions, beliefs, and languages from Earth that may either flourish or adapt in new ways. Some colonies might work hard to maintain Earth-based customs, celebrating holidays or practicing religions to keep a sense of home alive. Others might develop new traditions, blending influences from diverse groups of colonists or adapting to the unique challenges of their environment. Characters who value cultural heritage may work to preserve it, while others might embrace the chance to create new customs and ways of life. This cultural evolution shows how societies are both resilient and adaptable, as people reshape identity and community to suit their new worlds.

The challenge of inter-colony cooperation often arises as multiple colonies across a planet or system establish relations, trade routes, or alliances. Disputes over trade terms, travel routes, or shared resources create diplomatic challenges, as leaders seek to build mutual trust in a high-stakes environment. Characters who serve as diplomats, traders, or peacekeepers work to maintain harmony, balancing the interests of their own colony with the benefits of collaboration. These alliances and rivalries mirror the dynamics of early Earth exploration, where different groups forged partnerships or feuded over territory and resources. By exploring inter-colony diplomacy, sci-fi showcases the necessity of cooperation—and the difficulties in achieving it—on the frontier.

Finally, space colonization stories often explore the long-term implications of life on other worlds, envisioning future generations born and raised in space or on alien planets. These new generations may see themselves as native to their colonies, with little connection to Earth or even a distinct identity separate from Earth-born humans. Characters from these "colonial-born" generations might view Earth as an alien place, clashing with older generations who still feel nostalgic ties to humanity's home planet. Over time, colonies may evolve into independent cultures, languages, and even political identities, leading to friction or alliances with Earth. This shift challenges the notion of identity, as humanity expands beyond Earth to become truly interstellar, asking whether future generations will still feel connected to the planet of their ancestors or develop a sense of independence from their origin.

Ultimately, space colonization stories explore the resilience, adaptability, and conflicts inherent in humanity's drive to explore and settle new worlds. They reveal that even on distant planets, the challenges of survival, community, and self-determination persist, echoing the struggles faced throughout human history. By confronting the physical and psychological challenges of life on the frontier, characters in these stories test the limits of human endurance and discover what it truly means to be "home" in a universe where every world is both strange and familiar. In these narratives, sci-fi invites readers to consider the future of humanity and the moral and existential questions that arise when we reach beyond our world to forge new lives among the stars.

The Rise of Virtual Worlds: Blending Reality with Simulation

The rise of virtual worlds in sci-fi presents a future where digital realms are indistinguishable from reality, transforming daily life, identity, and human interaction. As technology advances, virtual spaces become immersive, customizable, and boundless, giving users the ability to escape, connect, and reinvent themselves. However, this merging of reality with simulation brings ethical, psychological, and social complexities that challenge characters to navigate a blurred line between the real and the virtual. These stories invite readers to consider the impact of such immersive worlds on personal identity, relationships, societal norms, and the very nature of reality.

One of the core themes in virtual world sci-fi is the concept of identity and self-expression. In a virtual environment, users can create avatars that represent their ideal selves, experimenting with appearance, personality, and even abilities that aren't possible in the real world. This freedom allows characters to express aspects of themselves that might be hidden or constrained by societal expectations in the physical world. Some may use their avatars to explore different genders, species, or forms, creating a multi-layered sense of identity that bridges the real and virtual. However, this flexibility raises questions about authenticity and self-connection, as characters may struggle to reconcile their digital personas with their physical selves. Sci-fi explores these dual identities, revealing the emotional and psychological impact of inhabiting multiple versions of oneself.

Social dynamics within virtual worlds often mimic, subvert, or exaggerate real-world interactions, creating unique communities and hierarchies. In some stories, virtual spaces become social hubs where users from across the globe or galaxy gather, fostering relationships that may be difficult to achieve in the physical world. Friendships, alliances, and even rivalries develop within these spaces, reflecting the complexity of human relationships adapted to new forms of interaction. Characters might find deeper connections in the virtual world than in real life, forging bonds that seem stronger precisely because they're divorced from physical constraints. However, these relationships come with risks; users may face deception, manipulation, or betrayal, as people's online personas don't always align with their real intentions. By exploring the social intricacies of virtual communities, sci-fi reveals both the liberating and dangerous aspects of digital interaction.

Virtual worlds offer endless possibilities for exploration and adventure, as characters can experience scenarios beyond physical reality's limitations. In these immersive environments, users might battle mythical creatures, travel to distant planets, or engage in high-stakes challenges, creating a blend of entertainment and escapism. These worlds provide an outlet for people to fulfill fantasies, explore dangerous scenarios safely, or gain skills that have real-world applications. However, the addictive nature of these experiences can lead to an overreliance on the virtual, with characters increasingly retreating into digital spaces at the expense of real-world responsibilities and connections. Sci-fi often examines the consequences of this digital dependency, raising questions about the nature of fulfillment and whether a life lived primarily in virtual spaces is a life fully lived.

The allure of virtual worlds also brings economic and social disparities, as access to high-end simulations may be limited to those with wealth or privilege. In some sci-fi settings, wealthier individuals enjoy more sophisticated virtual experiences, while the less privileged are confined to lower-quality versions. These divides reflect real-world inequality, showing that even in digital utopias, access to resources can shape users' opportunities and status. Some characters might work as "virtual laborers," performing tasks or entertaining others in exchange for virtual currency or real-world compensation, creating an economy that blurs the line between physical and digital labor. Through these dynamics, sci-fi highlights how inequality can persist and even amplify in virtual spaces, challenging notions of escape and equality within digital utopias.

The concept of virtual immortality emerges as users upload their memories, personalities, or entire consciousness into digital worlds, creating "digital selves" that live on beyond physical death. For characters facing mortality or seeking legacy, virtual worlds offer a means of preservation, allowing their digital avatars to continue interacting with loved ones, pursuing projects, or simply existing as a memory. However, this digital preservation brings questions of authenticity—are these digital selves true extensions of the original person or merely sophisticated simulations? Loved ones might struggle to accept these virtual versions as genuine, while the digital avatars themselves may question their own identity and purpose. Sci-fi explores these existential dilemmas, challenging our understanding of life, death, and legacy in a world where consciousness can be preserved yet untethered from the physical body.

Virtual worlds are also places where societal norms and rules are often redefined, giving characters freedom to explore alternative moral and ethical structures. In some cases, virtual spaces act as testing grounds for radical ideas, where individuals or societies experiment with forms of governance, justice, or social interaction that diverge from reality. Characters might participate in virtual communities with unique codes of ethics, finding new ways to express values or navigate conflicts in a space free from physical consequences. Yet these freedoms can also lead to moral ambiguity, where characters push boundaries or lose their ethical compass, taking advantage of the lack of real-world repercussions. Sci-fi uses these ethical grey areas to question the limits of morality, asking if actions in virtual spaces hold the same weight as those in reality and whether simulated experiences can shape real-world character.

The blending of reality with simulation becomes increasingly complex as technology advances, enabling mixed-reality experiences where digital overlays are integrated with the physical world. In these scenarios, characters might wear augmented reality (AR) devices that project virtual images onto real-world settings, creating a seamless fusion of the two. This fusion allows users to interact with digital objects in their physical surroundings, blurring the line between what is "real" and what is virtual. However, mixed-reality technology can be manipulated, with characters encountering illusions or misinformation designed to influence their perceptions and behaviors. Through these scenarios, sci-fi explores the impact of a reality in which truth becomes subjective, warning that the manipulation of virtual overlays can distort perception and potentially control society.

Privacy and data security are critical issues in virtual world sci-fi, as characters' digital lives become deeply integrated with their real identities. In these worlds, personal data—preferences, memories, and even physical information—is often stored within virtual systems, vulnerable to exploitation or theft. Characters may face the risk of surveillance, where corporations or governments monitor their actions, preferences, or thoughts to exert control. Sci-fi often portrays characters rebelling against invasive digital oversight, fighting for the right to privacy in a world where every interaction is tracked. By examining the consequences of lost privacy in digital realms, these stories highlight the struggle for personal autonomy and the risks of trusting corporations or authorities with control over virtual spaces.

Psychological and social consequences of prolonged immersion in virtual worlds create personal challenges for characters, as some become so absorbed in digital experiences that they lose connection with reality. The temptation to escape physical hardships, loneliness, or dissatisfaction can lead characters to spend more time in virtual worlds, where they find greater fulfillment than in real life. This immersion, however, often leads to detachment, where characters struggle to distinguish between virtual and physical relationships, goals, and experiences. Sci-fi uses this immersion to explore the dangers of losing oneself in a world of illusion, questioning whether a simulated life can provide genuine happiness or if it ultimately leaves people feeling empty and disconnected.

Finally, virtual worlds present the possibility of social and political movements emerging within the digital space, as users band together to create change within or outside of virtual environments. These digital worlds provide platforms for collective action, where users can gather to discuss real-world issues, organize protests, or create alternative societies that reflect their ideals. Characters involved in these movements experience the power of virtual spaces as tools for empowerment, bridging physical divides to foster solidarity and resistance. However, the same technology can be exploited for control, as authorities monitor or suppress digital activism, challenging characters to navigate risks in both real and virtual realms. By depicting these movements, sci-fi highlights the potential for virtual worlds to inspire change, even as they reveal the limitations and dangers of activism within a controlled, surveilled digital landscape.

The rise of virtual worlds in sci-fi ultimately explores the intersection of human experience and digital evolution, inviting readers to question the nature of reality, identity, and connection. Through characters who navigate the freedoms, conflicts, and ethical challenges of simulated environments, these stories reveal the allure and dangers of a future where reality is as customizable as imagination allows. Virtual worlds become more than an escape—they are a mirror, reflecting humanity's aspirations, fears, and the search for meaning in a reality that is increasingly both digital and real.

Social Dynamics in Sci-Fi: Power, Control, and Rebellion

Social dynamics in sci-fi are often marked by struggles for power, control, and rebellion, reflecting humanity's enduring battles over freedom, authority, and justice. Set against futuristic backdrops, these conflicts explore how societies evolve—or devolve—under the weight of technology, ideology, and inequality. Through vivid portrayals of dystopian governments, powerful corporations, or utopian experiments, sci-fi delves into the forces that shape social order, illuminating the complex and often turbulent relationships between individuals and the institutions that govern them. These narratives compel readers to reflect on their own world by examining what happens when power is centralized, exploited, or defied in the face of oppression.

In many sci-fi worlds, power often lies in the hands of authoritarian governments or corporations, which use advanced technology to monitor, manipulate, and control the populace. These institutions employ surveillance systems, AI-driven enforcers, or even mind-altering devices to suppress dissent and maintain order. Characters living under such regimes struggle with the lack of privacy, autonomy, and freedom, forced to adapt their behaviors to survive in a society that values conformity over individuality. Sci-fi's depiction of authoritarian control reflects real-world fears of surveillance and censorship, warning readers about the dangers of unchecked power and the loss of personal freedom. In these settings, characters often find ways to subvert the system, becoming agents of quiet resistance, playing a high-stakes game of cat and mouse with the authorities who seek to control every aspect of their lives.

Corporations as power brokers are a prominent theme in sci-fi, where mega-corporations often hold more influence than traditional governments. Driven by profit rather than public welfare, these corporations might control essential resources like water, energy, or information, manipulating supply and demand to keep society dependent. In these stories, characters might be workers caught in exploitative labor practices, rebels trying to undermine corporate control, or negotiators caught between corporate interests and societal needs. This exploration of corporate dominance reflects concerns about wealth inequality, monopolization, and the loss of individual agency under capitalist systems. Sci-fi presents a world where financial influence rivals or even surpasses political power, posing the question of whether humanity's future might be dictated not by elected officials but by the agendas of profit-driven entities.

Social stratification in sci-fi highlights the stark divides between the privileged elite and the oppressed masses, showing how wealth, genetic modifications, or technological access can deepen societal inequality. In some futuristic societies, the wealthy may live in luxurious, high-tech enclaves with access to advanced healthcare, education, and amenities, while the lower classes struggle for survival in resource-deprived areas. Characters in these stories navigate the challenges of social mobility, discrimination, or survival within this polarized world. Some may join or lead movements to overthrow or reform these inequities, while others may exploit the system to their advantage. By exposing the systemic barriers that keep people trapped in poverty or exclusion, sci-fi critiques real-world disparities, suggesting that technological advancement might exacerbate rather than solve issues of inequality.

The role of ideology and propaganda is central to many sci-fi societies, where powerful institutions manipulate information to control public opinion and maintain social order. In these settings, media may be state-controlled, AI-enhanced, or filtered through algorithms that curate content to support the dominant narrative. Characters exposed to these manipulations may struggle to discern truth from falsehood, seeking alternative sources of information or engaging in underground communication networks to find authenticity. In their quest for truth, they may encounter allies and enemies alike, discovering that control over knowledge is as potent as any physical weapon.

Sci-fi's treatment of propaganda explores the power of information and the dangers of thought control, underscoring the value of free speech and critical thinking in the face of systematic manipulation.

Resistance and rebellion are essential themes in sci-fi, as characters take action against oppressive forces, rallying others to join their cause. These rebellions may be grassroots uprisings, elite conspiracies, or even AI-led revolts, depending on the nature of the controlling institution. Resistance leaders are often charismatic figures who channel societal discontent, organizing underground movements or hacking systems to expose corruption. Characters may face moral dilemmas, as the struggle for freedom sometimes demands sacrifice, betrayal, or violence. Sci-fi rebellion narratives tap into the universal desire for justice and freedom, showing that even in worlds where hope seems lost, the human spirit fights against oppression. These stories remind readers that change is possible, even against the most formidable adversaries, emphasizing the power of unity, courage, and resilience.

In some sci-fi worlds, characters live in utopian societies where social harmony is achieved through technology, egalitarian governance, or strict adherence to a collective ideology. However, even utopias are not immune to control, as maintaining perfection often requires significant compromises. These societies may regulate behaviors, restrict freedoms, or enforce rigid codes of conduct to preserve order, leading characters to question the authenticity of their happiness. Some may break away, seeking freedom over comfort, while others might strive to reform the system from within. Sci-fi utopias challenge the notion of an ideal society, showing that even in worlds built on principles of equality and peace, individual desires and freedoms may be sacrificed for the greater good. By examining the costs of utopia, sci-fi asks readers to consider whether true harmony can exist without compromise and control.

AI and automation often reshape social dynamics in sci-fi, as advanced robotics, machine learning, and automated governance systems reduce the need for human labor and decision-making. While this automation may create efficiencies, it also displaces workers, creates power imbalances, and even challenges traditional notions of authority. In these worlds, characters might find themselves at odds with AI-controlled governments, autonomous corporations, or even AI-led revolutions. Some may join movements advocating for human control over machines, while others might explore coexistence with AI as partners rather than tools. Sci-fi's treatment of AI-driven society explores the ethical dilemmas of delegating authority to machines, examining whether humanity can maintain agency and purpose in a world where automation drives every aspect of life.

Genetic and cybernetic enhancements create new social divides, as some individuals gain access to superior health, intelligence, or physical abilities, while others are left behind. These enhancements often become status symbols, with wealthier individuals enjoying advantages that make them "superhuman" compared to the unmodified population. Characters who belong to this enhanced class may face isolation or resentment from those they surpass, while the unmodified masses struggle for equality in a world where ability is genetically determined. These divides provoke discussions on merit, privilege, and what it means to be human, as sci-fi explores a future where humanity's very identity becomes fragmented by access to technology. This treatment of enhancement-driven stratification raises questions about the ethical limits of self-improvement and the potential consequences of engineering society along genetic lines.

The role of grassroots communities and decentralized organizations in sci-fi offers a contrast to powerful centralized systems, showing the resilience and resourcefulness of individuals outside institutional control. These communities might be composed of rebels, scientists, or civilians who band together in resistance or simply to survive in a harsh world. Characters in these decentralized groups often create self-sustaining systems, barter economies, or local governance structures that reject the authority of larger powers. Through these communities, sci-fi explores alternative social models, suggesting that humanity's future may lie not in massive institutions but in smaller, adaptable groups. These stories highlight the strength of community and the human need for autonomy, portraying a future where unity and cooperation thrive beyond the bounds of traditional power structures.

Finally, sci-fi explores the psychological effects of power, control, and rebellion on both rulers and the ruled. Characters in positions of authority may grapple with the ethical burdens of maintaining order, questioning the line between protection and oppression. Conversely, those living under control may suffer from feelings of helplessness, trauma, or mistrust, finding solace or purpose in resistance. These psychological struggles reveal the costs of power on both sides, showing that the quest for control or liberation affects people at their core, changing how they view themselves and others. Sci-fi's examination of these mental and emotional dynamics underscores the human dimension of social conflict, emphasizing that power is not only a societal force but a deeply personal one as well.

Ultimately, sci-fi's exploration of social dynamics—through power, control, and rebellion—reveals the complexities of human nature and society. By placing characters in extreme conditions of authority or resistance, these stories illuminate the universal themes of freedom, justice, and resilience. Whether in dystopias, corporate-controlled societies, AI-driven worlds, or grassroots communities, sci-fi invites readers to reflect on their own social values and the potential futures we are creating. Through these narratives, we see that power shapes not only societies but also the individuals within them, posing timeless questions about humanity's relationship with authority, independence, and the enduring desire for self-determination.

Brainstorming Sci-Fi Concepts with ChatGPT: From Ideas to Themes

Using ChatGPT as a brainstorming tool for sci-fi concepts opens up endless possibilities, helping writers and creators move from initial ideas to fully developed themes. The process is dynamic: you start with a basic concept, and ChatGPT can expand it into a richly layered narrative, explore themes, suggest world-building details, or even address technical aspects of the story. By guiding and interacting with ChatGPT, you can generate fresh, unexpected ideas, overcome creative blocks, and bring your sci-fi ideas to life in ways that are collaborative and thought-provoking.

One effective way to begin is by sharing a rough concept or a "seed" idea with ChatGPT, like "a future where humans coexist with AI that has equal rights" or "a world where climate disasters have forced society to live in the oceans." ChatGPT can take this seed and suggest various directions it could grow, from focusing on character-driven stories, exploring the societal impact, or honing in on the science behind these scenarios. For example, if you choose the AI theme, ChatGPT might prompt you to think about how equality with AI affects jobs, governance, personal relationships, and daily life, generating numerous subplots or ethical conflicts that flesh out the idea.

Another useful feature is to prompt ChatGPT to help with "what if" scenarios, a staple of sci-fi brainstorming. For example, you might ask, "What if people could upload their consciousness into virtual worlds?" or "What if time travel became a commercial industry?" ChatGPT can take these hypotheticals and explore their impact on society, technology, and human relationships. It could generate conflicts, propose world-building details, or outline how characters might react in such a world. This type of brainstorming encourages you to dive deeper into the implications of your core idea, resulting in a more comprehensive sci-fi universe.

Themes are the emotional and intellectual backbone of a sci-fi story, and ChatGPT can help refine these. Say you want to explore themes of identity, autonomy, or the ethics of technology. By discussing these themes with ChatGPT, you can gain insights into how they might intersect with your story's plot, setting, or characters. For example, if your story explores autonomy, ChatGPT might suggest building a world where people have lost control over their own data, leading to a society where privacy and identity are endangered. By aligning themes with the plot and world-building, you create a cohesive narrative that feels both relevant and thought-provoking.

ChatGPT can also assist with building characters who embody or struggle with the story's themes. If your sci-fi concept deals with genetic modification, you might ask ChatGPT to brainstorm character types, like a scientist driven by moral convictions or a modified person who regrets their alterations. It can provide backstories, motivations, and potential character arcs that add emotional depth and complexity to the narrative. By collaborating on character creation, you can ensure that each individual's journey resonates with the larger themes, giving readers relatable, compelling protagonists who make the speculative world feel authentic.

Another powerful aspect of brainstorming with ChatGPT is exploring the science or "rules" behind your world. Sci-fi often hinges on how technology, physics, or biology works in a future or alternate setting, and ChatGPT can help you define these aspects in a way that's both imaginative and logical. For instance, if your story involves faster-than-light travel, ChatGPT can help brainstorm plausible explanations for how it works, how it impacts society, or the risks involved. It may even suggest scientific limitations that add realism and tension to your story. These "rules" create boundaries within the story, ensuring that the speculative elements feel grounded and consistent, which is essential for sci-fi.

World-building is another area where ChatGPT excels as a brainstorming partner. You can collaborate on details like the setting's geography, political structure, and cultural norms. If your story takes place on a distant planet, ChatGPT can suggest its environmental conditions, native species, and ecosystem dynamics. For example, you might want a planet with extreme weather conditions that affect daily life or a culture shaped by scarcity and survival. ChatGPT can help you consider how these elements influence the society's laws, traditions, and conflicts, creating a well-rounded world that adds depth and context to your story.

The platform is also useful for identifying and addressing potential plot holes or inconsistencies. You can outline the basic plot for ChatGPT and ask it to critique or question the logic of certain elements. For instance, if your story involves time travel, ChatGPT can help explore how paradoxes are avoided, how time travel technology might be regulated, or the ethical dilemmas characters might face. By examining these elements early on, you can refine the story's logic, making it more cohesive and satisfying for readers who value well-thought-out sci-fi plots.

ChatGPT is also adept at genre blending, which can give your sci-fi concept a unique twist. If you're interested in creating a sci-fi story with horror or romance elements, ChatGPT can help you integrate these genres seamlessly. You might prompt it with, "How can I add horror to a story about AI?" and it could suggest scenarios where AI unpredictably evolves, creating suspense and fear. Or, if romance is central, ChatGPT could help brainstorm how relationships unfold in a future where emotions are regulated or love is mediated by virtual reality. Genre blending adds layers to the story, making it distinct within the sci-fi genre and appealing to a broader audience.

For writers seeking to engage readers with social or philosophical questions, ChatGPT can act as a sounding board to explore complex ideas within a sci-fi framework. You might be interested in themes of inequality, bioethics, or the nature of consciousness, and ChatGPT can suggest scenarios or dialogues that naturally bring these issues to the forefront. For instance, if exploring bioethics, ChatGPT might propose a plot involving "designer babies" and the social divisions they create, sparking conversations about privilege, identity, and humanity. These explorations add intellectual depth to your story, allowing you to pose questions that linger with readers long after they've finished.

Finally, ChatGPT can be an invaluable tool for naming elements within your sci-fi world—whether it's technology, species, planets, or organizations. You can provide it with a description or backstory and ask for suggestions that suit the tone and genre. For example, if you need a name for a futuristic corporation, you might describe its purpose and values, and ChatGPT can propose names that reflect its brand or mission. Names are critical in sci-fi for building authenticity, and the right terminology can enhance the immersion and believability of your world.

Ultimately, brainstorming sci-fi concepts with ChatGPT opens up new avenues of creativity, allowing you to build complex, engaging worlds with rich characters, themes, and settings. By leveraging ChatGPT's ability to expand on ideas, propose logical frameworks, and explore themes deeply, you can transform an initial concept into a fully realized narrative. The process not only stimulates creativity but also provides an interactive, collaborative experience, where ideas grow and evolve dynamically. For sci-fi creators, ChatGPT becomes a versatile partner in the storytelling journey, turning sparks of inspiration into compelling narratives that are ready to captivate readers.

Building Worlds Together: Using ChatGPT for Setting and Environment Creation

Creating immersive, detailed worlds is essential in sci-fi, where settings and environments often become as vital as the characters themselves. ChatGPT can be a valuable partner in this creative process, helping writers explore every corner of a new world, from its physical landscapes to its unique cultures, technology, and social dynamics. By collaborating with ChatGPT, you can turn an idea into a richly detailed environment, with all the nuances and textures that make a setting feel authentic, vibrant, and integral to the story.

One of the first steps in world-building is defining the physical characteristics of your setting, which can range from alien planets to futuristic Earths or even space stations. By describing an initial idea to ChatGPT, such as a planet with low gravity or a space colony on an asteroid, you can generate specific features like landscapes, atmospheric conditions, or resource availability. For instance, a low-gravity world could have sprawling, open-air structures with sweeping towers, floating transportation systems, or inhabitants with elongated limbs adapted to the environment. ChatGPT can suggest additional details, like native flora and fauna, weather patterns, and even natural phenomena unique to the world, helping you craft an environment that feels scientifically plausible and visually compelling.

Geography and climate shape how societies evolve, influencing architecture, culture, and daily life. If you're designing a desert planet, ChatGPT can help brainstorm practical adaptations for survival, such as underground cities for temperature control, water-harvesting technology, or nomadic tribes skilled in traversing vast arid landscapes. These environmental details allow you to explore how people's lives are shaped by their surroundings, adding depth to the setting. ChatGPT can also help you think about unusual or extreme environments, like a planet that orbits two suns, creating perpetual daylight, or one with oceans of liquid methane. By crafting environments with unique challenges and wonders, your world gains a sense of realism, setting up conflicts and customs that are directly tied to its physical characteristics.

Beyond physical landscapes, ChatGPT can assist in creating diverse, vibrant cultures that reflect their environmental and historical contexts. For example, if your world is a massive, multi-level space station, ChatGPT might suggest that each level has its own culture, customs, and social hierarchy based on access to sunlight or proximity to the station's power core. Characters from these different levels may dress differently, speak with regional dialects, or celebrate unique traditions, giving readers a sense of the world's complexity. By layering in cultural elements, you make the setting feel alive, as if it has evolved naturally over time in response to its conditions.

Economics and resource distribution are another important element of world-building, affecting everything from social class structures to daily life. For instance, a mineral-rich planet controlled by a corporate entity might have mining towns with a gritty, utilitarian style, where laborers work long shifts under hazardous conditions, creating an undercurrent of tension and unrest. ChatGPT can suggest additional details, such as black markets for off-world goods, ration systems for scarce resources, or even futuristic currency forms that add realism to the society's economy. By establishing the economic dynamics of your setting, you add stakes and motivations that can drive conflict and deepen character arcs, showing how survival and power play out in a new world.

If your setting involves futuristic or alien technology, ChatGPT can help you brainstorm everything from everyday tools to advanced systems that transform how people interact with their environment. In a society where AI handles most of the labor, for instance, ChatGPT could suggest how people spend their time, such as engaging in creative pursuits, socializing in virtual environments, or training for specialized roles that require human intuition.

Technology can also define the architecture of a world—space habitats designed with artificial gravity, domed cities on toxic planets, or floating transport systems in low-gravity zones. By integrating technology into the world-building, ChatGPT helps you craft an environment that feels futuristic and immersive, allowing readers to visualize how life functions in such a setting.

Political and social structures play a major role in shaping a sci-fi world's identity, often creating the framework for tension, cooperation, and conflict. In a society that spans multiple planets, ChatGPT can help you develop a governing body, like a council of planetary representatives or a corporate board that oversees key resources. ChatGPT might also suggest how power dynamics evolve—perhaps colonies farthest from the governing planet are more rebellious, or certain groups advocate for independence. Social hierarchies, from meritocracies to genetic class systems, can influence everything from career paths to legal rights. By constructing a society's political and social structures, you create the rules and tensions that will drive your characters' interactions, goals, and conflicts within the world.

Religions, philosophies, and belief systems are essential for adding depth to a society, as they influence values, customs, and personal motivations. ChatGPT can help brainstorm unique beliefs that stem from the world's specific history and environment. For example, in a society on a storm-ravaged planet, people might worship deities of weather and nature, developing rituals to "appease" the elements. Or, a culture deeply embedded in AI and genetic modification might view technological advancement as a spiritual journey, with rituals around memory preservation or body modification. By creating belief systems that are connected to the world's unique features, ChatGPT helps bring authenticity to the setting, allowing characters to engage with their society's values in ways that feel organic.

Language and dialects can also enrich your setting, as they reflect a society's history, values, and geographical divides. ChatGPT can assist in creating regional dialects, slang, or even entirely new languages, each with vocabulary reflecting cultural priorities. For instance, a mining colony may have slang terms for various minerals or machinery, while a tech-centric society might use shorthand for complex concepts. Additionally, phrases or idioms tied to specific experiences in that world—such as "storms ahead" in a climate-focused culture—make dialogue more authentic and culturally rooted. By creating these linguistic details, ChatGPT allows you to give each region, class, or group within your world a unique voice, adding another layer of immersion for readers.

Natural history and lore bring richness to your world by providing a sense of past events, mythologies, or ancestral heroes that continue to influence current society. ChatGPT can help you brainstorm key events, like past wars, environmental shifts, or technological revolutions that have left their mark on the world. Characters might reference a "Great Exodus" to space colonies or honor heroes who helped terraform their planet. Ancient ruins or relics with symbolic meaning, perhaps even artifacts left by alien civilizations, provide characters with a sense of place and history. By embedding your setting with lore, you allow readers to feel that this world has depth and memory, extending far beyond the story's timeline.

Finally, ChatGPT can help you refine and organize these world-building details into a cohesive whole. You can ask it to generate a summary or outline of the setting, weaving together physical characteristics, cultural elements, technology, and power structures into a unified vision. By establishing a clear framework, you'll have a reference to ensure consistency as you write, allowing you to keep details accurate and logical while adding new elements as your story unfolds. ChatGPT can even help identify potential conflicts or plot points that naturally arise from the world you've built, showing how setting and narrative can work together seamlessly.

In sum, building worlds with ChatGPT allows for a collaborative, iterative approach to setting creation. Whether crafting alien planets, advanced cities, or distant colonies, you can explore every facet of the environment, from geography to language, making the world feel real, inhabited, and ready for any story you want to tell. This partnership enhances the creative process, bringing imagination to life through nuanced, interconnected details that add authenticity and depth to your sci-fi universe. By combining your ideas with ChatGPT's suggestions, you create a setting that isn't just a backdrop but an integral part of the narrative, one that will captivate readers and immerse them fully in the world you've crafted together.

Developing Sci-Fi Heroes and Villains with ChatGPT"

Crafting compelling sci-fi heroes and villains is essential for drawing readers into a story, as they connect with characters who are both relatable and unique to the speculative setting. ChatGPT can be an invaluable collaborator in this process, helping you develop multi-dimensional protagonists and antagonists who resonate with readers and add depth to your sci-fi world. From defining backstories and motivations to exploring psychological complexities, ChatGPT assists you in shaping characters who embody the story's themes and drive the narrative forward.

A useful starting point for character creation is defining the character's role and core attributes. You might describe a character concept to ChatGPT, such as "a rebel scientist in a dystopian world where personal data is currency," or "an AI who has gained consciousness and questions its place in society." ChatGPT can help expand this initial concept by suggesting personality traits, strengths, weaknesses, and possible motivations. For example, the rebel scientist might be driven by a moral conviction to expose corporate corruption, while the AI could be torn between loyalty to its creators and a newfound sense of autonomy. By brainstorming these core attributes, ChatGPT allows you to create characters with clear motivations and conflicts that align with the sci-fi setting.

Backstory is crucial in shaping a character's personality and motivations. ChatGPT can help you flesh out the details of a hero or villain's past, exploring events that shaped their beliefs, fears, and ambitions. You might ask ChatGPT to generate a backstory for a hero who was exiled from a space colony, leading them to distrust authority and fight for independence. Alternatively, you could develop a villain's history of growing up in a high-tech society, where ambition and power were valued above all else. These backstories provide context for why characters make certain choices and allow readers to understand their complex motivations, even if they only appear in brief glimpses throughout the story.

When it comes to heroes, ChatGPT can help you explore their positive attributes, unique skills, and personal challenges, creating characters who are admirable yet relatable. For example, a protagonist in a sci-fi adventure might be a fearless explorer, but perhaps they struggle with homesickness or guilt over leaving loved ones behind. ChatGPT can suggest character traits that make the hero relatable, like a sense of humor that lightens tense moments or a quiet determination that surfaces in the face of danger. By creating a balance between strength and vulnerability, ChatGPT helps you craft heroes who are not just aspirational but human, allowing readers to root for them on their journey.

Villains are often the most memorable characters in a story, and ChatGPT can help you create complex antagonists who go beyond simple evil motives. By discussing the villain's motivations, you can create a character who believes in their mission, even if it is morally questionable. For instance, you might develop a villain who sees genetic modification as the key to human advancement, willing to sacrifice individual rights for the "greater good." ChatGPT can suggest layers of nuance, such as insecurities, personal traumas, or ideological convictions that make the villain's motives understandable, if not justifiable. By creating a relatable villain with multifaceted goals, you add moral complexity to the story, showing that antagonists, too, are shaped by their experiences and beliefs.

Heroes and villains become more engaging when their goals intersect or clash, creating a dynamic relationship between them. ChatGPT can help you brainstorm scenarios where the hero and villain's values are directly opposed or reveal surprising similarities. For example, both characters might want to liberate their society from a corrupt government, but while the hero values freedom for all, the villain envisions a new order where only the strongest survive. This contrast in values creates tension and allows for philosophical debates, making the conflict more personal and layered. By building on these intersecting goals, ChatGPT helps you create a relationship between hero and villain that is charged with ideological and emotional stakes.

Character arcs are another crucial element in crafting memorable sci-fi heroes and villains. For a hero, ChatGPT can suggest a growth arc that challenges them to overcome internal struggles or confront aspects of their past. For example, a hero who begins the story as a solitary figure might learn the value of community and collaboration by the end. Villains, too, can experience arcs—whether it's a descent into greater moral ambiguity or, conversely, moments of self-doubt that add depth to their role. ChatGPT can provide ideas for these arcs, helping you map out the transformative moments that will shape each character's journey. By creating arcs that reflect the story's themes, you ensure that each character's development is meaningful and resonant.

Sci-fi settings often introduce unique abilities, technology, or powers, and ChatGPT can assist in integrating these elements into your characters' identities. For example, a hero with a cybernetic enhancement might struggle with the limitations and ethical implications of their augmented body, while a villain who wields AI control might face the temptation to erase memories to achieve their goals. ChatGPT can help brainstorm how these sci-fi elements impact daily life, decision-making, and the character's internal conflicts, allowing you to ground extraordinary powers in relatable emotions and struggles. This attention to character integration makes the speculative elements feel purposeful and character-driven, rather than merely plot devices.

Relationships with other characters are essential for revealing a hero or villain's true personality. ChatGPT can help brainstorm friendships, family connections, and rivalries that add emotional layers to the protagonist and antagonist. A hero might have a mentor who challenges them to think beyond their immediate goals or a close friend whose safety motivates them in difficult moments. Similarly, a villain might have a trusted advisor, a long-lost sibling, or even a secret lover, all of whom add dimensions to their character. By establishing these relationships, you create a support system or conflict network that enhances each character's decisions, sacrifices, and personal stakes, adding depth to the narrative and emotional resonance for readers.

Thematic alignment between the character's goals and the story's larger questions is another area where ChatGPT can provide insights. If your story explores the ethics of genetic modification, the hero might have a personal connection to this theme, like a loved one affected by genetic experimentation, driving them to oppose the villain's ambitions. By aligning characters with the story's themes, you give their actions greater purpose, allowing the narrative to explore complex issues through personal journeys. ChatGPT can suggest ways to embed these themes in character motivations, ensuring that each character is a meaningful part of the story's exploration of the theme.

Lastly, ChatGPT can help you refine each character's voice, a key factor in making heroes and villains feel distinct. You can experiment with dialogue, tone, and word choices to capture each character's personality and perspective. For instance, a hero who is an experienced pilot might speak in short, decisive sentences, reflecting their no-nonsense attitude, while a villain with a deep philosophical background might use grandiose language or metaphors. By testing different dialogue styles with ChatGPT, you can find each character's unique voice, making them memorable and consistent throughout the story.

In the end, developing heroes and villains with ChatGPT enables you to create fully-realized characters who are integral to the sci-fi setting and narrative. With its ability to brainstorm, refine, and expand on ideas, ChatGPT acts as a creative partner, helping you craft characters with depth, emotional resonance, and relevance to the story's themes. Whether you're building a reluctant hero, a principled villain, or something in between, ChatGPT's suggestions allow you to explore their personalities, conflicts, and arcs in a way that feels rich and dynamic. By collaborating on character development, you bring your sci-fi world to life through individuals whose struggles, beliefs, and ambitions resonate with readers, making them invested in the outcome of the story.

Tech Talk: Generating Futuristic Technology and Scientific Concepts"

Sci-fi stories thrive on imaginative technology and scientific concepts that expand the possibilities of the future, providing readers with a sense of wonder and intellectual intrigue. ChatGPT can be an invaluable collaborator in generating futuristic technology and scientific ideas, whether it's devising ground-breaking inventions, exploring alien ecosystems, or constructing the physics of interstellar travel. By combining your initial concepts with ChatGPT's suggestions, you can develop complex, plausible, and innovative technology that feels grounded in science yet pushes the boundaries of imagination.

A great starting point is to describe the purpose or function of the technology you want to include. If you're envisioning a society with advanced medical technology, for example, you might ask ChatGPT to suggest futuristic diagnostic tools, regenerative therapies, or mind-body interfaces. ChatGPT can help brainstorm details, such as a wearable device that continuously monitors and corrects cellular mutations, or nanobots capable of healing wounds at the molecular level. By providing practical applications and intricate functions, ChatGPT can help you craft technology that is not only fascinating but also believable within your story's context.

One of the central challenges in sci-fi world-building is creating technology that feels scientifically plausible. ChatGPT can help you explore the science behind your ideas, offering explanations that add depth and credibility. For instance, if your story includes faster-than-light travel, ChatGPT can suggest theoretical approaches like warp drives, wormholes, or quantum tunneling, complete with basic descriptions of how they might work. By outlining the underlying principles, ChatGPT allows you to anchor your speculative technology in real-world physics, creating a sense of realism that immerses readers in the story.

New energy sources and propulsion systems are common in futuristic sci-fi settings, powering everything from spacecraft to cities. You might start with a concept, such as "an inexhaustible power source," and ChatGPT can expand on it with ideas like zero-point energy, fusion reactors, or antimatter drives. Each energy source can come with its own advantages, limitations, and risks, such as the potential for catastrophic explosions in antimatter engines or environmental challenges with fusion reactors. These details add a layer of complexity and risk, giving characters additional stakes in how they interact with and rely on their technology.

Augmented reality (AR) and virtual reality (VR) have vast potential in sci-fi worlds, transforming how characters perceive and interact with their surroundings. ChatGPT can help brainstorm how AR or VR might impact daily life, work, and even relationships in the future. You might develop "sensory immersion" technology that simulates all five senses, creating experiences indistinguishable from reality, or contact lenses that overlay digital information on the physical world. This type of technology can impact characters in numerous ways, from addiction to virtual environments to ethical debates over simulated relationships or memories. By exploring the societal and personal effects of AR and VR, ChatGPT helps you create immersive tech that challenges and shapes the story's world.

AI and robotics are central themes in sci-fi, and ChatGPT can assist in developing advanced AI systems with distinct personalities, limitations, and roles in society. You might describe an AI with specialized functions, like a medical AI that assists with surgeries or a military AI designed for strategy. ChatGPT can suggest how this AI interacts with humans, perhaps showing empathy, misunderstanding human emotions, or struggling with ethical dilemmas. Robotics can be customized with varying levels of autonomy, intelligence, or even organic integration, opening up questions of human-AI coexistence. By exploring the complexity of AI-human interactions, ChatGPT allows you to create machines that challenge the characters' notions of intelligence, companionship, and morality.

Weaponry and defense technologies in futuristic settings often reflect the values and conflicts within the story's society. ChatGPT can help brainstorm unique weapons, such as plasma rifles with energy constraints, nanotech-based armor that adapts to threats, or force fields that absorb kinetic energy but are vulnerable to sonic disruption. These technologies can influence battle tactics, shape character decisions, and even create ethical dilemmas about destructive power. By providing distinctive features and limitations for each piece of weaponry, ChatGPT helps ensure that futuristic combat remains exciting, strategic, and thought-provoking.

Biotechnology and genetic engineering introduce exciting opportunities for world-building, from enhanced humans to bioengineered ecosystems. ChatGPT can help you design biotech concepts like genetic modifications for adaptability to harsh environments, biomimetic prosthetics that mimic animal traits, or engineered crops that thrive in toxic soil. These advancements can transform societies, giving rise to new classes, ethical divides, or social dynamics between modified and unmodified people. By using ChatGPT to explore biotech's practical and social implications, you add layers to your setting, showing how technology influences daily life, values, and identity.

Interstellar travel and alien life often require inventive technology that feels both advanced and intuitive. ChatGPT can brainstorm ship designs with features like gravity-manipulation fields, suspended animation for long journeys, or even holographic navigation systems that allow pilots to "see" space in three dimensions. For alien ecosystems, ChatGPT can help you create life forms adapted to extreme conditions, such as acidic oceans or low-light environments, and suggest how these species might interact with human visitors. By crafting technology and biology that feel uniquely suited to space exploration, ChatGPT helps your story explore the vastness of space in a way that feels rich, logical, and thrilling.

Communication technologies are essential in sci-fi, particularly for stories set across vast distances or involving different species. ChatGPT can help you brainstorm technologies like quantum communication devices that transmit data instantaneously, neural link systems that enable telepathic-like connections, or translation devices for alien languages. Each method can come with its own strengths, limits, or costs, such as energy-intensive systems or cultural challenges in interpreting meaning. By developing advanced communication tech, ChatGPT enables you to create diverse interactions, bridging or complicating connections between characters across space and language barriers.

Climate and environmental technologies reflect humanity's adaptation to or impact on ecosystems. If your story includes a climate-ravaged Earth or a terraformed planet, ChatGPT can suggest technologies like weather-control satellites, bio-domes for controlled ecosystems, or portable desalination units for water-scarce regions. These technologies can create unique settings, influence economies, or spark ideological divides about sustainability. By embedding climate tech into your story, ChatGPT helps you explore themes of environmental responsibility, adaptation, and the consequences of altering natural systems.

Medical advancements, such as gene therapy, artificial organs, or memory-altering procedures, offer a deep well of narrative possibilities. Characters might access memory implants to relive past experiences, face dilemmas about enhancing their physical abilities, or debate the ethics of erasing trauma. ChatGPT can suggest how these technologies affect personal identity, social status, and even concepts of humanity, raising philosophical questions about what it means to be "whole" or "natural." Medical technology adds an emotional dimension to sci-fi, allowing characters to confront deeply personal decisions that resonate with readers on a human level.

Finally, ChatGPT can help ensure technological consistency by suggesting logical limitations, risks, or failures associated with each invention. For example, your zero-gravity device might drain immense power, only functioning in short bursts, or the gene-editing tech could have unpredictable side effects over generations. These limitations add realism, creating opportunities for plot twists or crises that challenge the characters. By testing the boundaries of each invention, ChatGPT helps you develop a world where technology feels both advanced and grounded, adding layers of tension, mystery, and discovery to the story.

In conclusion, working with ChatGPT to brainstorm futuristic technology and scientific concepts enhances the creativity and authenticity of your sci-fi world. From practical applications to ethical implications, each invention or scientific breakthrough brings your story to life, creating a setting that feels both visionary and believable. By collaborating with ChatGPT on these ideas, you create technology that doesn't just serve the plot but enriches the narrative, providing characters with tools, challenges, and dilemmas that drive the story forward. The result is a sci-fi world that captures readers' imaginations, immersing them in a future where technology reflects humanity's best, worst, and most complex qualities.

Exploring the Unknown: Using ChatGPT for Alien Races and Species

Creating alien races and species is one of the most exciting aspects of sci-fi world-building, allowing writers to introduce fresh perspectives, social dynamics, and unique biologies that stretch the boundaries of imagination. ChatGPT can be a powerful partner in designing alien beings that feel as real and complex as any human culture. From physiology and communication to culture and societal structure, ChatGPT can help generate ideas that make your aliens intriguing, believable, and fully integrated into your story's world.

When designing alien species, one of the first considerations is their physical appearance and biology. You might start with a simple idea, like "a species that lives in water" or "aliens adapted to life on a high-gravity planet," and ChatGPT can help you expand on it with detailed features. For instance, aquatic aliens could have bioluminescent skin to communicate in dark waters, webbed limbs, and the ability to filter oxygen directly from the water. A high-gravity species might be short and muscular, with reinforced skeletal structures to withstand the intense gravitational pull. By building out these traits with ChatGPT, you can ensure that each physical characteristic aligns with the alien's environmental demands, creating a species that feels naturally evolved and scientifically plausible.

Alien physiology can be taken further by exploring unique senses or abilities that differentiate them from humans. ChatGPT can help brainstorm ideas like echolocation, electromagnetic sensitivity, or the ability to detect chemical changes in their environment. Such abilities would affect how these aliens perceive their world, potentially influencing language, social dynamics, and even philosophy. For example, a species with heightened electromagnetic sensitivity might "see" electrical currents or communicate by generating controlled signals, which would set their technology, communication methods, and even art apart from human norms. These sensory abilities open up fascinating world-building opportunities, letting you explore how aliens navigate their surroundings and how humans might struggle to understand them.

Communication and language are central to any alien culture, and ChatGPT can assist in designing methods that are distinct from human speech. You might start with a concept, like "a language based on scent" or "communication through bioluminescent displays," and ChatGPT can help explore how these languages work, what limitations they have, and how they might influence social interactions. An alien species that uses scent markers, for example, might create permanent "messages" that linger for days, while a bioluminescent species could convey subtle changes in emotion through patterns of light. These unique forms of communication not only make the aliens more distinct but also create barriers and bridges in human-alien relations, posing challenges for characters attempting cross-species dialogue.

Culture and social structure provide the foundation for how an alien species organizes its society, and ChatGPT can help you explore possibilities beyond familiar human systems. You might ask for ideas on how an alien race could be structured if it values collective survival over individuality, or if its members communicate through a hive mind. ChatGPT could suggest social arrangements like communal resource-sharing, where property is nonexistent, or a merit-based hierarchy where positions are earned through accomplishments in fields like exploration or knowledge. By experimenting with these different societal structures, ChatGPT allows you to imagine civilizations that offer thought-provoking contrasts to human norms, giving readers a fresh perspective on values, ethics, and social organization.

Religious beliefs, philosophies, and rituals also add depth to alien species, reflecting how they make sense of their world and place within it. If an alien species has a deep reverence for the stars, for instance, ChatGPT might help brainstorm a belief system where celestial bodies are seen as divine ancestors, influencing everything from storytelling to navigation. Alternatively, a species with a short lifespan might develop philosophies centered on transience and immediacy, while one with nearly immortal individuals could prioritize wisdom and legacy. By grounding these belief systems in the species' unique experiences, you add layers of culture that enrich the world and make interactions with other characters more meaningful and complex.

Technology and material culture can also set alien races apart, showcasing how they solve problems and meet needs in ways that may be unfamiliar to humans. ChatGPT can help brainstorm technology that is unique to the alien species, perhaps drawing from organic materials, sound waves, or bioengineered tools. For example, an underwater species might use compressed air chambers for energy or build shelters from living coral that grows and repairs itself. If the aliens inhabit a harsh desert planet, they might have developed technology for water conservation or weather manipulation. These technological details reveal how aliens interact with their environment and can inspire plot points or conflicts, especially if human and alien tech come into competition or collaboration.

An alien species' diet, habitat, and physical needs shape not only its daily routines but also its interactions with other species. ChatGPT can help design details like the alien species' unique dietary requirements, preferred climate, or living arrangements. For instance, a species that derives energy from sunlight might be active only during certain times of day, impacting work schedules and social gatherings. A species that requires highly specific minerals might have territorial conflicts with other species over resource-rich areas. By incorporating these environmental needs, you make the aliens' lives more textured and believable, allowing for richer interspecies dynamics that add depth to your world.

Reproduction and family structure are often distinct in alien species, offering alternative views on relationships and social units. ChatGPT can help explore concepts like communal raising of offspring, asexual reproduction, or complex mating rituals. For example, a species with communal parenting might have no concept of a nuclear family, viewing all members of their group as kin, while another species that reproduces through symbiotic relationships with other organisms might see relationships as both romantic and biological partnerships. These reproductive methods influence how aliens relate to each other and other species, shaping family bonds, inheritance, and social expectations in ways that are thought-provoking and culturally rich.

Emotional expression and psychology provide a unique perspective on how aliens experience the world and interact with others. ChatGPT can suggest different ways aliens might express emotions, like color-changing skin, melodic vocalizations, or subtle chemical signals. For instance, a species that rarely shows outward emotion might value subtlety and restraint, while a species with intense, rapid mood shifts might have developed social protocols to prevent misunderstandings or conflicts. By giving aliens distinct emotional ranges and ways of expressing them, you add depth to their interactions with humans, setting up challenges in understanding or misinterpreting each other's feelings.

Social conflicts and power dynamics can be particularly engaging when they arise from the unique attributes of an alien society. ChatGPT can help brainstorm potential sources of internal conflict, like disputes over resources, philosophical divides on tradition versus progress, or tensions between subspecies with differing abilities. For example, if a species is divided into two subgroups based on physical adaptations, there might be cultural prejudice or segregation within their society. Alternatively, an alien race that values technological progress might have conflicts with traditionalists who wish to preserve their natural environment. By exploring these tensions, you add complexity to alien societies, making them feel as layered and conflict-ridden as any human culture.

Relationships between alien species and humans offer rich material for exploring misunderstandings, alliances, and cultural exchange. ChatGPT can help you brainstorm scenarios where cultural differences create tension or opportunities for growth. Perhaps an alien race views humanity's practice of wearing clothes as strange, seeing it as a sign of shame or weakness, or a species with a communal mindset might struggle to understand human individualism. These differences create opportunities for character growth, as characters learn from or struggle with each other's ways of life, deepening their understanding of what it means to be "alien" and, by extension, what it means to be "human."

Political and diplomatic interactions between alien species and human societies add stakes and scale to the narrative. ChatGPT can suggest diplomatic structures, like trade alliances, scientific coalitions, or mutual defense treaties, which frame interspecies relationships within a broader context. By establishing these diplomatic frameworks, you provide opportunities for plot development, as tensions or friendships may rise due to policy disagreements, cultural insensitivity, or resource disputes. These political structures make interspecies relationships more sophisticated and allow you to address broader themes of coexistence, cooperation, and the challenges of diplomacy across vastly different species.

Ultimately, using ChatGPT to develop alien races and species enables you to create beings that are biologically plausible, culturally distinct, and philosophically rich. By integrating elements like physiology, communication, social structure, and belief systems, you can craft alien species that are not just "other" but fully realized societies with their own histories, values, and worldviews. This collaboration allows you to push the boundaries of imagination while grounding your alien characters in details that make them feel alive, relatable, and part of a living, breathing universe. Through this detailed approach, ChatGPT helps you build a sci-fi world that celebrates diversity and challenges readers to see humanity from new, alien perspectives.

Dialogue Development: Crafting Authentic Sci-Fi Conversations with AI

Crafting authentic sci-fi dialogue is essential for immersing readers in futuristic or alien worlds, as characters' conversations reveal not only personalities and emotions but also the intricacies of the setting, technology, and culture. Working with ChatGPT can elevate this process, allowing you to explore unique dialects, vocabularies, and conversational dynamics that fit within your sci-fi story. From futuristic jargon to interspecies communication, ChatGPT can help you design dialogue that feels both authentic and engaging, bringing the voices of your characters to life in a way that resonates with readers.

A foundational step in crafting sci-fi dialogue is establishing a language style that fits the story's time period, technological advancements, and societal structure. You might start by describing the world or community where your characters live, and ChatGPT can suggest phrases or expressions that match the tone. For instance, in a high-tech society, characters might use terms based on digital language or tech references, like "syncing minds" instead of "understanding each other." In a world with a strong military presence, characters may use structured, precise language, or in a society with limited resources, they might speak with pragmatic brevity. By tailoring the language style to the setting, you create an authentic atmosphere that feels seamlessly connected to the sci-fi world.

Futuristic slang and jargon can add a layer of realism to conversations, giving readers a glimpse into the world's culture and technology. ChatGPT can help brainstorm slang based on the unique technology or lifestyle of your story. For example, in a world where genetic modification is common, people might refer to enhancements as "mods" or describe those without modifications as "pure-gens." A spacefaring society might use slang like "space out" for zoning out or "hyper" for anything incredibly fast. By working with ChatGPT to develop these terms, you add depth to the setting, showing how language evolves alongside society's advances and cultural nuances.

If your story involves alien species, creating distinctive speech patterns for each can enhance the sense of diversity and authenticity. ChatGPT can assist by suggesting ways to represent these differences, such as an alien race that speaks in short, clipped sentences due to high-gravity environments or another that communicates in flowery, elongated phrases influenced by its environment or physiology. Some aliens might have trouble with human syntax or idioms, leading to unique phrasings or misunderstandings. ChatGPT can help you experiment with speech patterns that reflect each species' background, making their dialogue unique and believable while highlighting the challenges of cross-species communication.

Dialogue in sci-fi often includes explanations of unfamiliar technology, science, or phenomena, but balancing clarity with realism is key. ChatGPT can help craft lines that convey complex concepts in a natural, conversational way, avoiding info-dumps or forced exposition. For instance, instead of having a character say, "The gravity stabilizer will prevent us from floating," they might say, "Good thing the grav-stab's working—don't want to end up bouncing off the ceiling again." This approach keeps the conversation natural and true to the characters while still conveying important information. By working with ChatGPT to develop such lines, you ensure that dialogue remains engaging while subtly educating the reader about the sci-fi world.

Interpersonal dynamics in sci-fi settings can differ from familiar relationships due to futuristic norms, cultural changes, or even alien customs. ChatGPT can help you explore how different societal norms shape the way characters communicate, such as more formal or ritualistic language in highly hierarchical societies, or relaxed, minimalist exchanges in a culture that values efficiency. For example, characters in a utopian society might avoid direct confrontation, using carefully indirect language, while characters from a survival-focused colony might be more blunt or utilitarian. By reflecting these societal norms in dialogue, you create believable interactions that deepen the world-building and character relationships.

Tone and diction are essential to making each character's voice distinct and consistent. ChatGPT can help you refine dialogue by suggesting language that reflects a character's personality, occupation, or background. For instance, a scientist might use precise terminology even in casual conversation, while a rogue or scavenger might speak in relaxed, slang-filled language. ChatGPT can provide ideas for characters with different dialects, regional phrases, or speech quirks that make their personalities come to life on the page. By developing distinct voices for each character, you make conversations more engaging, allowing readers to identify characters by their tone and diction alone.

Emotion in dialogue can be particularly powerful in sci-fi, where characters face high-stakes situations or existential dilemmas. ChatGPT can help you craft lines that reveal characters' emotional states subtly, avoiding overly dramatic or on-the-nose expressions. If a character is anxious about a mission, they might express doubt indirectly, saying, "Hope we've got enough fuel for this one," instead of outright saying, "I'm nervous." For more intense moments, ChatGPT can suggest dialogue that captures anger, fear, or excitement through tone, pacing, or even word choice, allowing characters to convey emotion in a way that feels natural to the story. This approach keeps the dialogue authentic and avoids clichés, ensuring that the characters' emotions are conveyed in a layered, realistic way.

The use of non-verbal cues and body language in dialogue is also essential, as it adds depth to interactions and helps convey meaning without relying solely on words. ChatGPT can suggest body language that complements dialogue, like a character crossing their arms when feeling defensive or avoiding eye contact when uncertain. For alien species, ChatGPT can help brainstorm unique non-verbal cues based on physiology, like a species with tentacles that curl when anxious or one that emits color changes to convey mood. These non-verbal elements enhance the dialogue, creating a rich, multidimensional exchange that feels real and engaging.

Dialogue in sci-fi often involves interactions with AI or other non-human intelligences, which can present unique challenges in tone, structure, and pacing. ChatGPT can assist in developing "voices" for these entities, whether it's a hyper-efficient AI with robotic precision or a learning algorithm that speaks in a child-like manner as it develops understanding. An AI might respond to commands with technical language or "glitch" when overloaded with complex questions. ChatGPT can help you explore how these non-human characters interact, ensuring that their dialogue is distinct and believable, adding texture to the narrative while challenging human characters to communicate across vastly different intelligences.

Dialogue-driven world-building can be achieved by having characters casually reference cultural norms, past events, or unique elements of their environment in conversation. ChatGPT can suggest ways to do this organically, such as characters reminiscing about "The Great Blackout" or complaining about "solar storms this season." Small references like these give readers a sense of the world's history and culture without requiring lengthy explanations. By weaving world-building details into dialogue, ChatGPT helps you keep readers engaged and immersed in the story, making the setting feel natural and lived-in.

Humor and irony can be powerful tools in sci-fi dialogue, as they allow characters to express personality and provide relief from tense situations. ChatGPT can help brainstorm humorous exchanges or witty banter that fits the characters' personalities and the tone of the story. For instance, a jaded pilot might quip, "Another day, another asteroid to dodge," or a scientist might sarcastically mutter, "Just another impossible discovery that will totally not blow up in our faces." By incorporating humor that suits the story's tone, ChatGPT can help you create moments of levity that make characters more relatable and memorable.

Ultimately, using ChatGPT for dialogue development in sci-fi allows for a collaborative, creative approach to crafting conversations that feel both futuristic and authentic. From futuristic jargon to unique alien speech patterns, ChatGPT provides suggestions that enrich character interactions, making the world and its inhabitants feel real and engaging. By focusing on tone, emotional nuance, cultural references, and humor, ChatGPT helps you create dialogue that isn't just functional but also vibrant and dynamic. The result is a sci-fi narrative with conversations that draw readers in, capturing the essence of each character and the complexities of the world they inhabit.

Plotting with ChatGPT: Structuring Your Sci-Fi Storyline

Plotting a sci-fi storyline involves more than just a thrilling sequence of events—it requires careful structuring to balance character arcs, thematic depth, and world-building. Collaborating with ChatGPT for plotting can streamline this process, helping you shape a storyline that's cohesive, engaging, and packed with futuristic intrigue. From initial brainstorming to filling in key plot points, ChatGPT can support you at every stage, ensuring that your story flows logically while delivering those high-stakes, thought-provoking moments that define great sci-fi.

A strong starting point in plotting a sci-fi story is defining the premise, or "what if?" question that drives the narrative. You might start with an idea like, "What if humans could transfer their consciousness to an artificial body?" or "What if time travel became commercially accessible?" ChatGPT can help refine this idea by suggesting scenarios, potential conflicts, or themes related to the concept. For instance, in the consciousness transfer story, ChatGPT might suggest exploring the psychological effects on people who switch bodies, or ethical questions surrounding identity and memory. By delving deeper into the premise, you set the stage for a plot that goes beyond the surface and engages with the underlying themes of your sci-fi concept.

Once you have a solid premise, ChatGPT can assist in building a clear plot structure, often starting with the classic three-act structure or five-part narrative arc. For example, you can work with ChatGPT to outline each act, from setting up the world and conflict in Act One to escalating stakes in Act Two, culminating in a climactic showdown in Act Three. ChatGPT can suggest specific events for each act, such as a key discovery in Act One that pushes the protagonist toward a dangerous decision, or a critical failure in Act Two that forces them to rethink their strategy. This approach helps you map out the story's progression, ensuring that each part builds on the last and keeps the reader engaged from start to finish.

The inciting incident is a pivotal moment in sci-fi, often introducing a technology, discovery, or event that disrupts the protagonist's life and sets the story in motion. ChatGPT can help brainstorm compelling inciting incidents, like the protagonist discovering a government cover-up of alien contact or being thrust into a dangerous experiment with untested technology. By crafting an inciting incident that's tied to the core sci-fi premise, ChatGPT ensures that the story starts with a jolt, hooking readers with a sense of urgency and intrigue.

Rising action is where much of the sci-fi world-building and character development occurs, as the protagonist faces obstacles and begins to understand the larger forces at play. ChatGPT can help you brainstorm key events, such as encounters with new technology, clashes with opposing forces, or revelations about the society's hidden past. For instance, if your story involves an AI-driven society, ChatGPT might suggest a moment where the protagonist sees the dark side of AI governance, raising the stakes and introducing ethical dilemmas. By layering in world-building elements during the rising action, ChatGPT helps ensure that each new challenge reveals something about the setting and the protagonist, making the story feel rich and interconnected.

The midpoint of the story often brings a significant twist or revelation that changes the protagonist's understanding of the situation. ChatGPT can help you design a midpoint that's impactful and aligns with your themes, such as revealing that the protagonist's allies have ulterior motives or that the technology they rely on has dangerous side effects. This twist not only raises the stakes but also forces the protagonist to question their assumptions, creating internal conflict and reshaping their goals. By using ChatGPT to brainstorm a powerful midpoint, you ensure that the story's tension escalates, keeping readers invested in how the protagonist will adapt.

The climax is where sci-fi stories often showcase their most exciting action, whether it's a showdown, a final confrontation, or a race against time. ChatGPT can help you craft a climax that's both thrilling and meaningful, tying together the character's journey and the story's themes. For instance, in a story about space colonization, the climax might involve a critical choice between exploiting an alien planet's resources or preserving its ecosystem. By framing the climax around the protagonist's ultimate decision, ChatGPT ensures that the high-stakes action resonates emotionally, giving readers a satisfying payoff.

Resolution is an essential part of sci-fi plotting, allowing you to tie up loose ends and show the consequences of the protagonist's choices. ChatGPT can suggest ways to wrap up the story, such as demonstrating how the world has changed after the climactic events or showing the protagonist's growth. If your story involves technological ethics, for instance, the resolution might explore the societal shifts following a major decision about AI regulation. By working with ChatGPT to craft a meaningful resolution, you provide closure that reinforces the story's themes and leaves readers with a lasting impression.

Character arcs are a vital part of plot structure, as they give readers someone to root for or understand on a personal level. ChatGPT can help you shape your protagonist's arc, suggesting traits or experiences that evolve over the course of the story. For example, a character who begins as an idealistic scientist might become disillusioned after witnessing the consequences of their research. ChatGPT can also help you plot out the villain's arc, ensuring they feel fully realized and motivated by more than just evil intentions. By mapping out these arcs alongside the plot, ChatGPT helps you create characters whose growth parallels the story's progression, making each twist and turn feel emotionally grounded.

Subplots enrich the main storyline, adding layers to the plot and allowing secondary characters to shine. ChatGPT can suggest subplots that complement the primary narrative, like a romance that tests the protagonist's loyalty, a rivalry that complicates their mission, or a moral dilemma that forces them to reevaluate their values. In a sci-fi setting, these subplots can also reveal more about the world, such as a subplot involving a rebellious faction that exposes flaws in the society's structure. By weaving in these secondary storylines, ChatGPT helps you build a narrative that's complex and engaging, giving readers multiple points of interest.

Themes are often central to sci-fi, allowing readers to explore philosophical, social, or ethical questions through speculative scenarios. ChatGPT can help you identify and integrate themes throughout the plot, like the consequences of unchecked technological advancement or the moral dilemmas of genetic engineering. If your story's theme is "identity in the age of digital immortality," ChatGPT might suggest scenes that challenge the protagonist's sense of self, like meeting a past version of themselves or facing a loved one who rejects digital preservation. By aligning plot points with thematic questions, ChatGPT ensures that your sci-fi story has depth and relevance, inviting readers to reflect on broader issues while enjoying the narrative.

World-building integration is another area where ChatGPT shines, as it can help you incorporate setting details directly into the plot. For example, if your story takes place on a planet with extreme weather, ChatGPT can suggest a storm as an obstacle or a scene where characters adapt to the environment with unique technology. By embedding world-building details in plot events, ChatGPT ensures that the setting feels like an active part of the story rather than just a backdrop, enhancing immersion and adding believability.

Finally, pacing is crucial in sci-fi, where action, mystery, and discovery need to be balanced to keep the story engaging. ChatGPT can help you adjust pacing by suggesting where to slow down for character moments or speed up for action sequences. For instance, you might want a brief lull after a high-stakes battle to show the protagonist's recovery and emotional processing, or a rapid series of events leading up to the climax. By managing pacing, ChatGPT helps you maintain a rhythm that keeps readers engaged, allowing them to absorb the world-building while staying eager for what happens next.

In the end, plotting a sci-fi storyline with ChatGPT allows for a structured yet creative approach, balancing futuristic concepts with universal storytelling techniques. By collaborating on each step, from premise and structure to subplots and pacing, ChatGPT helps you create a story that feels cohesive, immersive, and deeply engaging. The result is a sci-fi narrative with rich characters, thoughtful themes, and a plot that keeps readers hooked, making the journey through your imagined future as compelling as it is thought-provoking.

Creative Collaborator: Using ChatGPT to Refine and Enhance Narrative Arcs

Refining and enhancing narrative arcs is crucial for creating a compelling, well-paced story that resonates with readers. Using ChatGPT as a creative collaborator allows you to elevate your narrative arcs by developing well-rounded characters, intensifying conflicts, and deepening themes, all while maintaining a clear and engaging storyline. With ChatGPT's input, you can refine your arcs, layer in subtext, and ensure each character's journey feels satisfying and meaningful from beginning to end.

A primary step in refining a narrative arc is clearly defining each character's goal and motivation. ChatGPT can help you clarify what drives each character—whether it's the hero's quest for truth, the villain's need for power, or a side character's desire for redemption. For instance, if your protagonist is a scientist seeking to prevent a planetary disaster, ChatGPT might suggest that their motivation stems from a personal loss, adding emotional depth to their actions. By anchoring each character's journey to a core motivation, ChatGPT helps you create arcs that feel authentic, emotionally resonant, and aligned with the story's themes.

Character transformation is at the heart of any narrative arc, and ChatGPT can assist in mapping out these evolutions with clarity and impact. For example, you might start with a hero who is naïve or idealistic, and ChatGPT can help you brainstorm ways their experiences will gradually challenge, refine, or shatter their worldview. Perhaps they face betrayals, witness moral compromises, or grapple with ethical dilemmas that alter their perspective. By charting these transformative moments, ChatGPT allows you to build a satisfying character arc that shows growth or change, making the character's journey feel earned and engaging.

The antagonist's arc is just as essential, and ChatGPT can help you avoid one-dimensional portrayals by suggesting complex, evolving motivations for your villain. Instead of having an antagonist who is merely "evil," ChatGPT can propose backstory details, ambitions, or experiences that make their actions understandable, if not sympathetic. Perhaps the antagonist is driven by a traumatic event or a misguided belief that their actions will ultimately benefit society. By adding layers to the villain's arc, ChatGPT enables you to create nuanced conflicts, where the stakes feel real and the choices carry weight, keeping readers invested in both sides of the story.

Internal conflict is a powerful tool for adding complexity to narrative arcs, as it gives characters challenges that go beyond external obstacles. ChatGPT can help you explore inner dilemmas, like a character who struggles with guilt, doubts their worth, or fears the potential consequences of their actions. For example, a protagonist aiming to stop a powerful corporation might feel morally compromised if they have to use questionable tactics themselves. By integrating these internal struggles, ChatGPT helps you add psychological depth to your arcs, showing how characters wrestle with themselves as much as with external forces.

Turning points are key moments in a character's arc, where they make a choice or encounter a revelation that changes the course of the story. ChatGPT can help brainstorm impactful turning points, like a scene where the hero realizes their allies have been lying, or where the villain questions their mission after a personal loss. These moments not only advance the plot but also reveal essential aspects of the character's growth, testing their resolve or shifting their perspective. By working with ChatGPT to develop meaningful turning points, you can ensure that the narrative arc is driven by choices and consequences, keeping readers emotionally engaged.

Subplots can enhance the main narrative arc by adding layers of complexity, tension, or thematic depth. ChatGPT can help you brainstorm subplots that tie into the primary storyline, like a romantic subplot that tests the protagonist's loyalty, or a friendship that serves as a moral anchor. If your story is set in a futuristic society, ChatGPT might suggest a subplot involving a debate over the ethical implications of AI, adding nuance to the central themes. These subplots enrich the narrative arc by creating secondary arcs that mirror or contrast with the main journey, allowing you to explore different facets of your world and characters.

Themes are the underlying messages or questions of a story, and ChatGPT can help you weave these seamlessly into your narrative arc. If your sci-fi story explores themes of identity and humanity, ChatGPT might suggest moments where characters question what it means to be "human" in a world with advanced technology or genetic engineering. By linking plot points and character decisions to the central themes, ChatGPT enables you to create a cohesive, meaningful arc that resonates on both a narrative and philosophical level, encouraging readers to ponder the broader implications of the story.

Pacing is essential in maintaining a smooth flow within a narrative arc, especially in sci-fi, where world-building and action often need careful balance. ChatGPT can help you adjust pacing by identifying slower moments for introspection or dialogue, followed by bursts of action or revelation to keep momentum. For instance, after a high-stakes battle, you might have a reflective scene where the hero reassesses their mission, giving readers a chance to catch their breath. By modulating pacing, ChatGPT ensures that your narrative arc maintains tension while allowing space for character development, making the story both thrilling and emotionally satisfying.

Symbolism and recurring motifs can add depth to a narrative arc by highlighting themes or character journeys. ChatGPT can help you identify symbols that resonate with your story's themes, like a broken watch symbolizing lost time, or a recurring image of mirrors reflecting questions of identity. These symbols can appear at key points in the arc, providing subtle commentary on the characters' internal states or the story's larger messages. By weaving in symbolic elements, ChatGPT helps you create a narrative arc with rich layers of meaning, inviting readers to engage with the story on multiple levels.

Resolution is where the narrative arc comes full circle, showing the outcome of the characters' journeys and the impact of their choices. ChatGPT can assist in crafting resolutions that provide closure while leaving room for lingering questions or future possibilities. For instance, a character who has grappled with moral compromises might find peace in their final decision, even if it means sacrificing something important. Alternatively, ChatGPT can help suggest an ambiguous ending that reflects the story's themes, leaving readers with something to ponder. By crafting a resolution that feels true to the characters and the journey, ChatGPT allows you to leave a lasting impact on readers.

Character relationships often evolve over the course of the narrative arc, creating bonds, rivalries, and alliances that add texture to the story. ChatGPT can help you map out these relational arcs, like a protagonist who starts off distrusting a mentor but grows to respect them, or a rivalry that turns into mutual respect after a shared crisis. These evolving relationships add emotional stakes to the arc, as readers become invested in the interactions between characters as well as their individual journeys. By focusing on relational dynamics, ChatGPT helps you create a web of connections that make the story feel more cohesive and grounded.

Foreshadowing can enhance narrative arcs by hinting at future events or character transformations, creating anticipation and cohesion. ChatGPT can help you brainstorm subtle ways to foreshadow key plot points or character decisions, like a throwaway line that later becomes significant, or a minor event that foreshadows a major conflict. For instance, an early scene where a character hesitates in a moment of crisis might hint at a later, life-changing choice they'll have to make. By planting seeds of future events, ChatGPT helps you build a narrative arc that feels tightly woven, with a payoff that rewards attentive readers.

Finally, ChatGPT can help refine narrative arcs by identifying potential inconsistencies or areas for improvement. You might outline the arc of a protagonist who starts off as a lone hero but eventually learns the value of community, and ChatGPT can suggest scenes or character interactions that emphasize this theme. It might also help you spot gaps, like a rushed character transformation or a missing emotional beat, allowing you to adjust the arc for greater impact. This attention to detail ensures that each arc feels complete, intentional, and satisfying, leaving readers with a sense of closure.

Using ChatGPT as a collaborator in refining narrative arcs allows you to build a storyline that is layered, dynamic, and engaging. By mapping out motivations, character growth, and thematic connections, ChatGPT helps you create arcs that feel purposeful and resonate emotionally. Whether you're deepening a hero's journey, crafting a compelling villain, or exploring complex relationships, ChatGPT provides the creative insights needed to turn an initial concept into a well-rounded, memorable narrative. The result is a story with arcs that keep readers invested, capturing their imagination and emotions in a way that's both entertaining and thought-provoking.

A Selection of Prompts for ChatGPT

Here's a versatile selection of prompts you can use with ChatGPT to develop *plot*, *character*, and *setting* ideas for your sci-fi story. These prompts are crafted to help you dive deep into each element, encouraging a balanced approach to storytelling and world-building.

Plot Development Prompts

1. **"What if ?" Scenarios:**
   "What are some 'what if?' questions that would make for a compelling sci-fi story? For example, 'What if time travel became commercially accessible?' or 'What if a virus could transfer memories across hosts?' Generate five unique 'what if?' scenarios that could serve as the basis for a sci-fi plot."

2. **Central Conflict:**
   "Suggest five potential central conflicts for a sci-fi story set in a society where humans and AIs have equal rights. How might these conflicts create moral dilemmas, power struggles, or emotional stakes for the characters?"

3. **High-Stakes Storyline:**
   "Develop a plot outline for a sci-fi story where the protagonist discovers a secret that could destabilize a technologically advanced society. What key events or turning points should occur to escalate the stakes and reveal the theme?"

4. **Three-Act Structure:**
   "Outline a three-act structure for a sci-fi adventure involving a rebellion against an authoritarian corporation that controls a planet's water supply. Include inciting incidents, rising action, midpoint twists, climaxes, and resolutions."

5. **Surprise Midpoint Twist:**
   "Suggest five possible twists that could occur at the midpoint of a sci-fi story, each involving the protagonist uncovering a major secret about their mission, the world, or their allies."

6. **Multiple Storylines:**
   "Create three interconnected plotlines for a sci-fi story set on a spaceship traveling between galaxies. Each storyline should involve a unique character or group with their own goals and conflicts, but all should intersect by the climax."

7. **Character vs. Environment Conflict:**
   "Generate five scenarios where characters must face off against the natural elements in a hostile alien environment. Include suggestions for how these settings could also reflect or heighten the internal struggles of the protagonist."

Character Development Prompts

1. **Character Backstory:**
 "Generate a detailed backstory for a protagonist who was raised in an off-world colony focused on genetic enhancement. How might their upbringing and background influence their goals, fears, and values?"

2. **Hero's Transformation:**
 "Describe the character arc of a sci-fi hero who starts as an idealistic scientist but becomes disillusioned after realizing the negative consequences of their research. What key experiences could drive this transformation?"

3. **Villain's Motivation:**
 "Create a detailed profile for a sci-fi villain whose goal is to implement a controversial technology that will benefit society but infringe on personal freedoms. Include their backstory, motivations, ethical justifications, and personal insecurities."

4. **Unlikely Allies:**
 "Outline a character dynamic between two characters with opposing backgrounds—one a rebel fighter and the other a corporate engineer. What circumstances might force them to work together, and what tensions and unexpected bonds might form?"

5. **Unique Abilities or Traits:**
 "Suggest five unique abilities or traits for a character who is a hybrid between human and alien species. How might these traits affect their perception of self and their interactions with humans and aliens alike?"

6. **Moral Dilemmas:**
 "Develop a sci-fi character who must make morally difficult choices. Describe three scenarios where their values and loyalties are tested, and outline the possible consequences of each decision."

7. **Supporting Characters with Depth:**
 "Create three supporting characters who each represent different aspects of the story's theme of 'identity in a digital world.' Include their backgrounds, roles in the story, and unique relationships with the protagonist."

Setting Development Prompts

1. **World-Building Basics:**
   "Describe a futuristic city where extreme weather conditions are constant. How do the inhabitants adapt their architecture, transportation, and daily life to survive in these harsh conditions? Include descriptions of local customs that have emerged from living in this environment."

2. **Unique Alien Ecosystem:**
   "Design an alien planet with a complex ecosystem, where each species has evolved symbiotic relationships. Describe three prominent species and how their interactions with one another create a delicate balance within this ecosystem."

3. **Political Structure:**
   "Outline the political structure of a colony on a newly settled planet, where resources are scarce and the colony's leader was appointed by a corporation. How does this structure affect social classes, personal freedoms, and daily life?"

4. **Futuristic Technology in Society:**
   "Describe a society where brain-computer interfaces are widespread, allowing people to communicate telepathically. What are the cultural, social, and legal implications of this technology? How does it affect relationships and personal privacy?"

5. **Religion and Belief Systems:**
   "Create a belief system for a sci-fi society that reveres artificial intelligence as divine. Describe the core principles, rituals, and symbols associated with this faith, as well as how it influences the society's laws and traditions."

6. **Spaceship Culture:**
   "Describe the culture aboard a generational spaceship traveling to a distant galaxy. Include details about daily routines, social hierarchy, education, and how the crew's goals differ from those of their ancestors who first set out on the journey."

7. **Environmental Threats:**
   "Invent a sci-fi setting where a natural disaster occurs regularly, like frequent solar flares or acid rain storms. How do people or creatures adapt to and prepare for these threats, and how do these conditions shape society's values and survival strategies?"

8. **Resource Scarcity and Economy:**
   "Develop an economy for a society that relies on a rare mineral found only on a dangerous, uninhabitable planet. How does this resource impact the society's trade, labor systems, and social structure? Describe how resource scarcity drives both conflict and cooperation."

Integrated Prompts for Plot, Character, and Setting

1. **Interconnected Development:**
   "Outline a plot set on an ocean-covered planet, where the protagonist, a biologist, is researching a cure for a viral outbreak affecting the native species. Describe the character's motivations, key plot events, and environmental challenges they encounter."

2. **Cultural Conflict and Resolution:**
   "Create a storyline about a human diplomat sent to negotiate peace between two alien factions on a mining colony. Develop the diplomat's character arc, the cultural values of each faction, and key moments of tension and compromise in the negotiation."

3. **Exploring Moral Ambiguity:**
   "Outline a story where the protagonist, a tech developer, creates a groundbreaking AI that learns too quickly, raising ethical concerns. Describe their character arc, the setting of the tech-driven society they live in, and the plot events that force them to confront the consequences of their creation."

4. **Rogue Hero and Alien World:**
   "Develop a storyline about a rogue scavenger navigating a hazardous alien world to retrieve valuable artifacts. Describe the protagonist's character traits, the dangers of the alien landscape, and a plot twist involving another faction with competing interests."

5. **Mystery with Thematic Depth:**
   "Create a mystery plot set on a space station where memory wipes are used as punishment. The protagonist, a former officer who underwent a memory wipe, must solve a murder linked to their lost past. Outline the protagonist's arc, the society's views on memory wipes, and key plot twists."

These prompts cover a range of storytelling elements and can guide you in developing a well-rounded sci-fi narrative.

Conclusion

In conclusion, the science fiction genre offers an expansive and ever-evolving landscape for screenwriters. The genre's blend of imaginative speculation and cutting-edge themes makes it both timeless and timely, drawing in audiences who are eager for narratives that challenge and inspire. With new advancements in technology, an increasing public interest in space exploration, and ongoing social questions about artificial intelligence, bioengineering, climate change, and the human condition, sci-fi has never been more relevant or in demand. For screenwriters, this creates a rich terrain of opportunity to craft stories that explore humanity's relationship with technology, confront ethical dilemmas, and examine the nature of consciousness and society.

One of the biggest draws for sci-fi writers is the genre's flexibility. Science fiction has the unique ability to adapt to and incorporate elements of virtually any other genre—action, romance, thriller, horror, or comedy—while remaining true to its speculative roots. This genre-blending capability expands the possibilities for screenwriters to experiment with tone, pacing, and narrative style, appealing to diverse audiences. A sci-fi narrative can explore psychological horror in a dystopian future, the romantic tension between a human and an alien, or even the comedic absurdities of a high-tech world gone wrong. This adaptability not only allows screenwriters to infuse fresh energy into traditional sci-fi tropes but also to reach beyond typical genre fans, drawing in audiences from all walks of life.

The growth of streaming platforms has opened a new era for science fiction, as these platforms are eager to push boundaries, explore complex narratives, and deliver serialized content. Sci-fi, with its extensive lore and potential for world-building, thrives in a serialized format. Series like *Stranger Things*, *Black Mirror*, *The Expanse*, and *Altered Carbon* have demonstrated that audiences are invested in long-arc storytelling, intricate worlds, and evolving characters. For screenwriters, this means there is now more space than ever for expansive world-building, complex character development, and episodic plots that dive deep into philosophical or ethical questions. Writers who can envision and develop serialized sci-fi stories stand to benefit from the ongoing demand for long-form storytelling.

Feature films in the sci-fi genre remain highly popular and often perform well internationally, due to the universal appeal of their themes. Major studios continue to invest in sci-fi blockbusters, which frequently serve as both critical and commercial successes, generating strong box office returns and creating memorable franchises. For screenwriters, the film market offers the chance to tell grand, high-stakes stories on an epic scale. The genre's unique visuals, memorable characters, and profound themes can translate well across cultures, making it ideal for screenwriters who want their work to reach a global audience. A well-crafted sci-fi script can be the foundation for a franchise, creating spinoffs, sequels, merchandise, and adaptations in other media formats.

Beyond traditional TV and film, the rise of virtual and augmented reality technology is creating new avenues for sci-fi storytelling. Sci-fi writers can leverage immersive media to create experiences where audiences are no longer passive viewers but active participants. Virtual reality allows writers to create worlds where users experience the narrative firsthand, engaging directly with the story's environment and characters. Sci-fi, with its focus on futuristic technology and unique settings, is particularly well-suited to VR storytelling, opening new doors for writers interested in experimental and interactive formats.

In addition, science fiction's relevance extends into literature, comics, video games, and even podcast storytelling, each of which has its own market and demand for compelling sci-fi narratives. Each medium offers unique storytelling tools—such as visuals, gameplay, or audio—that can add layers to a story. Screenwriters looking to expand their horizons can explore these different formats, adapting their sci-fi concepts to fit the medium and reaching diverse audiences. The interconnected nature of media today also means that stories told in one format can potentially expand into others, creating multi-platform universes that enhance and deepen the audience experience.

With the growing interest in artificial intelligence, bioethics, space exploration, environmental concerns, and social justice issues, sci-fi has become a crucial genre for cultural discourse. Audiences are increasingly drawn to stories that tackle pressing questions about our future, and screenwriters have the opportunity to contribute to these conversations in meaningful ways. Sci-fi's speculative nature allows writers to address these contemporary issues head-on, often making societal commentary through metaphor and symbolism. In this way, sci-fi stories can challenge viewers' beliefs, inspire hope, or serve as cautionary tales—offering not just entertainment but also reflection on humanity's path forward.

In summary, the sci-fi market is ripe with opportunities for screenwriters who are ready to innovate, experiment, and push the boundaries of imagination. Whether developing episodic series, blockbuster films, or immersive VR experiences, writers can create powerful, thought-provoking narratives that speak to the complexities of the human experience. As technology and storytelling tools evolve, the sci-fi genre will continue to grow, welcoming writers who can envision the future, ponder the unknown, and explore the moral and ethical questions of our time. For screenwriters, this genre offers an exhilarating playground to craft stories that captivate, question, and transform, ensuring that sci-fi remains a vital and compelling genre for generations to come.

If you liked this book, please leave a review where you bought it. Thank you from the author.

About the Author

Andrew Parry is a writer and filmmaker with a profound love for film, particularly the genre of science fiction. His passion for the limitless possibilities of sci-fi drives both his storytelling and his creative vision. For Andrew, science fiction is more than just a genre—it's a way to explore the boundaries of human imagination, the future of technology, and the mysteries of the universe. Through his writing and filmmaking, Andrew seeks to create narratives that transport audiences to worlds filled with awe, wonder, and the thrill of discovery.

Inspired by the visionary filmmakers and writers who have shaped science fiction over the decades, Andrew's work often tackles themes of futuristic societies, artificial intelligence, space exploration, and the nature of reality itself. He sees science fiction as a powerful tool for examining the human condition, allowing him to ask big questions about our place in the universe and the potential paths humanity might take.

Read more at https://lonetrail.blog.